D0394721

THE ART OF THE CON

How to Think & Like a Real Hustler and Avoid Being Scammed

R. Paul Wilson

Foreword by Frank Abagnale Jr.,
author of *Catch Me If You Can*

LYONS PRESS
Guilford, Connecticut
Helena, Montana
An imprint of Rowman & Littlefield

Lyons Press is an imprint of Rowman & Littlefield

Distributed by NATIONAL BOOK NETWORK

All interior photos by Jason England

British Library Cataloguing-in-Publication Information available

Library of Congress Cataloging-in-Publication Data available

ISBN 978-1-4930-0060-9

∞™ The paper used in this publication meets the minimum requirements of American National Standard for Information Sciences—Permanence of Paper for Printed Library Materials, ANSI/NISO Z39.48-1992.

To Julie, Connor, and Cameron—
for keeping me honest

Contents

FOREWORD

For five years I lived as an impostor. I pretended to be a pilot, a doctor, a teacher, a lawyer, and a peace officer. I taught myself how to defraud companies out of large sums of money and became so good at lying, both in person and on paper, that I might have continued my descent into dishonesty until there was no coming back.

Thankfully, I was caught. I paid my debt to society and found that my natural ability for deception could be used legitimately. I discovered that I could use my abilities to help society by advising government agencies or corporations and, while my five years as a forger makes for a great story, an engaging book, and a successful movie, my real achievements in life came once I learned how to re-direct my talents toward detection and prevention.

The more the public knows about how criminals think and operate, the more difficult it becomes for fraudsters to succeed. We live in an unethical society where the teaching of ethics is rarely found in schools and colleges. I believe a better understanding of what is right could help the next generation recognize when something might be wrong, and I regularly advocate better education regarding the art of deception.

People need to be proactive to protect themselves. The world today is over-saturated with information and personal data that can easily find its way into the wrong hands. Social media continues to expand, technology evolves at a staggering rate, and people have learned to share too much about themselves online, where it might one day be used by a potential employer, a bank, or a scammer.

The methods and strategies used in con games are often the foundation for financial fraud or questionable business practices. Even if you never fall victim to a con game, the principles Paul identifies in this book can be found wherever businesses or individuals attempt to deceive or defraud.

This book provides invaluable insight into how professional deceivers think, and it will hopefully encourage you to protect your interests in all walks of life because whether you're traveling, conducting business, or playing poker, it never hurts to have a little "grift sense."

Frank Abagnale Jr.
July 2014

Part One
RAP SHEET

*L*ook around. Do you see a mark, a sucker, or a fish? Perhaps you're in a bookstore or an airport or just sitting at home. Wherever you are at this exact moment, I guarantee you are close—very close—to the potential victim of a con game. The world is filled with people who are looking for their next "mark." The truth is, we have all fallen for some form of deception in our lives and we all know someone who has been badly conned. A con game is a criminal act of deception where the objective is to separate a victim from something of value. It can be carefully played over time or be a quick, cunning trap designed to win, steal, or defraud.

The book you are holding is about how cons work, how con artists think, and how ordinary honest people—like you—can learn how to recognize a scam before it's too late.

Your first lesson begins right here. I'm going to teach you how to spot a potential "mark," someone who could genuinely fall for a scam. It's simple: *Look in a mirror.*✓

After thirty-six years of research, study, obsession, and practice, I still look at my reflection and remind myself that to someone, I'm just another mark, waiting to get clipped. As the old saying goes, if you're playing cards and don't know who the sucker is, it's you. What matters is how quickly you realize that it's time to walk away from the table.

I learned my first scam when I was eight years old. It wasn't a money drop or a lost ring game or even a proposition bet. It was a simple sleight-of-hand maneuver that allowed me to cheat at the game of Gin. That was the first step on a road that has taken me around the world and allowed me to study the art of the con without ever resorting to a life of crime.

My journey has been a unique one. A childhood fascination grew into an adult obsession that would eventually help me build a singular career, first advising for film and television, then working in front of the camera to execute real cons on real people. Since 2005, I have arguably pulled more scams than anyone, and along the way, I have learned more than I could ever have hoped or expected. In this book I will share those experiences to reveal the secrets of how and why con games work. I will take you inside con artists' minds and show how these criminals manipulate innocent people into handing over their hard-earned money. With a better understanding of these principles, you will learn to avoid con games and recognize the signs of deception. My primary goal is to turn you into a "tough mark."

My journey began on Gibson Terrace, a row of tenement flats in the Fountainbridge area of Edinburgh, Scotland. While spending weekends with my grandparents as a child, I played cards constantly. One day, after losing for what seemed like the hundredth time, I started "rabbit-hunting": turning over cards, looking for the one I needed.

My grandfather smiled. "Looking for the four of diamonds?" he asked, but I ignored him and kept turning cards. "It's on the bottom," he told me.

I stopped and looked at him. He was smiling from ear to ear. Turning over the pile, I found the four of diamonds right where he said it would be. It's not much of a card trick, but I was completely baffled. How could he possibly have known?

The next time I carefully watched him shuffle, running cards from hand to hand in the overhand style. He dealt the cards as I collected my hand, still watching to see if he peeked at the basement. He didn't but I lost again and, again, he named the bottom card as I turned over the stub. How was it done? I had to wait weeks before he would tip the secret.

As it turned out, my grandfather had learned how to hold the bottom card in position during a shuffle. Glimpsing the card early on allowed him to shuffle, deal, and set without ever returning his gaze to the pack. This would later prove to be one of the easiest ways to control cards during a shuffle and, in the hands of a skilled gin player, it can guarantee an unbeatable edge, making the cheater lots of money. Except my granddad was not a professional, nor was he particularly good compared to my grandmother who—whether granddad knew the bottom card or not—could beat him nine times out of ten with her eyes shut. I would later learn that not all sleights are automatic winners. Some simply give the crooked player an advantage that'll pay off in the long run. Others are a complete lock and steal every penny at the table but are far more dangerous, requiring greater skill and courage on the part of the cheat.

That first card move ignited in me a lifelong passion for sleight of hand, magic, and con games. Shortly after, I saw the movie *The Sting* with Paul Newman and Robert Redford and I was completely hooked. There I was, eight years old and hungry for anything I could find about con games, cheating, and manipulation. But since I spent much of my time in a tiny Scottish apartment, there were few opportunities for me to find that kind of information, especially back in the 1970s. Over the years, I found the occasional book teaching magic tricks and a series of card manipulation booklets by Jean Hugard, but I would later learn directly from some of the finest exponents in the world.

Since those first experiences at my grandparents' house, I have eagerly sought out any information about cheating, con games, or ways to beat the system. By the time I reached my mid-twenties, I had spent most of my life perfecting sleight of hand, performing magic, and studying the art of deception. I was greatly influenced by "The Professor," Dai Vernon, one of the most important magicians of the twentieth century. The Professor helped define a new approach to close-up magic, inspired by lessons he had learned from cheaters who used similar skills at the card table. Vernon spent much of his life seeking out crooked gamblers or con men; his tales of ne'er-do-well characters from that world fired my imagination and cemented my desire to learn everything I could on the subject.

I have always been particularly interested in con artists. Characters like Count Victor Lustig, Yellow Kid Weil, Titanic

Thompson, Soapy Smith, and Charles Ponzi filled my imagination with possibilities. These people were crooks, certainly, but they were also heroic in a way, seemingly deceiving countless victims with cunning, inventing strategies that were almost magical to me. Today my library of books, pamphlets, magazine articles, and newspaper reports concerning con artists and their methods is extensive but by no means complete, though I'm fortunate to have access to much larger collections around the world.

Despite my lifelong fascination, I have never felt the desire to make a living stealing from people. That's not to say I haven't crossed the line from time to time. I've found myself uncomfortably on the wrong side of that line on several occasions but have resisted the temptation to go further. Some might say that this is a weakness on my part, a fear of getting my hands dirty, perhaps. I would argue that it takes much greater strength of character to resist the urge to make easy money and stronger character to recognize the true cost of a life lived in the shadows. This creates a dilemma: Having a sincere interest in con games that you cannot, in good conscience, practice means that no matter how much you read, discuss, or study, there is no way to truly understand how con artists think or why con games work. It's like being fascinated by the ocean without ever getting your feet wet.

Con artists come in all shapes and sizes and from every walk of life. There's no way to identify one unless you recognize the actions of a master deceiver in advance or when it's too late and your money's long gone. Most con men are naturally gifted with the skills to manipulate people and situations, weaving webs of complex simplicity and charm to convince anyone of anything. The ability to con people is accompanied by other traits that are almost universal to con men: an automatic detachment from the consequences of their actions, a lack of empathy for the victim, and no sense of guilt or responsibility whatsoever. Without these qualities a human being wouldn't last long as a grifter. I'm proud to say that while I have developed an ability to think and act as a con artist, I have never lost my sense of right and wrong and have managed to stay (mostly) on the right side of the law.

My television career started in 2002, right after working on the film *Shade*, written and directed by my friend Damian Nieman. I had been initially hired as an expert consultant on cheating methods and con games but soon found myself with a small role in the film, spending a week on camera with Stuart Townsend, Mark Boone Jr., Gabriel Byrne, and Jamie Foxx. From there I was hired as second unit director and by the time production was over, I was hungry to do more. Damian and I developed a number of ideas for television, including a drama series and a reality concept where I would pull cons, attempt heists, and even cheat casinos. We bounced around Hollywood for a few months pitching these ideas until, eventually, one of them was picked up.

The Takedown was produced by MPH for Court TV in New York. Each episode featured me and a team of experts trying to beat casinos, rip off companies, and even steal art from a busy art gallery. A lot of the show was filmed in Nevada with the blessing of the gaming authorities thanks to the fact that the on-camera performers were magicians and had no criminal background. The show did good business, but by the time a second season was prematurely announced, I had already moved back to the UK and was working for the BBC.

The Real Hustle began in 2005 and continued for eleven seasons until 2012. I was approached in 2004 to help write and develop the show after creating and producing *The Takedown*. *The Real Hustle* sought to combine the genre with a "Candid Camera" format where multiple scams would be shown in a single episode.

The principles I had learned and developed producing my first show in America proved essential when working on *The Real Hustle* for the BBC. For *The Real Hustle*, I would be presented with the opportunity to perform a greater number of scams and perhaps have the chance to gain a better understanding of why they worked. After a lifetime of study, I was a natural for a show like this, but I could not have predicted how much I was going to learn about the art of the con.

By the time I started the first season of *The Real Hustle*, I was pretty sure of myself. I have friends who have come directly from the world of cons, and over the years, they have rewarded me with inside knowledge, information, and insights that you won't find in any literature. Their objective was never to analyze or study what they were doing. At best they might question the ethics of their actions, but when asked to explain the reasons why scams work, their answers were all too predictable. People are greedy or stupid or naive and all a grifter needed to do was set the trap and wait for pigeons to land.

I have always had trouble believing that. It confused and frustrated me that the public held the same view about those who fall victim to con games: that they are motivated by greed, taken advantage of because of stupidity, or are foolish about the ways of the world. Perhaps these doubts kept me from cynically taking my own sheep to market. It wasn't until I found myself in the back of a truck, holding fistfuls of cash, that I fully understood that these con games really worked, that there was a great deal to discover about why they worked and that, despite all my years of study, I had so much more to learn.

This book will reveal the lessons I've learned from these experiences. It will share my insights into the mechanics of cons and scams, from crooked carnival games to big cons that steal billions from innocent people each year. Along the way you will develop your own "grift sense" and learn to identify the elements of a confidence trick, no matter how it might be re-invented or dressed up. You will learn how to protect yourself, your family, and your colleagues with a few simple rules and discover how society can identify a scam much sooner and defend those most vulnerable. In short, I am going to break the grifter's golden rule: "Never wise-up a mark."

LESSONS IN LARCENY

I stood in the back of the truck, holding tightly to a length of coarse rope as we turned the corner a little faster than expected. Boxes slid across the floor and bounced off the wall beside me. The rope, tied to the wooden slats that lined the interior, groaned as it took my weight, suspending me at a sharp angle until the driver straightened out and I was pushed back with a few of the lighter boxes tumbling after me.

I was nervous. I had rehearsed this many times, obtained the necessary props, and considered every possible outcome. Everything seemed to make sense before I had closed the shutter and given the signal to drive away. As the truck got closer to our destination, the doubts began to creep in. What if this didn't work? What if the books were wrong? What if I couldn't pull it off?

The truck slowed and maneuvered into position, ready for a clear getaway. I checked my clothes, tightened the band on my apron, and repositioned the boxes ready for the pitch. The engine stopped and someone walked around to open the shutter as a radio in the driver's cab confirmed that cameras were rolling. A lever popped, the shutter was thrown up, and light poured in. There was no going back.

London's Chapel Market is a very busy place at ten o'clock in the morning. Stall holders fill the street with clothes, food, toys, and assorted gadgets designed to improve or enhance the lives of anyone with a little cash to spare. We had parked beside a cafe, on the corner so that the main flow of people was passing the open rear end of the truck. I handed a roll of plastic bags to my assistant and pulled a couple of boxes even closer to the opening. Behind me, stacked to the roof, were boxes for PlayStations, Xboxes, DVD players, and LCD televisions. These were the bait. All we needed now was the fish.

"Ladies and gentlemen!" I said, filling my gut with air to project as far as I could without shouting, gaining maximum volume without strain.

"Ladies and gentlemen, welcome to Chapel Market, where you find real bargains for real people." A few people stopped. Others glanced over as they walked by. Some slowed their pace a little. Remembering a lesson from my youth, I kept talking as if a thousand people had stopped to hear. "Here at the market, you know that you are guaranteed to find the very best prices for the finest merchandise. This isn't Oxford Street. This isn't Regent Street where you pay as much for the name on the bag as you do for what's inside!" More people had stopped and the crowd was starting to fill out.

I reached into the first box and pulled out a personal grooming kit, sealed inside clear, brittle plastic. "Come a little closer, there's room for everyone. Here at the market we guarantee the very best bargains and, this morning I'm here to offer you all a deal you will never find at those big shops on the high street.

Who knows what this is? It's a men's grooming kit. Ladies, this little kit is sure to clean up those dirty fingernails, trim those beards, and shave that stubble. It comes in its own case and is ready to wrap for Christmas or that special birthday boy. How much would you pay for something like this downtown? Fifty? Twenty? If you're really, really lucky, maybe fifteen quid. Here, at the market the price is—wait for it—two pounds!"

That got their attention. I could see people reaching for purses and pockets but I wasn't finished. I pulled a women's grooming kit from the box and put that beside the other one. "We also have a lady's kit for the same low price and, as part of today's special promotion we are selling both—both of these kits for the same low price of just two pounds. That's two pounds for both kits! Put your hands in the air if you have two pounds and, remember, we guarantee you'll be satisfied and we guarantee you'll be happy!"

Hands flew up as we passed out oversized bags with two kits already inside. I pulled another box toward me as the crowd eyed the boxes of expensive merchandise still stacked against the back wall of the van.

"Now, let me ask you something." I was getting into it now, finding my rhythm. "Who would say that two grooming sets for just two pounds is a fantastic bargain? Show me your hands. Now, here at the market, we want to be sure everyone is happy so, if you are happy with your purchase, put your hands in the air and shout 'I'm Happy!'" Everyone does. More people join the crowd; I turn to my assistant and say "Alex, everyone who has their hand in the air—give them their money back!"

The crowd was baffled as everyone who bought a kit was given a full refund. I pull out a set of twenty pens from another box. They look expensive behind the plastic wrapping—the kind a businessman might carry. I pull one from my pocket to use as an example.

"Now, I want you to look at this. You've all seen pens like this. This is a high quality writing pen that would be at home in any suit pocket or briefcase. It's a perfect gift for anyone and, if you buy it on the high street it would easily cost you fifty pounds. I'm not asking fifty pounds. I'm not even asking twenty or ten! The price you pay today is just five pounds but I'm not just going to give you one—I'm going to give you twenty! That's right, twenty beautiful pens—twenty fantastic gifts—for just five pounds! And remember, I guarantee satisfaction and I guarantee you will be happy!"

The crowd blushed with money as everyone with a bag held out their cash in return for the large plastic packages, filled with pens. We even gave out grooming kits to anyone who missed them first time around.

"Twenty pens for a fiver? Where else but the market do you get a deal like that? Now, remember, I guarantee satisfaction and I promise you will be happy so let me hear it: Who's happy?" The crowd shouts back and more people gather to see what's going on. "Put your hands in the air if you're happy, keep your hands up. Alex, if they're happy, give them their money back!"

Five-pound notes were passed back to everyone. I suddenly found myself wishing we had more people to manage the crowd, but I pressed on and removed a large glass vase from its box.

"This is something you have all seen before, probably in the bigger shops—the ones with the biggest prices. It's a vase, perfect for all those times your husband buys you flowers." The crowd laughs. I noticed that Alex was still distributing five-pound notes from the last round of sales. The crowd was bigger than we had anticipated and it crossed my mind that we might be in serious trouble if the engine didn't start or we couldn't make a clean getaway. "This is the real deal, made from genuine Italian glass!" I snapped my finger against the cheap vase to create a ringing sound that seemed to prove something—but it didn't matter; I could see that they already wanted to buy.

"Who wouldn't expect to pay sixty or even a hundred pounds for this in one of those shops? Not at the market! Here, we guarantee satisfaction and we guarantee to make you happy. Who has ten pounds for me?" This time the hands were in the air instantly and Alex started passing large colorful boxes containing cheap, poorly made vases. Again I settled the crowd down and asked "Who's happy?" The crowd shouted back "I'm Happy!" and I smiled, getting deeper into the role. I shouted back "We guarantee satisfaction and we guarantee that you will be happy—Alex, give them their money back!"

This time I waited until everyone had their money before reaching back for a handheld game system. Alex pointed to another box, and with the crowd watching, I pretended to remember something. Replacing the game, I reached into another large box and produced a wristwatch inside an impressive presentation case (in actual fact, it was cheap "slum," a lookalike of more expensive watches that cost less than one US dollar when bought in large quantities).

"Ladies and gentlemen, I almost forgot one of our biggest bargains. Now, this is a gentleman's watch and we have several different styles. You might recognize this one, it's exactly the same as those watches you see in magazines and sold to people with more money than sense. This is not one of those watches—but you'd have to be an expert to know the difference! This very same model is sold less than a mile away for over sixty pounds and I have to admit that, even for that price, it's a real bargain. Here at the market we are here to give you the very best products at the very best prices. If I told you this was forty pounds you'd think these were stolen—they're not but when you hear the price you're going to be stealing these from me. Not eighty, not sixty, and not even forty. These watches, in the case, with the guarantee . . . are twenty pounds and remember, we guarantee you will be happy."

Hands filled with money shot toward us. Alex fought to take all the cash and hand out the watches. Before we knew it, every watch we had was gone and we could have sold many, many more. Alex's apron was stuffed with twenty-pound notes. I turned back to the crowd. "Isn't that what coming to the market is about? A watch like that for twenty pounds? Who is satisfied?" Hands fill the air. "Who's happy?"

Everyone shouts back "I'm happy!" and I reached up and grabbed the handle for the shutter.

"If you're all happy," I said, "then we're happy!"

I pulled down the shutter with a crash, sealing us inside the van. The engine started and we drove quickly away leaving the stunned crowd behind us, our pockets full of money. I looked around at the empty boxes. If we had more merchandise, we could have sold it all. If we were doing this for a living, we'd be making money hand over fist—but this was not my biggest revelation that day. One of the most important lessons I would ever learn about cons was yet to come, when we returned to face the crowd and give them back their money.

This was not my first experience working a pitch. For two years, in my late teens, I spent many weeks and months on the road following "DW," a professional pitchman (also known as a "Grafter"), as he set up new pitches then left me to continue selling while he found new locations to work. That product was the infamous Svengali Deck, a special pack of cards that could, in the right hands, perform miracles. Cards can be made to appear in any location, the deck could be seen to be normal or, with a riffle of the cards, transform so that every card was exactly the same. Each deck came with two free additional tricks for reading minds and winning money, all presented in an oversized copy of the card box.

At first, I was reluctant to follow DW's orders. I didn't want to follow his presentation to the letter and only perform the tricks according to a strict script. Like most young men in their late teens, I thought I knew better, so I ignored those instructions and developed my own routine, which I was much happier with—

until it became painfully obvious that I wasn't selling enough decks to cover my expenses, let alone make a profit. Finally, I wised up and returned to the pitch that DW had originally taught me. Having built my confidence over a couple of weeks, the pitch was suddenly much more effective. People began to respond and sales increased sharply. It proved to be a wise move because DW returned one day, unannounced, to watch me work. Later, he took me for lunch and gave me some important advice: "This is not a magic show. It's a game and the name of the game is to make them want what we're selling. If you show off, you lose."

It's a game.

I remembered that, so when DW taught me how to build a crowd, how to hold them, and apply subtle pressure to make a sale, I listened. He told me, "If you learn, you'll earn" and I did both. Eventually I landed back in Scotland and ran a pitch for many months. I gained a great deal of experience about how to speak to an audience, work a crowd, and press their buttons for the desired response. Ever since, I've had a real appreciation for grafters. I've learned to observe how they construct presentations, layering every conceivable positive aspect of a product until the crowd is smothered in reasons to buy. I have studied how they manipulate groups of people into reacting without giving them a chance to think or consider their options. I've seen pitches for knives, chopping devices, miracle cleaning products, cookers, household gadgets, Saran Wrap dispensers, magic tricks, sunglasses, and even towels.

Mark Mason, a master pitchman, told me that towels were his favorite pitch of all time and that he would drive hundreds of miles to make a killing pitching towel sets at weekly markets. When I spoke to him, he slipped effortlessly into his old routine, verbally recounting each type of towel, the color options, the sizes, the thickness and quality of the cotton, that they always "washed soft" and that, for the same low price, they would receive two sets of any color they desired—and a third free set of white towels. "You know, for guests!"

There is a real art to the pitch that I've always admired. A great pitch can be an excellent bit of theater where the product is the star of the show. Often, the same item can be bought cheaper elsewhere, but it's an honest enough game most of the time. It graduates to being a scam when the result is not what the buyer expects, the crowd is manipulated by dirty tricks, or the seller lies or deceives to secure a sale.

A crooked pitch presents people with items they don't really need in such a way that almost anyone might be convinced to buy. Some might argue that the pitch we made from the back of that truck in Chapel Market barely qualifies as a con game since each individual item was sold in exactly the same way that a legitimate pitchman might sell it. This may be true, but a pitch becomes a scam when lies are presented and people are manipulated in order to take their money. This simple version of a Jam Auction, from the back of our truck, was just that. We hooked the crowd with apparently free merchandise and the unspoken promise of better items to come. It was almost a legitimate pitch but these small deceptions made it cross that fine line.

Jam auctions or Mock Auctions have been around for a very long time. In the late 1920s Walter B. Gibson published a series of newspaper articles concerning con games or "bunco" that proved to be both enlightening and entertaining. One of those articles, "Inside Information on Jam Auctions," described the pitch scam that we pulled in Chapel Market. When speaking publicly I often related this scam so it was naturally one of the first con games I wrote for the TV show. People always laughed when I revealed the punchline to the scam but, as it turned out, I really didn't understand it at all.

Jam auctions are rarely subtle affairs. In the UK they are usually called run-out joints, where crowds of people are attracted to a windowless salesroom, often in the back of empty high street stores. Victims are tempted by sales notices promising high-end merchandise for incredibly low prices. It may seem too good to be true, but curiosity will cause many to come along and see what's on offer. Once everyone is inside, the long process of wearing down people's defenses begins. Naturally, the scammers do not advertise that the sale will take upward of ninety minutes, nor that it will be held in a crowded room without natural light and only one apparent way out. But, of course, these things make people easier to control and are essential elements of the scam.

A modern run-out joint begins once everyone is sealed inside the auction room. A barker, standing on an elevated podium, begins by showing the types of products on offer: game systems, televisions, Blu-Ray players, and so on. He tells the crowd about the auctioneer who will eventually conduct the sale and conditions the crowd to bid quickly so they don't miss out on the best bargains. In the sales I've witnessed (before I became recognizable from television and was routinely ejected), no actual merchandise is sold during this phase of the scam. Instead, the role of the auctioneer is built up and the crowd's anticipation is fueled by the sight of the "flash" (products used as bait).

Once the build-up is concluded, the auctioneer arrives: usually a powerful character, he is sometimes funny and charming, other times rough and forceful in his presentation. The sale often begins with a couple of items quickly shown and offered for incredibly low prices. Someone in the crowd always bids immediately and gets passed his/her merchandise for examination and to confirm that the item is genuine. The PlayStation might be real; the person buying it certainly is not. He or she is a shill (sometimes referred to as a "capper") whose job is to snap up the real stuff and keep the marks from winning anything of actual value.

After these items are "sold," the shill opens the box and examines the goods for the benefit of the people close by. The fact that these items are genuine gets quickly absorbed into the crowd; more hands jump into the air each time, but those people always lose out to other lucky buyers who are somehow quicker. This process continues in various forms with all sorts of stories and scenarios played out for the crowd who, by the end of this charade, has been on their feet for well over an hour. Finally, some wonderful product is introduced in an impressive box, filled with solid-looking items familiar to the crowd, now hungry for a bargain.

I've seen many items sold this way but one of the most memorable was an SLR "Olympic" camera. The name of the camera itself was deliberately close to "Olympus," one of the finest manufacturers in the world, and the box was red and white and much like packaging used by that brand. As a keen photographer, I immediately identified these deliberate similarities, but to the other people watching, it must have looked like the real deal. From my position at the edge of the crowd (hiding my face from the bouncers), it certainly looked the part and I could feel people preparing to bid quickly. This is when the procedure changed; the room was about to get stung.

The auctioneer repackaged the camera and placed the box in front of him as he recounted the features and the enormous prices being charged for cameras just like this one "down the street." This time, he did not invite bids or call for hands in the air. Instead, he named a price and asked anyone with enough cash to hold it in the air to prove they were serious bidders. Fistfuls of money shot up into the air. Suddenly, people from the back of the auctioneer's storage room pushed their way into the crowd holding laminated coupons as the auctioneer barked instructions at them to collect the cash. Each buyer was handed a coupon in return for their money and told to keep holding it in the air.

In the back, boxes of cameras were being prepared for distribution as the man on the podium held everyone's attention, congratulating everyone who was holding a coupon. A few stragglers were admonished for not taking advantage of this opportunity. Most eventually conceded and handed over their money. One of the helpers leaned into me as I stood to the side, but I held my ground, refusing to be bullied. Behind me, I could hear the doors to the street being opened, and without warning, the auction was over. People were traded red and white camera boxes for coupons as they were hustled up the stairs and onto the street. I was pushed along but managed to get a good look at the speed with which coupon holders were given their merchandise and sent packing.

Outside, I watched as the shills made their way down an alley to rejoin their fellow hustlers. Meanwhile, the honest victims were left to discover the true value of their purchase. Each camera was nothing more than a cheap, brittle shell with a limp plastic lens. A working mechanism could be detected but I doubt it would produce an image of any value. People became upset; some seemed ashamed. Most victims just walked away, accepting their losses. At the doorway, a couple of people tried to complain. Out of earshot, I couldn't hear what they were told by the imposing doorman but I knew the story all too well. All sales were final. No refunds. There was a sign to that effect, and if they didn't like what they bought, that was their problem. There certainly was a sign that explained these rules in accordance with the exact letter of the law. It was slightly bigger than a postcard and pasted to the wall behind the crowd as they watched the auction. The only real opportunity to notice it was when everyone was being forced to leave and by that time, of course, it was already too late.

During pre-production for *The Real Hustle*, we infiltrated a full-scale run-out joint armed with hidden voice recorders. As was typical by this point, I was immediately spotted and politely asked to leave. Alex remained unchallenged and returned two hours later with the recording and a brand new camera. We constructed our own script based on that auction and sold the same camera, and a dozen just like it, from an empty shop on Manchester's High Street. Afterward we interviewed everyone, while I took extensive notes about the experience.

I played the "barker," roping the crowd and building up "Mr. Harvey" the auctioneer, played by Alex. As an actor, Alex was keen to play this role based on—and named after—the same hustler we had recorded weeks before. Alex was brought up in English boarding schools and went from there to drama school in London. His cartoon Cockney accent held up for most of his performance, slipping to his polite upper-middle-class self every now and then, but the script he memorized worked perfectly. As I had learned selling trick cards years before, a refined pitch— even a crooked one—works wonders. The real Mr. Harvey had no doubt learned the scam, graduated to run his own crew, and applied proven principles to his own line of patter. I'm pretty sure he would be less than happy to see his pitch played out for millions of viewers on our TV show, so after the broadcast, I retired from watching jam auctions.

How did that first jam auction in Chapel Market open my eyes? What were the factors that made me realize how much there was to understand? Until I was given the opportunity to actually perform these cons for television, I regarded them the way anyone with a serious interest in the subject would. I had an encyclopedic knowledge of the actual scams, but if asked to explain how and why they worked, my answer would have pointed to the cunning of the hustler or the gullibility of the mark.

Almost everything one reads on the subject makes the same point, taking great pleasure in recording the details of these confidence tricks without touching upon the human factor. The list of different con games is almost endless and new cons appear every year, but they're mostly just old wine in new bottles. I'm by no means the first to recognize that most modern scams are easily traced to older progenitors; nor that, like jokes or stories, scams can be easily categorized. What shifted was my perspective. Suddenly, I was looking at these scams from the other side of the table.

In the back of that truck, I was staggered by just how effective our con had been. By simply acting out a scam described in an article written decades before, we were holding handfuls of twenty-pound notes. If we had more time, more merchandise, and fewer scruples, this could easily have become a very profitable career. It struck me then that it was not our expert cunning that helped make this money: We had only ever pulled the scam once! Was it the gullibility of the crowd? We were certain that those people would be extremely upset as we negotiated to return to the scene of our crime. The producers, however, reported a completely different story.

Once we, the "hustlers," had made a safe getaway, the producers would typically approach our victims and let them off the hook. Many times, this had to be done very quickly before real panic set in and emotions got too high. I never envied the victims at that moment, but almost every time, it was a relief to learn their property or cash was safe. This was different. First, our runners had a tough job gathering everyone who'd bought from us because none of them felt conned in any way. They were all happy. They were all satisfied. This changed once people had some time to think about it, but even then, they were content. Incredibly, many refused to take their money back and preferred to keep the merchandise! On our return, there was no animosity, so I asked a couple of people what they felt when we rolled down the shutter and drove off. Mostly they were just disappointed that the sale was over before I got to the Xboxes and televisions at the back of the van. This really made me rethink everything.

There were two seasons of *The Real Hustle* between the back of that truck and the full-scale run-out joint we played in Manchester. By that time, I was already beginning to identify how each scam seemed to work in terms of deceiving people. I understood that scams could be played softly to walk a profit without waking up the marks or used to hit people hard and leave them stunned on the sidewalk. I could see that these two versions of the jam auction not only shared certain principles, they actually manipulated the crowd in exactly the same way, taking them down the same paths and walking them off the same cliff. The only real difference was how big a fall awaited the victim.

It was then clear to me that there was a real structure that could be identified and used to understand how and why scams work and to more effectively protect the public. Instead of exposing hundreds of con games based on analogous principles, I could reveal the fundamental concepts at the heart of all con games, so that no matter how they might be re-invented, people would be able to see past the illusion and recognize the hallmarks of deception.

About now, you might begin to worry that this information could be abused in the wrong hands, that I have created a blueprint for con men to follow. As I have pointed out many times before, informing con artists has never been my goal, nor has it been necessary: They already know how to con people. The scams I expose already exist in the real world and could easily be learned from the same sources that I have used over the years. Informing the con man is a non-issue, but informing the victim can genuinely change things for the better. Informing the public is the only way to protect people from these crimes; I can assure you that con artists are much more concerned about potential marks learning their methods than they are in need of ideas. The only reason any con game was ever successful is that the victim did not recognize it as a scam until it was too late.

My intention is to put you into the mindset of a hustler, to make you think like a thief and see through the eyes of a swindler. It's much easier to recognize ingredients once you've cooked with them yourself, and this book will give you a taste of how it feels to pull a con. If that motivates you toward a life of crime, know that you need to have more than a little larceny in your heart to be a successful grifter, and I can't take responsibility for any qualities or character traits that would allow you to act upon such feelings. Nor can I be blamed for the time you are almost certainly going to spend behind bars, because almost every con artist eventually gets caught.

By sharing what I have learned, I am not trying to convince you that you are now no longer a potential target, nor am I promising you will always be able to recognize a scam before it's too late. Instead, my aim is to encourage a better understanding of how and why these methods work so that the game becomes much harder to play from the con man's side of the table. In essence, I'm out to even the odds.

SCAMS AND SCAMMERS

The first time I saw the Dancing Dolls was as a child at Ingleston Market, just outside of Edinburgh. A man sold them from a gap between two stalls, squatting on the floor while surrounded by curious passers-by. The dolls were cut from thick card: a simple head and body made from one piece with string for arms, a bead for hands, and string legs with cheap, weighted magnets for feet. Each doll was sold inside a clear plastic bag with a cardboard label stapled to one end, sealing the package shut.

The seller would pass them around, allowing people to see how simple they were, then, taking them back, he would squat and hold a doll upright so the feet dangled below the doll and touched the floor. He would then slowly let go of the cardboard torso, but instead of collapsing, the doll remained upright, as if somehow brought to life. It would then appear to dance as the body swayed and hopped in opposite directions to the arms and legs. People pushed and shoved to see the little dolls as another seller began passing out packages with identical contents, asking only a few pounds for each one. They always seemed to sell out quickly and the sellers were then nowhere to be found. I watched them pitch these dolls many times, and over the years, I've seen the same dolls in many different guises: Mickey and Minnie Mouse, Bart and Lisa Simpson, even cutouts of political figures. But they all had one thing in common: They didn't work.

I've seen the dancing dolls con played all over the world, mostly in markets or on the street, and the secret is quite simple: The seller has a line of invisible thread hidden within a cassette player, which plays the music that supposedly causes the dolls to dance. In fact, the dolls have a tiny notch cut into the cardboard, which is used to suspend them on the thread, which is attached to a nearby wall. The motor that drives the cassette also rotates the thread in a circular motion so that the dolls appear to hop up and down to the rhythm. This has the added advantage of ensuring the line of thread does not constantly occupy the same point in space. While already hard to see, the thread is rendered completely invisible thanks to this movement.

Interestingly, the guy who sold them when I was younger did not use a music player at all. He simply placed them on the floor as he bent down and the dolls danced. Recently, on a visit to Madrid, I noticed a crowd near Plaza Major. Walking up, I spotted the familiar movement of paper dolls dancing between the legs of a man, squatting at the center of the crowd. He was completely surrounded and clapped his hands to make the dolls dance. Just as I remembered, there was no cassette player or boom box but the dolls still danced. I immediately understood how this version (no doubt the original method) worked. Between his knees was a line of super-thin elastic, almost impossible to see unless the viewer is very close. When he squatted, his knees would stretch the line between them, allowing him to place the doll. By clapping and singing he created enough body movement to translate to the doll, which appeared to move in concert with the beat.

What was never clear to me was how people *thought* they supposedly worked. The most common explanation the dishonest salesmen would give was that the vibration from the speaker somehow caused the thick paper to defy the laws of physics. When I was younger, the reason had something to do with heat from the seller's hand. He would hold the doll between the palms of both hands, then bend down and cause the doll to dance. Of course, none of these reasons make any sense. But they do help to illustrate an important point, what I would consider the key to the success of most scams: wishful thinking. The very idea that these dolls would work might even be more powerful than showing them dancing. The demonstration merely quashes any doubts and convinces the unwary to listen to their inner voice that wants the story to be true. Somehow, people who buy the dolls seem to accept whatever reason they are told as to how the dolls dance and happily hand over their money. When we decided to pull this scam for the TV show, I immediately saw an opportunity to explore this further.

We set up in London's Oxford Street, with Alex and Jessica-Jane Clement on camera, selling the dolls. The most interesting part for me came afterward, when the victims were interviewed on camera. In advance we had written multiple excuses for the dolls' talents: magnets, special inks, nanotechnology, vibration from the music, and even heat-activated layers within the cardboard. We also concocted ways to "recharge" the dolls: put them in the freezer, place them on top of a microwave oven, leave them in sunlight for an hour, or heat them between your hands for five minutes. Alex and Jess did a sterling job with this, throwing out different reasons and methods to people as they bought the dolls.

As victims left with their purchases, our runners intercepted them so they could be interviewed by our co-conspirators, posing as a news team. We wanted to know what they had bought, which they gladly explained to us. We then asked "how do they work?" and listened to them repeat what they had been told. As they told us this, most people began to slow a little and actually *consider* what they were saying. By the time we asked them to tell us how the dolls could be recharged, they realized just how preposterous it all sounded. One lady enthusiastically told us about the dolls and how they worked until, mid-sentence, she simply stopped and visibly deflated. She looked at the package and then up at me and said, "These don't work." Repeating our lies caused people to realize how ludicrous they were and this experiment proved something to me that has become essential in my research: When it comes to con games, bullshit is sometimes easier to taste than to smell.*

Many might argue that the dancing dolls are nothing more than an amusing deception—a bit of sharp practice with a touch of magic. This way of thinking is not only wrong; it can

---

* This is not always true. Some scams force the mark to invest in a lie by repeating it to a third party, but this requires careful handling and depends on context and timing.

be dangerous. In another guise this same scam has been used to steal millions of dollars and potentially cost thousands of lives.

Confidence tricks are an integral part of human history. From the first moment we were able to share ideas or convey knowledge, the door for dishonesty swung open, and as the ways in which we communicate continue to grow and expand, criminal minds cast larger nets to catch more fish than ever before. Many of the scams that have become familiar on the Internet are based on cons that are hundreds of years old. The principles remain the same but the story—and the means by which that story is told—has evolved and adapted in that time.

My objective is not merely to share these con games but to illustrate exactly how and why they work: to break them down, pull them apart, and expose the mechanics at the heart of every major con game. I do not pretend to be a psychologist, a criminologist, or an academic. I consider myself a lifelong enthusiast and expert in the ways and means of the con artist with unique experience executing and examining these scams without having to cross the criminal line.

To begin, let's agree on a few simple terms. In the literature dedicated to this genre, the words "con" and "scam" typically prove to be synonymous. In some cases, experts refer to certain crimes as a "con game" and to others as a "scam," but as you read more and more these terms become interchangeable with both words simply referring to crimes of deception.

Indeed, there are many words that can be used to describe the act of theft by deceit: fraud, hustle, racket, double cross, double deal, flimflam, cheat, rip-off, shakedown, sham, sting, sucker game, and even shell game. Many might try to distinguish each of these by allotting certain types of con to each word. A hustle, for example, generally refers to a con game where the victim is cajoled into making a wager based on the false belief that his ability or knowledge outweighs that of the hustler. As a street term, this might be correct; but for our purposes, they're all con games and they come in every conceivable shape and size. Even if we were to poll a thousand professional grifters, crossroaders, scufflers, con artists, and scammers, they would never be able to agree on what's actually what. In this book, I will call a con a scam; a scam a fraud; a fraud a play; a play a swindle and so on. These are all tricks of a sort, dodges of a kind, and are all types of con game. I may occasionally lean on my own language preferences, but remember that by any other name, a scam still stinks.

It's important to establish what kind of crime falls under this verbose umbrella. It is a common misconception that a con artist uses charm as a mugger might use a knife. There's much more to it than that. Con artists are by no means averse to using violence, though often as leverage to help direct their victim toward a desired outcome. It is the act of *manipulation*, whether subtle or overt, that distinguishes the con artist from other crooks.

So, what is a con game?

After years of consideration, I find that the following definition applies to the majority of scams: *A confidence trick creates or distorts a scenario, then manipulates how the victim perceives his options and potential rewards.*

The key ingredient is deception, in all its forms. Using any means, from subtle suggestion to bald-faced lies, the con man somehow misleads the victim by internal or external influences. Con games are a matter of carrot and stick, whereas a mugging, burglary, or theft is arguably "all stick." The size and shape of the carrot changes from con to con, but the principles used to construct these scams are surprisingly limited. Even so, a victim may find it difficult to recognize a scam because, to stretch the metaphor further, the donkey only ever sees the carrot.

It is also important to understand what kind of person makes a successful con artist. Although we have established a simple definition for most types of scam, creating a similar catch-all definition would be almost impossible for the perpetrators. If con games can come in all shapes and sizes, from dishonest street sellers to corrupt financiers running billion-dollar Ponzi schemes, how can there be a sure way to recognize a swindler? The sheer wealth of different con games would suggest there isn't one type, but after a lifetime of observation, I have identified a few qualities that are common to anyone attempting to gain or steal by means of deception.

Grifters, hustlers, or fraudsters come from all walks of life. You are as likely to find them in so-called polite society as you are in the back alleys of any major city. Sadly, that means they look just like you, me, and everyone else, so while there are no physical characteristics that identify a swindler, there is one common factor: *the way they think.*

Often, hustlers are the kind of people who take no responsibility for the consequences of their actions. They have little concern for the circumstances of their victims and they lose little sleep worrying over foolish matters such as morals, ethics, or fair play. To a grifter, everyone is a sucker just waiting to be taken and if they don't take your money, someone else will. Common excuses—I've heard them all—include "it's the victim's own fault for getting involved," "they didn't need to hand over their money," and, my personal favorite, "they won't do that again," somehow implying that the con artist is teaching the mark a lesson and therefore doing them a favor. As riverboat gambler Canada Bill Jones once said, "A sucker has no business with the money in the first place."

This disassociation from guilt or responsibility can come in many forms. Denial and self-delusion help to create the important element of detachment, which is essential to the success of a fraudster. Having deceived and manipulated hundreds of people, I would have become an emotional wreck without the comfort of knowing the victim would always be reunited with their property. On several occasions I felt truly terrible when I was able to take advantage of people's feelings, hopes, and dreams—even though I knew the con wasn't real. There was a critical moment in many of these cons when I felt suddenly in control and able to take the mark wherever I pleased. When this happened, my producers and I would have to be extra careful about bringing them back to reality. For some victims, the fall would be really hard, almost damaging, so most of our producers became adept at bringing people down gently. We developed strategies solely to protect our marks so they would not be too upset. The con may have been fake but the emotions the mark went through were still real. Such considerations are nonexistent in the world of real cons and scams. The harder they fall, the farther they roll, and the less likely that they will be to pursue.

It should be clear by now that con artists cannot be recognized by the way they look or talk nor by the way they dress or behave. A person's background or breeding, real or invented, is no assurance of honesty; judging someone by one's own moral limitations can be an expensive mistake. Trying to identify a con artist this way is like trying to determine someone's job by the shape of their ears. That's not to say there aren't common traits that might arouse suspicions, but until compared to actions and intent, there's no way to be sure. Our objective here is to recognize the con game rather than the con man.

Many books exist that describe hundreds of scams and I recommend them to anyone with a sincere interest in the subject. The problem is that con games evolve over time. How often have you heard a joke, only to recognize it after the punchline? A different setup, altered details, and the way of telling can make a simple joke seem different or new, but like a well-proven scam, the punchline often remains the same.

Naturally, if you recognize a particular scam, you should immediately walk away. Once you are caught in the web of a con, weaved by an expert con artist, it can be incredibly difficult to wake up and smell what's being shoveled. Many people walk up to Monte games fully aware that they're a scam, but still get caught up in the action and leave with empty pockets. It's like watching a *Rocky* movie before getting into a ring with Mike Tyson; you might know what's coming but you're still going to the hospital. Con artists are better at conning you than you are at not being conned. Remember, they have played this game before and you are almost certain to lose—even if you know what's going on.

Society often makes the mistake of giving con games a lower priority than more immediate and sensational crimes, but the ramifications of scams can be severe and extremely damaging. It is not unusual for victims to shoulder full responsibility for being fooled, as if they are to blame for losing their own money. Perhaps this is a natural reaction, but it is also one of the key reasons that con games continue to flourish. Grifters depend on their victims to feel this way, knowing that the shame of being conned usually discourages a mark from reporting the crime.

Writer, actor, and magician Ricky Jay is a genuine expert on the subject. His work in the field is both illuminating and entertaining, but I have grown to disagree with his assertion that a confidence trick is a "soft crime."* Certainly, some scams are softer than others. Being swindled by a carnival game might merely bruise the ego, but giving away one's life savings has driven some victims to suicide. Being threatened with a knife in

---

* It might be argued that con games are a soft crime for the perpetrators.

a back alley, even assaulted, is traumatic, but there is a sharper edge to personal guilt or lost self-respect. Many victims internalize this suffering and withdraw from family and friends. It's like comparing slashed tires with sugar in your gas tank: The subtle attack can be the most damaging over time.

Information is the most powerful weapon against con artists. My shows, *The Real Hustle*, *The Takedown*, and *Scammed*, all sought to entertain the audience and educate them by osmosis. I firmly believe that we succeeded in our goal of making ordinary people more aware, of giving them tools to spot these scams before falling victim. But journalists continued to ask me the same question in almost every interview: Aren't I teaching people how to con other people? You might ask the same question as you read this book. Will it provide further education to the criminally inclined?

My answer is simple: *Con artists already know how to con you.* Scams have been spreading like viruses for centuries, and today, anyone can learn countless new con games with a simple Google search. Hustlers do not need my help to rip you off, but what they do need—what they absolutely depend upon—is the ignorance of the general public about how they operate. An informed public is a protected public. It's a simple equation and it bears repeating. In the history of con games, the only reason a con has ever succeeded is because the mark did not realize he was being conned.

How big the problem is depends on your perspective. The occasional crooked street game may seem like nothing more than a nuisance, but some can wipe out fortunes or destroy trust and reputation. Sustained attempts to defraud foreign visitors could contribute to a declining tourist industry while regular attempts to con people on the Internet might seriously impact a country's image, as Nigeria (now synonymous with a famous online scam) has learned in recent years.

Con games continue to evolve and find new victims. The rewards for the fraudster can be enormous, but the ramifications for the victims can be much more serious than merely financial. In 2007, businessman James McCormick began selling a bomb-detection kit, designed to be used as a way to effectively locate explosive devices. The device was offered to both the military and civilians, selling for up to forty thousand dollars each. It featured a gun-like grip with a retractable antenna that folded back into the device. Samples of suspected substances were placed into a jar, then transferred to a card, which was inserted into the handle. McCormick claimed the device could detect explosives and other materials from over one kilometer (3,260 feet), even underwater or from the air, and pre-programmed cards were supplied to detect everything from ivory to one-hundred-dollar banknotes.

The method McCormick claimed he used to supposedly program these detection cards was fascinating. A substance was placed into a glass Kilner jar, along with a paper sticker, which would then "absorb the vapors" before being placed onto a card and inserted into the device. McCormick's detector would then, he claimed, compare chemicals in the air to those on the sticker, giving the user a visual indication of concealment.*

---

* Morris, Stephen; Jones, Meirion; Booth, Robert (23 April 2013), "The 'magic' bomb detection that endangered lives all over the world." *The Guardian* (London). Retrieved 23 April 2013.

This is nothing more than a dowsing system* and has no scientific merit whatsoever. In fact, even someone who believes in dowsing might question these claims. The simple truth is that James McCormick knew perfectly well that this system would never work. It was a scam from the beginning.

In war-torn regions, Improvised Explosive Devices (IEDs) are one of the most dangerous weapons faced by civilians and professional soldiers. Finding and disposing of these devices can be a deadly business and McCormick saw this as an opportunity. Combining a feasible story with a desperate need allowed him to sell thousands of useless devices to governments, companies, and individuals. He made eighty million dollars from sales, selling six thousand devices in Iraq alone. There are no figures to estimate how many people may have died while relying on this device but I suspect the number to be depressingly high.

McCormick was able to secure contracts to supply the device to governments around the world. Once he had one major client, he was able to use that client's patronage to convince others that he was a legitimate businessman. While I discourage blaming the victim in most cases, I believe the British government had ample resources to conduct even the simplest of tests on this equipment. Incredibly, McCormick sold them hundreds of units and used this to support his claims with other clients. The UK government may be guilty of neglect in this regard, but that is nothing compared to the irresponsibility of the Kenyan

---

* Dowsing is a centuries-old method of detecting water, underground structures, or precious materials using sticks, metal rods, or pendulums (among other methods). Scientifically speaking, it's hogwash.

government. Three days after McCormick was found guilty and sentenced, the Kenyan police demonstrated their magic detection devices for reporters, apparently proving that they worked exactly as McCormick claimed. Even after the device was fully exposed as an adapted twenty-dollar golf ball locator, the Kenyan authorities publicly insisted that they were effective at locating drugs, explosives, and firearms. This proves only that it's easier to cling to a lie than face the depressing truth and all that it implies.

When confronted in 2010 by one of his salesmen, McCormick told him, "They do exactly what they are meant to do: make money." This is all a con man cares about. Free from remorse or regret, McCormick simply kept selling his "bomb detectors" without any regard for the consequences.

Compare this awful fraud to the almost amusing dancing dolls scam and we find that exactly the same principles are at work. Both scams depend on a feasible working method and both feature demonstrations to prove that the products work, but whereas the dancing dolls scam depends on novelty to attract buyers, McCormick's scheme took advantage of a genuine need for safety and protection. He identified a situation that demanded a solution, one which people would be willing to pay a great deal to have. McCormick created a bogus device, concocted a story around its abilities, and was overwhelmed by demand from potential victims.

Con games are everywhere and even the simplest hustle can be transformed into a big con with a little imagination. James McCormick may never have seen a dancing doll seller, but his objectives and methods were exactly the same. To be able to recognize the elements of a scam, we need to look deeper into how it unfolds. Virtually all cons have four phases: the hook, the line, the sinker, and the cool-out.

THE HOOK

*P*rotection is not just a matter of spotting a scam before getting involved; it's equally important to recognize one from within. Con games evolve over time and anyone can be suckered in by the right story; but if you spot the hallmarks of a scam before it takes you, then it might be possible to walk away without losing a penny. This knowledge can also be invaluable when helping others who are likely to get scammed or already entangled in a con man's web.

My bookshelves groan with the weight of past volumes, exposés, and reminiscences by retired con artists, police officers, federal agents, and bunco men. I have books by academics and magicians who, like myself, were fascinated by the genre, interpreting its history and characters from their own peculiar or entertaining perspective. Strange stories, facts, and personalities fill these pages and have sold quite a number of copies.

As it turns out, writing a book on con games can be quite easy. Many are merely a rewrite (sometimes a blatant rip-off) of already existing material. For hundreds of years, authors have filled their pages with poorly veiled facsimiles of past texts. This counterfeit creativity can be mapped over the years as new authors appear to recycle the same old stories for each new generation because scams make great stories; like good jokes they often feature a fascinating setup followed by a strong punch line. People love clever ideas and tales with a twist, so the constant interest in swindles is easy to understand.

Most books relate their selection of scams with a little commentary or theory thrown in. Such cautionary tales hope to protect the reader by revealing these tricks and supposedly teaching how to avoid falling victim in the future. The problem is that this simply doesn't work. One of the key reasons that people enjoy reading stories about con artists is that they feel detached from the action. They see the hustler as a clever fox and the victims as gullible chickens waiting to be plucked. The details of each story are often embellished, re-ordered, or simply invented to be more entertaining—it's designed so that the readers enjoy the ride without actually remembering where they've been.

When I first started speaking to businesses, educators, and law enforcement about con games, my approach was much the same as the contents of my library. I selected scams from a smorgasbord of criminal history, reconstructed them in my own words, and learned how best to tell them in an effort to entertain and inform my audience. The chances were excellent that if any con man happened to pick someone from that audience and attempt one of those scams, he'd come up empty because the mark would recognize what he was up to.

The problem with this approach is that con games evolve with the times. Once a particular scam becomes well known, con artists can either move to the next town and ply their trade anew or begin a completely different con game, as yet unknown to the public. Most scams can be dressed up in a variety of disguises and re-invented thousands of times to produce the same result: "Get the Fucking Money," or GTFM. As I will illustrate later in this book, some con games can even be repeated on the same victim! Reading about con games in a book is clearly not the same as being the target of one. It's the difference between watching a racing car from the bleachers and being locked in its trunk.

It seemed to me that a fresh approach for a book on con games would be to use these scams as examples to illustrate the *underlying principles* that make con games effective. Together, we're going to ask why they work and learn how to identify a scam before it's too late. Along the way I will share my own experiences as a con artist, examine the many types of con game, and discuss exactly how I got each mark to "pop."

After working on *The Real Hustle* for a couple of years, I began to analyze my notes from each of the scams we had pulled. The concept of breaking the con down into "hook, line, and sinker" came to me when I first used it in a talk for a credit card company in Miami. It was a simple way to illustrate how I felt con games worked; a convenient illustration of the core principles that I was starting to recognize.

At that time, I felt that there was much more to find and that the list would expand as my understanding and experience deepened. To that end, I began to add to the list, but as we continued to film these scams, I grew to understand that almost everything important could be categorized by those first three phases. Eventually, I added the "cool-out" (also known as the "blow-off") to the sequence, and, from this point I began to see how these applied to each and every scam that I'd pulled.

The Hook—Get them interested in the bait.

The Line—Build their desire, sell the story, and establish rapport.

The Sinker—Close the deal.

The Cool-Out—Get them to accept their losses.

Some con games are all about the hook, others are about keeping the mark on the line, and some are nothing but a fast sting, sinking the victim immediately. The cool-out, while not always possible, is often inherent to the type of scam but usually needs to be either baked into the con or carefully applied after the sting.

It is how each of these phases is played that determines the success of the con artist, and I hope to illustrate exactly how a hustler plays this game and responds to the challenges or concerns of a potential victim.

To illustrate these hook, line, and sinker elements, I will walk you through the con game I designed for The History Channel TV show *Scammed*. It's an excellent example because the principles used can be identified in almost any type of con game. Along the way we'll pull several scams together, trying to anticipate every outcome to better understand what a con game feels like from my side of the table.

Uncle Barry

He was not an easy mark. Charming, intelligent, and witty, Uncle Barry was nobody's fool. His nephew, Randy, had secretly set him up for *Scammed*, a two-hour special for The History Channel. My mission was to expose the world's most famous scam by targeting an American businessman. To do this I had to re-invent the game, tailor it to my mark, and pull it off in just forty-eight hours. I had worked out the sting and the best way to reel him in, but setting the bait was going to be risky, as it always is. During pre-production, I was hoping for someone who would bite quickly—but Barry was way too smart for that.

The Nigerian Prince scam is, by now, very well known to anyone with an e-mail account. The idea is simple: A foreign national wants you to hold onto a large amount of money in return for an irresistible percentage of it "for your trouble." The only catch is that, for a variety of reasons, the person receiving the money, the mark, must pay a few legal costs, transfer fees, or put up his own cash as a show of good faith. Whatever the details might be, it amounts to this: The mark must pay his own money under some pretext in the hope of receiving a much bigger sum in return.

It's not a new con game. Over two hundred years ago it was known as the "Spanish Prisoner," where wealthy suckers were convinced they could pay a ransom or fund a voyage to receive the lion's share of a ship loaded with treasure. Boiled down to its base elements, it's the perfect example of a classic con game that might seem ludicrous from the outside, but from the perspective of an entangled victim, perfectly plausible.

My challenge was to re-invent this scam—which would be well known to Barry in its "African prince" disguise—and prove that it could still work if the details were changed. While I had constructed a powerful story and a dramatic sting to get the money, I had to be very careful about how I got our mark to play the game. Just saying, "Hey Barry, want to make a hundred grand?" wasn't going to cut it.

We met over breakfast in Charleston, South Carolina. I played the part of a businessman who brokered large money transfers from overseas. According to my story, I employed US citizens to accept funds into their own accounts, hold them for an agreed period, then, once the legal requirements were satisfied, transfer the money back to the owner's US bank, minus a very attractive percentage. Barry seemed to accept all of this at face value; he only asked a few simple questions as we chatted over coffee and orange juice. We agreed to meet later that day so I could talk to them about working together.

Once Randy and his uncle were gone, I looked to our secret camera position where my producers were watching and said, "We're in trouble."

Reading a mark is an acquired skill. After hundreds of con games I have learned to recognize the hallmarks of a difficult customer. Over breakfast, Barry was calm and friendly but volunteered very little. He rarely leaned forward, which forced me to do too much of the talking.

The situation we had engineered for Barry was simple. He had come to Charleston to assess a potential business deal for his nephew, Randy. Randy was secretly setting up his uncle but would take no part in convincing him to hand over his cash. During the setup, I would need to switch the deal so that Barry would invest his own money. A great deal of work had gone into not tipping Barry off while making sure he could get the money at a day's notice. Everything hinged on how I set the bait, and if Barry didn't bite, we would have come a long way for nothing.

The trouble was that Barry's demeanor during our first encounter was friendly but guarded. He didn't volunteer anything I could use as leverage. He absorbed everything I offered by way of information, giving very little in return other than a few jokes and some charming repartee. The production crew agreed we were in trouble, but for a different reason. When I had left the table for a few moments during the meeting, the producers heard something that made it seem unlikely that our mark was going to bite.

With Uncle Barry, I had my work cut out for me. From the beginning, our objective had been to find a mark who would give me a real challenge. Easy meat can mean easy money, but in my experience, if it's all too convenient then the television audience would quickly dismiss it. If they regarded the victim as foolish or gullible, then they might think *that's* the reason why the con worked. In order to properly illustrate the power and potential of this scam, I needed a worthy adversary and I knew I had more than I bargained for when Barry sat down to breakfast.

While I was at the table, Barry chatted about the quality of the orange juice, the weather, and how much he loved living in the South but gave almost nothing away regarding my business proposal. As soon as he was alone with Randy, that changed. Once I was out of earshot, Barry turned to Randy and said, "This has got Mafia written all over it."

The production team was convinced that this was the end of the road. They were already considering backup options (other potential marks we could bring in at a day's notice) but I was not worried by Barry's words: quite the opposite. My concern had been that Barry was simply not interested and would resist any attempts to pull him deeper into the scam; as soon as I learned what Barry had said to his nephew, I knew that the bait was set and our mark was definitely interested.

The team must have thought I was insane. Barry was as good as gone in their mind, but I had done this many times before; the fact that Barry sensed something "off" was not important. The crucial point was that despite suspecting something fishy, possibly illegal, he still agreed to meet later to find out more. This told me everything I needed to know about our mark: He was willing to roll the dice.

Despite his facade of indifference, I knew Barry was interested. This wasn't a sure thing but our mark was definitely nibbling the bait. We needed to play him carefully, build his confidence, quash his concerns, and satisfy his curiosity. Then we would reel him in.

The hook is the most important element of any con game. Without it, the con artist would have nobody to con because the hook is the means by which the victim becomes involved and starts down a road that will eventually take him over a cliff. The ability to rope someone into a scam is prized above all else. Being able to think and act under pressure, to talk your way out of any challenge, or look a pigeon in the eye as you calmly take his money are useful skills—but they're all ultimately worthless unless a mark is in play.

Professional con artists, from online bottom feeders to high-end fraudsters, are all looking for the perfect way to attract more victims. In some cases, the hook is the main problem to be over-come. In other scams, the hook is just the beginning, the first step on a winding path to an unsuspected destination, and once someone becomes involved it can already be too late.

The Bait

The most important element of the hook is the bait. For years, I've told my audiences that there's one all-encompassing truth that lies at the heart of all con games: *If I know what you want, I can take everything you have.*

What people want can be broken down into desires, aspi-rations, and essentials. These could be specific to one person or common to everyone, but once a mark's needs have been identified, the con artist has a reason to approach and leverage to use. The bait is often the most important distraction in a con game. Even the most suspicious potential victim must listen to the voices in his head that want, hope, and need an opportunity to be real. No matter how many questions need to be answered, the con artist knows that somewhere inside the mind of his target, there's an unwitting accomplice to the scam, nudging the mark ever closer to the prize.

A powerful element of the hook is the suggestion that there might be something illegal or illicit. This can be rendered down to an honest opportunity as the result of an unfortunate, unexpected, or unknown situation, but the very fact that this doesn't immediately scare off the mark can be powerful leverage later on. For many, the merest notion that something might be illegal is enough to make them walk away, but if the mark is still listening, then the hook is probably working.

There's no use offering the latest and greatest laptop technology to someone who doesn't own a cell phone or trying to sell land to someone who can't afford a mortgage. The bait must be a juicy carrot, big enough to distract from the harsh reality of the stick. That carrot can be something of value to the general public or tailored specifically to one unlucky victim. Advertising cheap electronics will attract suitable victims, as will a fake casting call or a bogus modeling agency. The scammer introduces the bait knowing that the victim is already interested or can guess what the target wants or needs.

The nature of the con dictates how best to rope a mark. Some people need to be encouraged at the beginning but become motivated as soon as they are introduced to the bait; others need to be almost forced into the game. Many scams simply depend on the bait to attract suitable victims, but in many cases, the way that the mark is introduced to an idea dictates their perception for the rest of the con. Therefore, the approach is crucial to a successful swindle. There are three types of hooks used in most con games: the Big Hook, the Soft Hook, and the Straight Hook.

The Big Hook

By far the easiest way to identify a mark is to set up a trap and see who falls in. Simply making something available and spreading the word is enough to attract anyone who's interested. Marrying the bait to the perfect mark becomes a numbers game that depends entirely on what the con artist is pretending to offer, sometimes attracting people without ever having to engage them directly. The success of this kind of hook is often determined by location and timing.

The jam auction, for example, succeeds because it offers well-known items that are already desired by a large number of people. A list of items distributed in a good location with lots of passing traffic is enough to get the unwary into the room. Once the doors are closed and the pitch has begun, most people succumb to well-proven techniques, but the actual hook requires nothing more than a few hired hands, a handful of leaflets, and the promise of cheap PlayStations. A big hook is set for anyone to bite. You throw it into the biggest crowd available and someone will take the bait. Most Internet scams qualify as big hooks because it's all about the percentage of potential marks who respond. Ninety-nine percent of people might not be taken in by an e-mail promising riches, but if the scammer sends a million e-mails, the remaining 1 percent can prove to be incredibly profitable.

The Soft Hook

There are many ways to present someone with an opportunity, and the soft hook attempts to use subtlety to get the mark into the game. Depending on their desire for the bait, this can be anything from an overheard phone call or a passing remark to a cleverly constructed scenario where information is fed to the mark or left where they are sure to find it.

We once targeted people in a cafe near a well-known London antiques market. While waiting to be served at the counter, I spoke on the phone to someone, telling them that I had spotted a piece of "Hollingworth Blueware," worth thousands of pounds, but I didn't have enough cash for it. I gave my imaginary friend directions and ordered a cup of tea. People within earshot soon began to wander out of the cafe and walk toward the market.

Within minutes they were at our stall and looking at a blue plate that had cost us pennies. The phone call got people interested enough to go to the stall, but they were still naturally cautious. Jess played the part of the stall owner, and rather than give them a long story about the plate, we decided to keep it simple and let the marks convince themselves. It worked every time. After each victim bought his plate, we simply replaced it with a duplicate and waited for the next eavesdropper to arrive.

The objective of a soft hook is to have the marks chase the bait, and many of the most effective scams convince the victims that they are in the driver's seat. Once the marks show an interest and start following the prize, they are hooked. But an experienced hustler knows that they are not yet committed to anything; come on too strong and they might easily break away.

The Straight Hook

When time is short or subtlety has failed, the direct approach works best. Whether offering something for sale or giving the mark a choice, the straight hook quickly comes down to a "yes or no" proposition. That's not to say that a refusal is the end of the story; often it's just the beginning if the hustler has a particular angle or some useful leverage. Walk-up scammers approach people on the street to ask for money under some pretext and come right out with their bullshit story about a kid in the hospital or being stranded without gas. They find out in seconds what kind of mark they're dealing with, but in the face of a refusal, they don't always give up, instead trying a new direction. Often a softer approach is most effective after the mark has said no.

A well-structured walk-up scam introduces the scenario up-front and quickly filters out those who refuse to stop or get involved. Once someone stops to listen, the hustler adds more detail before asking for money for a taxi or a train, to pay a restaurant bill, or even a gambling debt. Many people quickly refuse, often lying to say they have no money. This is a natural defense mechanism; in fact, the scammer expects it and is prepared to redirect.

In the UK, I've encountered many walk-up hustlers with all sorts of stories. Late at night, in the heart of London, a guy dressed in cyclist's Lycra carrying a helmet and a messenger bag asked me for help because his bike had been stolen. He even had the broken bicycle lock as evidence of the crime. All he needed was money to get home. I gave him all the change I had and watched him approach another group. I wasn't fooled; to the contrary, despite being certain that he was lying, I genuinely appreciated the trouble he'd gone to for a handful of coins. I found out for sure that he was a scammer when two nights later he approached me in a different part of town with the same story. I advised him to find a different brand of lock as he wasn't having much luck with the one he showed me. He didn't miss a beat, shifting from his stolen bike story to another one about trying to raise money to visit his mother. I could have been there all night as he tried one angle after another, so in the end, I walked away.

Thanks to the success of *The Real Hustle* and becoming recognizable on television, I've developed a temporary defense against walk-ups like this one. One evening, on Shaftsbury Avenue, a guy hits me with a story about his son being in the hospital. As is typical, his objective was to get the story out before I could walk away, but halfway into the details he stopped and tilted his head to look at me properly. Recognizing who I was, he said "never mind" and walked quickly away.

The Pigeon Drop

Sometimes a scam begins with a softer approach but builds to a straight choice for the mark. This becomes a hit-and-run scam once the mark gets wrapped up by the situation. An excellent example of this is the classic Pigeon Drop scam, which gives the victim a "take it or leave it" decision that's hard to walk away from.

Our setup was in a pub near London's South Bank area. Due to the pressures of filming a hidden camera show and the limited time we had to control our mark, the scam needed to be squeezed into a much shorter time frame than was normal, and in order to capture every detail, the entire affair would take place in one location. Nevertheless, the elements of the scam remained true to the classic "drop."

Jess sat alone in the bar, waiting for my signal, while Alex took up a large booth near the corner. He was well dressed with a briefcase and a handful of bogus business cards. I stood near the bar and waited for our mark to settle down and get comfortable. When the time was right, I gave Jess the signal and our little drama began.

Within minutes, Jess was yelling at someone on her phone, something about an airport and it not being worth the risk. Finally she stormed off, shouting that she was "leaving it" as she exited the pub. I waited for a while to let the dust settle before I went to the restroom. On the way back I noticed a bag near where Jess was sitting and very close to where our mark was talking to his friend. I picked up the bag and asked the mark if it belonged to him. It didn't but it gave me the chance to converse for a while before I suggested the mark look inside for some sort of name or address. The bag was full of money. Thousands of pounds stared back at the mark as I reacted but observed his response carefully. Looking around I said, "you know we could hand this into the bar or the local police station but I'll bet all that money that we'll never get a penny if the bag isn't claimed." This prepared the mark for what was to follow, but more important, it tested him to see if he was interested in the money and willing to take action to secure it. He immediately agreed that handing it in was a bad idea. That was not common sense talking—it was greed.

The mark was now following the hook and all I needed to do was convince him to bite. I began to explain that we could take it to the local police station and share any reward or split the money if it was never claimed, but that I was uncertain of exactly what to do. Luckily, my friend "the lawyer" was sitting in a booth nearby. We all approached Alex and I introduced the mark. As we explained our situation, Alex took a moment to pass out his phony business card and flash his lawyer's wig (what lawyers wear in UK courts), which "just happened" to be in his briefcase.

The Pigeon Drop depends on encouraging the sucker to hold onto the cash in return for a good faith deposit that proves he will split the big bag of money when the time comes. Variations use a diamond ring or even a gold brick, but the key is to create a reason not to divide the prize then and there. As per my crooked predecessors, the reason I had concocted was loaded with legal mumbo-jumbo. Alex explained that we were within our rights to keep the money if no claim had been made to either the bar or the local police within two weeks. He went on to say that we could keep the money but that it must not be split up or divided in any way. It was vital that the money be kept together so it could all be returned if claimed. Under these circumstances, we could either keep all of the money or demand a 40 percent reward if the owner came forward.

After we explained what we'd heard Jess say on the phone, Alex nodded knowingly and informed us that the money was going to be taken out of the country and she obviously chickened out. Nobody would come to claim it, Alex told us, but it was essential to keep the cash together as described so the money could legally be ours.

Now the mark could smell the score and was genuinely excited, but who was going to keep the money? Alex suggested that I hold the money, but since we both had a claim, I would need to give the mark a large sum as security, say five hundred pounds. I replied that I didn't have access to that kind of cash, and we all thought about it for a moment. The hook was right there, waiting for the mark to go for it. So far, we'd merely been building up the story until he was utterly convinced; now the trap door was waiting for him to take one more step. The opportunity was there if he wanted to grab it. This approach is an open hook, and when devising these scams I always prefer to allow the mark to come after the deal *on his own*. If that fails, then the straight hook is offered.

"Then how about you?" Alex asked. "Can you get access to five hundred pounds?"

The mark nodded.

"Then why don't you keep the money? I'm happy to act as a witness. If you exchange your details and meet at my office in two weeks, I'll happily oversee the transaction. Does that sound fair?" The mark agreed. He was excited, looking like he couldn't wait to get away with the cash. In his mind, he was probably already spending his share. He might have even been considering ways to keep it all for himself.

As I walked him to the ATM, Alex switched the bag for a duplicate full of newspaper. When the mark left, he could barely believe his luck until a television crew stopped him around the corner and asked the bewildered victim to look in the bag. His elation was short lived.

This scam has worked for decades and depends entirely on keeping the victim focused on the prize. Many who have fallen for this probably never intended to return to divide the cash. Temptation is a powerful force that few of us can resist in the heat of the moment. If you offer steak to a hungry man, there's a good chance he's going to eat.

The closed hook is best employed once a mark is convinced that the opportunity is genuine, but while a quick "yes" is preferred, the experienced con artist knows how to redirect a refusal. Had this mark turned down Alex's suggestion, then we might have reasoned with him for a while or pulled the money away, toying with him until he took action to secure it. It's a lot like dangling a piece of string in front of a cat. She might appear disinterested, but if you persevere and play the game just right, eventually she'll pounce.

On television shows, my objective is to convince someone to commit and to hand over their own money or property, but time is limited: We rarely attempt to steal more than someone has immediate access to, or could be convinced to bring along.

I've often heard that this kind of con game is old-school and isn't played like this any more, but in Kansas in 2009, this exact con was being pulled all over town by two female hustlers, taking thousands of dollars from each of their victims.

Just the Ticket

Let's consider a fairly common confidence trick, but put ourselves into the role of a con artist and apply a few simple strategies to ensure success. For this scenario, we'll employ elements from the Pigeon Drop: a natural switch, a soft hook, and, if that doesn't work, we'll try a straight hook.

In summer 2013, I was in Louisville, Kentucky, for a festival that happened on the same weekend as a very large concert that attracted hordes of teenage girls. Outside the venue were hundreds of girls and their parents hoping to pick up tickets for a decent price. As I walked past the concert hall, I saw dozens of potential marks and began to theorize about how a hustler might prey on their situation. How would you do it? Setting aside your principles for just a moment, how would you try to fleece someone if you knew exactly what they wanted and were willing to pay for it?

Selling fake tickets narrows the potential victims to those willing to pay to see a particular event or show. Many bogus websites have appeared over the years to take advantage of concerts and sporting events. These provide a fake front for a genuine product and allow scammers to take advantage of the disparity between the limited number of tickets and the large demand from excited teenagers. A bogus website simply needs to look the part and function as expected to take your money. This usually happens long before the date of the show so that the fraudsters can reboot their business under another disguise. The protection offered by many credit card companies means you might not lose your money, but many ticket sellers now ask for payment by other means to minimize their own risk. Be extremely cautious, for example, when anyone asks you to make payment via a wire-transfer service for any type of transaction.

This type of ticket fraud isn't much of a scam. It simply takes advantage of something that's in demand and a believable delay in delivering the product. A more traditional con game would be to sell actual tickets on the day of the event. We know that there will be plenty of people looking to buy tickets and that those tickets sell for very high prices from scalpers. Fakes can be extremely convincing, but as technology advances, it becomes more and more difficult to get past the turnstiles unless you're holding the real deal. As scammers, getting inside the venue is not our problem; but we do need a convincing product or we'll never get the money.

First, we need some real tickets. These can be stolen, purchased legitimately, or bought from a friendly scalper. We could even con someone out of the genuine article. Scammers have intercepted people just after buying their tickets and pretended to work for the box office. They explain that they've sold them the wrong seats but offer much better seats in return. The scammer keeps the tickets and walks them back to the front of the line, then leaves to enter the office through a side door. They never return.

Another strategy is to wait outside the venue for a group of fans—anything up to a dozen—and pretend to be part of the crew looking for suitable people to come backstage. Under some pretext, the hustler would convince the group that they can watch the whole show from the VIP area and exchange their real tickets for convincing but entirely fake "All-Access" passes. The real tickets would then be sold to other unsuspecting fans who would later find themselves sitting in stolen seats.

Let's say we have obtained a pair of real tickets long enough in advance to make some half-decent copies. These fakes might not fool anyone on their own, but the mark won't see them until it's too late. In addition, we would obtain some envelopes and print the logo of a well-known ticket agent on all of them. We put the genuine tickets in one envelope and the copies in another. Now all we need is someone who really needs to see the show.

Consider for a moment how you would act in this situation, as the buyer. What are your questions? How do you make sure they're real or not stolen? Unless you are intimately familiar with the tickets being sold (which is rare), it's very difficult to identify a fake. A few years ago I watched an interview with an anti-fraud detective who placed a fake ticket beside a real one. On camera, he commented that "it's hard to believe that someone could fall for this" but this attitude fails to consider that the victims may never have seen a real ticket, let alone had one to compare. It's also possible that the tickets they purchased were absolutely real when they examined them, as you will see.

A rank hustler will simply farm out fake tickets to anyone who takes them at face value. In many cases, this is a charmless, by-the-numbers fraud that depends on the victim not to ask too many questions. A more sophisticated scammer would take fewer chances, make more money, and be a lot more convincing. In order to do this, he needs to understand how the victim will think during the transaction.

Walk-ups can be difficult. Approaching anyone cold with a proposition activates people's defenses and puts them on guard. In this scenario, this is less of a problem since walking around outside the venue shouting "Tickets!" will attract people desperate to see the show. Of course this also places the seller in the easiest spot for police or a wised-up sucker to find them but in the days or hours leading up to a big event, there are many opportunities to approach and sell our bogus tickets.

For this scam, we will make the mark come to us; we will quickly answer any suspicions, gain her trust, and apply the simplest but most common strategy to secure the victim's money. All we'll need is a cell phone.

In Louisville, the city was lousy with teenage girls excited to see their favorite band. By lunchtime the restaurants were full of obvious targets, most of whom probably already had a ticket but might be accompanied by someone who did not or would know plenty of people who might want one. These are perfect marks for this scam because they have access to a real ticket, and since we have gone to the trouble of securing the real thing, we should play this to maximum advantage. We actually want the suckers to compare our tickets to their own.

I go for a smart, casual look with jeans, shirt, and a suit jacket to project the right image. I'm in my early forties so I'm perfect to act as the father of a fan who can't make the show. This should be something that will resonate with the victim, perhaps even gain her sympathy without raising questions. There's nothing a con artist won't say to get your money, but it's important not to play our hand too strong or we'll attract suspicion.

Walking from one place to another, it's easy to find groups of people who might be interested, and a little time spent observing and listening can pay dividends. Once we've identified our target, it's time to make a phone call. My end of the conversation might go like this:

Yes, yes. I picked up the tickets. I don't know what to do. I asked some people outside but they all have tickets. I'll probably have to wait until tonight and hope there's someone then. What? I have no idea, I've never tried to sell tickets before! I'll wait and see but if the office calls, I have to go. Maybe she can get her money back. Okay, I'll call.

This conversation with my imaginary wife regarding tickets for my imaginary daughter is all for the benefit of anyone in earshot, and it will either attract their attention or soften my approach if I still need to do the legwork.

Next, I order a soft drink and wait to see if I have anyone's attention. In most cases I would have singled out a suitable target and would know very quickly if she were interested. They would either come up to me or might be discussing what they heard. Sometimes all I need to observe is that they stop to listen to my call, but once I hang up, I need to wait and see what happens.

Softening the approach can be an important step, especially with those who tend to especially dislike cold calls and unexpected interruptions. There's a certain band of society that resists outside human interaction generally. How many of us don't even know the names of our closest neighbors? For this type of person, making a connection requires an understanding of what will engage the mark.

Giving them a little information in advance about who and what you are can be used against you. The most important objective, from the scammers' point of view, is to ensure they identify with you somehow and believe that you don't want anything from them. That's especially important in a simple scam like this. We could easily just walk from bar to bar and keep asking groups of people if they want to buy tickets, and this is how many hustlers operate. The problem is that they attract attention and they activate suspicion. With a little grift-sense we can narrow our target search, encourage trust, and perhaps even sell our fakes to people who *already have tickets*.

The best-case scenario after our phone call is that someone who needs a ticket walks up and engages us directly. This is perfect for our needs as it puts the mark in the position of establishing herself first and clearly indicates that she has been hooked by the bait. If this doesn't happen, we still have a powerful option available to us, which is to ask her advice. This ploy doesn't need us to establish our story with the phone call, but it becomes more powerful when the intended victim thinks she already knows something about my situation.

Let's take the difficult path. No one approaches me but I sense genuine interest in my predicament from the next table: a middle-aged woman of above average means with her daughter and two of her friends. I have no doubt they all have tickets to the show, but we can still secure a sale. Here's how I would proceed:

I stand up while checking my phone and adopt an image of impatience. In my mind, I have been summoned to the office for some sort of work emergency and I won't be able to wait around to sell my daughter's ticket. I'm not going to say any of this unless I need to, but human beings are able to sense body language; putting myself in this frame of mind can be a powerful psychological ally. I have prepared my story but I avoid scripting anything too clearly as this can sound false and memorized. Instead I try to clearly understand the scenario and stick to that story.

Here's how things might pan out when I walk up to the mark:
ME: Excuse me.
MARK: Yes?
ME: Sorry to bother you but do you happen to be going to the concert tonight?
MARK: Yes, we are.

ME: You wouldn't happen to know anywhere that would buy my daughter's tickets? A record shop or . . . I don't know.

This is a soft hook. In one, clear sentence, I've told them I have tickets for sale and suggested an explanation for where they've come from, but I've done it *without making a direct offer.* Instead, I've asked for advice and I'm watching to see if anyone appears interested.

MARK: She can't go?

ME: Excuse me?

I heard her the first time but making people repeat something gives me a better read on their level of interest.

MARK: Your daughter can't go?

ME: She broke her collarbone. Hockey. The ticket company wouldn't refund them so I had to pick them up for her.

Here I play for sympathy but not too strong. That's a personal choice, but professional scammers have no shame in proclaiming their imaginary children, grannies, or partners as dead if it might lead to a profit.

MARK: How much were they?

More like a nibble than a bite but it's enough. I know they already have tickets so this question is more about my veracity. They're definitely interested.

ME: Let me check. Where's the price?

I take out the envelope and look at the genuine tickets. I show them to someone so they can spot the price for me, but more important, I've put the tickets into their hands, which makes it much harder for them to refuse if they really want them. If I'm lucky, someone at the table needs a pair of tickets, but the bait is already on the table and there's more than one way to hook our fish.

Let's imagine they don't jump at the chance right away. The soft hook is almost played out.

MARK: There will be people outside the concert, later. I'm sure you can sell them there.

ME: No, I need to get to work. You don't know anyone who wants to go?

If they did, I'd suggest calling them to see if they wanted my tickets, but it's important not to hang around too long. I have one last chance to get the money.

ME: Outside the concert, do they sell these for the normal price or charge more?

MARK: They charge a lot more. Last year they were charging three hundred dollars!

Here comes the straight hook:

ME: You guys are going to the show. Do you want to buy these and sell them tonight? You can make a lot of money—or sell them to someone who deserves to see it without getting ripped off.

It's now a direct take it or leave it proposition. I've worded it so it speaks to both their desire to make a profit and to their conscience. They could make a lot of money or they could let someone have them for a fair price and avoid being scalped. It's important not to let this moment become awkward. Some potential marks may automatically say no while others are still considering the idea as I'm putting the tickets away and thanking them for their time. As I go to my pocket, I switch the envelope with the real tickets for one containing fakes. This is a simple switch that anyone can physically pull off but takes real skill to perform naturally, without attracting suspicion. I've seen actors and magicians fall to pieces and suffer the shakes in these situations; deception, even when it seems easy, is extremely difficult in the heat of the moment. With enough experience and a little sleight of hand, a scammer could switch the tickets without replacing the envelope in his pocket. It's even possible without the envelope at all, but that would leave the fakes in the open and a good con artist would prefer to avoid that.

This little scam can be repeated a dozen times in as many different places, each scoring the face value of the real tickets. If two tickets cost $150, then we're close to two grand for a couple of hours of work. Finally we scalp the real tickets to someone for double their price and we're on our way to a steak dinner.

In this example, I've deliberately played out most of the likely outcomes, but if I choose my marks carefully and relate to them effectively, the road tends to be much smoother. Once I've made it clear that I'm unable to use or sell the tickets, chances are excellent that they will try to *convince me* to sell.

What can we learn from this? How does putting ourselves in the hustler's shoes help us? The first thing we know is not to judge an offer by how the other person looks. A genuine, honestly acquired ticket might come from anyone. We also know that even if the ticket is real, it might be exchanged for a fake when we're distracted, but even if we hold on to the ticket, it might turn out to be stolen.

There are so many ways to work a con like this one that the only real defense is to not get involved and to politely decline any unsolicited offers, even if it's something you really, really want. In a con game, it's not just a matter of what you are being offered; the *circumstances* of that opportunity may be just as fake as the prize. None of us believe we can be easily manipulated, but con artists know this and can use this belief as a powerful weapon against us.

Individual circumstances play a large part in the hook part of the process. In the ticket scam we know that on one particular day there will be a large number of people who either want to see a show or know lots of people who do. With the Pigeon Drop, we know that people need money and are easily attracted to an opportunity once they believe the circumstances. Real-life con artists prey on almost any situation where they can identify a clear need or desire, and they have no standard of common decency. After a natural disaster, they pretend to raise money for those in need; they trawl obituaries to steal from the recently bereaved; they offer phony cures to desperate people with real diseases.

In all cases, the hustler is taking advantage of what the victims want. In Charleston, Uncle Barry wanted to protect his nephew and check out a potential business deal. Despite his air of indifference, I knew he could smell a potential opportunity but wanted to know a lot more. If his suspicions about me laundering money for the Mob were confirmed in any way, he was sure to walk away, but I had prepared a very convincing journey for Barry. Once he agreed to come along for the ride, he was hooked.

THE LINE

$\mathcal{M}$y driver picked up Uncle Barry and Randy at their hotel and drove a few miles out of town to Lowndes Grove, a historic South Carolina landmark that's often rented out for weddings and private events. The large white house at the heart of the property overlooks an enormous lawn, gardens, and a nearby dock. It was the perfect location to introduce Barry to one of my investors.

We had rented the place for just two hours—a small price to pay for millions of dollars in credibility. Inside, the house was almost empty, ready for any kind of function or event, so we set up a few pieces of patio furniture on the grass. By the time we arrived, John and our southern belle, Angie, who was almost wearing a tiny bikini, were in character as a wealthy business-man and his beautiful wife.

As he pulled into the estate and drove around the front lawn, Barry's reaction was everything I'd hoped for. He was sold on John's wealth from the moment he passed through the gates. But the game was still ours to lose. A slip-up or crack in the story might easily ignite Barry's suspicion. Charming, intelli-gent, and casual about his wealth, John was the consummate international investor, soon making Barry feel welcome and respected. Nothing was left to chance; we kept Barry focused on the surroundings, especially Angie's figure as she lay nearby, soaking up the sun.

After a few introductions, John quickly shifted the conversation toward business, giving Uncle Barry a short history of his foreign land investments and why he needed to move money out of certain countries using my services to minimize any financial loss. Barry then explained what he did for a living and was starting to be much more involved in the conversation. This was a different Barry from the one I'd met in the morning. Thanks to no more than a rented house and a tiny swimsuit, in a few short hours, Barry had opened up.

Our objective at this meeting wasn't just to lend credibility to my story; it was to begin playing Barry in an effort to make him play back. I also wanted to address his concerns about money laundering and my business having "Mafia written all over it." I saw this as an opportunity to give the deal further veracity by turning the tables on Barry.

Once the usual pleasantries were out of the way, I shifted the conversation toward one of my biggest concerns about new clients like Randy and his Uncle Barry. Apologizing in advance, I asked them both if they had a criminal record. This question served several purposes, but its primary goal was to test Barry's reaction. Would he revert to the quiet, shrugging sphinx I'd shared breakfast with, or would he assure us that he was a suitable candidate?

This is an important test because the question is both direct and potentially offensive. Any response at all can be used to either redirect or manipulate the mark into a deeper commitment. Had he become angry, I would have diffused the situation quickly while watching to see if he was using that reaction as a way out. Many people use high emotions as an escape route or a means to avoid certain subjects, but they also use demonstrative feelings such as anger to support their position, especially when their reputation or position is questioned. I was prepared for this, but Barry's response was much friendlier. He laughed, assured us of his spotless record, and made it perfectly clear that he wanted to know more. The purpose of this meeting was to shift Barry into the position of wanting to impress us. After building Barry's confidence to this point, all I needed was for him to take a few baby steps in our direction and he was on his way to being conned.

While I explained a few details about my money transfer system, John appeared to catch up on e-mails before standing to excuse himself. John bid us farewell and returned to the house with Angie. The meeting was over, but Barry was inching closer to the prize. The story was starting to work and in the car, monitored by our hidden cameras, Uncle Barry told Randy, "This is some serious money." Next, I needed to build on these foundations until the time was right to make Barry an offer he wouldn't refuse.

In addition to Lowndes Grove, we had also rented a local store that was a bank at one time, complete with an impressive vault and a door that weighed several tons. The location was perfect, just a short walk to the real bank with escape routes in four directions. A little set dressing and a few bad checks to pay for it all and we could quickly create a convincing backdrop for anyone who became tangled in our web. I'd invited Randy and his Uncle Barry along for a more formal meeting and to perhaps get the ball rolling, but my real objective was to put the deal onto the table and force Barry to take the reins away from his nephew. I had much less time to play the mark than I needed, so there was a real chance he might break away if I came on too strong.

The office was incredibly convincing, fully furnished and dressed with some homemade certificates. The shelves of the safe were stacked high with photocopied money from around the world and under the desk were two duplicate flight cases ready for the sting. After hiring a few locals to play small parts in our little play, the stage was set and ready for my audience of one. Our actress, Robin, had prepared for her role as a regular client who'd received several large amounts of money in the past. When Barry arrived, we made sure he had a few moments to chat with her before being whisked away to conclude our latest transfer. This gave Barry and Randy a few moments to take in the sights as large amounts of money were counted from the cashier's cage for Robin to take to the bank. If a picture is worth a thousand words, then a convincing "big store" might be worth a million dollars. Sometimes this can backfire when actually seeing the cash turns an interesting idea into a frightening reality; Uncle Barry immediately began to feel things were moving too quickly.

After a brief chat, I sent Robin on her way and invited Randy and his uncle to join me. I had two goals in this meeting: to explain the deal and to secure interest from Uncle Barry. All I needed was the simplest gesture of commitment to lean upon, but if Barry couldn't stand the heat, the whole game was a bust and I didn't have the luxury of time. Hidden cameras and production crews are extremely expensive and it's not feasible to follow a con for weeks without an enormous bankroll. Had this been the real deal, I'd have fifty marks lined up for months, all singing my "free money" song before taking them down simultaneously and heading to the Bahamas.

In Charleston, I had two days and one chance to fleece my mark. After explaining to Barry about international money transfers and unusual tax laws, I was forced to ask if he would be interested. The answer was exactly what I was afraid of. Barry felt he hadn't had enough time to absorb everything and was stalling the process, which is the smart thing to do; I had no choice but to increase the pressure and hope Uncle Barry didn't run for the exit. My phone rang and I stepped into the back office to take an imaginary call. With Barry and his nephew still in earshot, I pretended to talk to a money-receiving client who was letting me down. I shouted and I swore, but as I yelled at myself down an empty line, it soon became clear that there was nothing more I could do. I hung up and returned to my potential mark, who had been listening to the whole thing.

Now was my best chance to get Uncle Barry into the game. All I needed was for him to show a little interest, but, as soon as I was back at the desk, he continued right where we left off. Seemingly concerned about my fake phone call, I acted distant and unable to concentrate; I then offered to take Randy and Barry out for dinner to talk further. By way of explanation, I commented on my delinquent client who was not going to be in Charleston in time to receive John's transfer. Genial to the last, Barry joked that he'd be happy to take the money; I quickly latched onto this passing remark as a way to make Barry an offer. This was a big mistake.

Appearing to be inspired by Barry's joke, I asked him outright if he could get twenty thousand dollars before the end of the day. Right away, my mark was reeling and I knew this meant a refusal. I'd played him too hard and too fast and the more I tried to keep moving forward, the harder Barry hit the brakes. Still friendly and keen to stay involved, Barry just couldn't throw down such a large amount so quickly without compromising his business instincts. Before I could redirect, he was walking out the door with his nephew. Barry had just been wisecracking and I'd hit him with too much, too soon.

The whole scam was beginning to collapse. In the back room, the producers, who had been monitoring every second, as the British say, were having kittens. The whole production sat on a knife's edge, because if we had to bring in another mark, it was going to cost a fortune. This time, I had to agree that things weren't looking good.

But just as we were considering plan B, our cameraman on the street reported that Uncle Barry was coming back.

Line Dancing

The line is about adding layers to the story, like piling comforters onto a mark until he's warm and cozy, and most important, unable to move under the weight. The longer you play a mark, the greater the risk of them waking up or chickening out, but the extra time has a benefit as well; it also offers a chance to increase the stakes and nurture deeper faith in the lie. Along the way there are many tiny hurdles to guide the victim over before they have confidence in the deal that's being offered. Later, when trying to explain what happened, the victim often describes these hurdles piled on top of one another, like an enormous height that only a fool would jump from. This is where the real con game is played.

The hook is about getting the mark involved. The line is about building that interest into something impossible to resist. The con artist uses a variety of methods to grow the commitment, which is determined by the con man's story and his deepening relationship with the mark. An experienced scammer knows how to manipulate the victim's perspective, clamping down or stepping back as needed. Con men are adaptable, but once even a rank grifter has successfully muddled through a con game, he simply repeats the same line for the next sucker. Hustlers know from experience what the most likely outcome will be because people's actions are sadly predictable when presented with proven scenarios.

The Story

One of the most powerful aspects of a great con game is how it often *uses the truth to support a lie.*

In 1920s Paris, Count Victor Lustig, one of history's most notorious con artists, spotted a newspaper story suggesting that repairs for the Eiffel Tower could be too expensive and that the government might decide to scrap the monument. Lustig, who knew the tower was never originally intended to be a permanent landmark, saw an opportunity to construct a powerful lie based on verifiable facts.

He adopted the role of a French bureaucrat, entrusted with the delicate task of arranging to disassemble the tower, and contacted several scrap merchants with the offer of a lifetime, nicely printed on official-looking headed notepaper.

Each merchant was told to keep the situation secret for fear of public outrage, and distracted by enormous potential profits, they all agreed. Lustig received a quote from each of these businessmen to buy the tower and even convinced them to pay a healthy bribe or two. After building their confidence, Lustig picked out his best mark, accepted his offer, and bought a ticket to Austria to escape with the money. After a few weeks, it became apparent that the mark, André Poisson, had not reported Victor to the French authorities, perhaps too ashamed to admit being conned. Lustig seized on this opportunity and returned to Paris, selling the Eiffel Tower to five more suckers before fleeing to the United States once the police were finally called.

All of this hinged on a simple story, which was based on fact. The Eiffel Tower was never intended to be a permanent part of the Paris skyline, was badly in need of repair, and according to a single line in a newspaper report, the government apparently had considered selling it for scrap. All of this was true and could be easily checked or demonstrated, allowing a master con man to invent an entirely false scenario with an attractive prize and the chance to hit several marks simultaneously.

Once a mark's attention has been secured, the con man will try to satisfy and manipulate his curiosity. People are bound to have concerns or be naturally suspicious, but their desire for the bait will continue to drive them forward as long as there's fuel in the engine. If I were to say "there's scientific proof that *Star Trek*–style teleportation devices were now real and already being manufactured," this might spark a mark's interest, but if I can't follow that up with a plausible explanation that both holds his attention *and* deepens his interest, then he will likely dismiss it and walk away. The quality of proof that I need varies depending on a mark's existing knowledge or beliefs, but even with someone who really knows a subject, there are ways to keep him on the hook and following the line.

The lie needs to be carefully constructed, difficult to disprove, and hidden within folds of fact and truth. Blatant lies may work when the con is short and the mark is under constant control, but when the line is longer and the mark has time to think about things, the fraud needs to be carefully camouflaged.

I needed to give Uncle Barry a plausible reason for transferring large amounts of money to a third party, which is a key element of the well-known Nigerian prince or 419 scam. I already had the location and my phony office, but how could I convince this businessman that a stranger would send him a large sum of money and let him keep 40 percent? The answer turned out to be buried in US tax law. Any transaction of ten thousand dollars or more is automatically referred to the government, and even if it's a gift, taxes may be taken from it. This does not apply to international monetary gifts, for which there is no tax liability. This explained how my clients could accept the funds but not why John would send them with such an enormous loss.

So I made up a story based loosely on fact. Foreign investors sometimes find it difficult to move money out of certain countries. To protect John (and my bullshit story) I couldn't say what the countries were, only that the penalties for sending money out were crippling unless they were being sent to a separate entity. An essential part of the deal was that John had to be able to illustrate that he was paying for the privilege elsewhere and had no direct connection to the receiver. In short, losing 40 percent in the United States would save John from losing 70 percent abroad. I also told Barry that this only works within certain limits, so that John has to undertake dozens of transactions to release all of his money.

I had all the trappings of a genuine financial expert, someone who knows what he's doing and has been doing so successfully for a long time. The setting and the situation were a perfect marriage for my story. If you're an accountant, a stockbroker, or a banker, your tongue might be clicking loudly as you read this or perhaps you're shaking your head so violently that you might cause yourself an injury. This scam isn't for you, obviously, but I'd bet a cup of coffee and a fresh doughnut that you could easily convince a layman to buy it.

It's remarkably easy to tell a lie when it is accompanied by something real that appears to support that lie. Con artists have a talent for spotting facts that can be distorted in their favor. The believability of a good scam depends on roping the right mark and telling him something he is either inclined to believe or can be convinced of using proven techniques that have a powerful influence over anyone under the right circumstances.

The process goes something like this:

$$X + Y = Z$$
$$X = \text{a fact}$$
$$Y = \text{a lie (that in some way relates to the fact)}$$
$$Z = \text{a desire}$$

I know people want Z.
They know X is true.
Y can be used to make Z seem real or attainable.
Therefore I can feasibly prove that X plus Y equals Z.

Borrowing the truth is easy, but it has to be complemented by a falsehood to be effective. The truth can be used to support a scam or distorted until it leads the mark to the wrong conclusion. Consider all of the fad diets that use science to support their unsubstantiated claims. Whenever there's a news story about a theory relating to weight loss, it's only a matter of time before it is being sold as fact for three easy payments of $39.99. Science is an easy tool for anyone who wishes to support a questionable theory or back up an outright lie for the public; it's almost certain that the public or the media will not dedicate long hours to verify anything. If I wanted to prove any claim, I could simply pull random equations from the Internet and use a search engine to compile seemingly related data that might feasibly support whatever I'm trying to sell. I can guarantee that the simple quantity of apparent "facts" would be enough to convince many people that it could be true.

As an expert in a couple of fields, I am used to seeing these subjects misrepresented in the media. Since I understand these topics enough to see through gaping holes, fallacies, or agenda-driven biases, I'm perfectly placed to comment on the accuracy of what's being written. The problem is, as any expert will tell you, no one wants to hear the boring truth when the lie is fascinating. I've grown to be suspicious of almost anything that I read, and if something interests me, I'll do a little research to see if the story holds up. Along the way I am constantly stumbling upon perfect scenarios for a con game. Diet pills claim to help you burn fat "as part of a balanced diet" but one could argue that it's more likely to be the improved diet that helps people lose weight than the powdered snake-oil being peddled.

Healthier regime (X) plus unproven supplement (Y) equals guaranteed results (Z).

Recently I read some fascinating research about how sugars and fats affect the body and that the combination of these can be as addicting as cocaine. Immediately I conjured the idea of a pill that would counteract this addiction and allow people to eat without succumbing to these urges. Naturally, directions for use would stipulate that my worthless placebos be used "as part of a balanced diet." Diet scams perfectly illustrate how people's desires outweigh their common sense, since if a genuine, safe, and scientifically proven method of easy weight loss was discovered tomorrow, it would be bigger than Viagra.

Hiding in Plain Sight

A con artist can introduce information from any source that the mark would accept as believable; that information can either misrepresent the truth, be manipulated to support the scam, or entirely manufactured. There are several ways to feed the victim what he needs to know or control exposure to any contradictory information. A con artist can use facts that are obvious, easily available, or he may have to point them out himself. However, the hustler can also be more subtle—planting the information in a way that the mark comes to believe he's learned something on his own. In this case, the mark may believe he has exclusive knowledge that he can use, perhaps as leverage. In some cases, con artists would even orchestrate conversations within earshot of their victim, feeding them proof or additional information to give the mark greater confidence.

This strategy has been used by companies who pay actors to loudly discuss their hotel, restaurant or other services on a busy train. One possibly apocryphal story concerns a creative screenwriter who spent days traveling up and down elevators and eating in restaurants filled with Hollywood types, discussing an incredible new script that's "doing the rounds." By the following week, his agent was overwhelmed by requests to read it.

A powerful strategy is for the con artist to only tell the mark what's true (X) and have him receive the false information (Y) from another source. If the source that's feeding the lie appears to be completely separate, then the mark's inclination is to believe the story. Once upon a time, a con artist might have planted a story in the newspaper or even printed duplicates with information added purely for their mark; today it's extremely easy to design a believable website filled with anything a hustler needs to convince a mark. Links can point to genuine sources or to other bogus sites to verify any lie or exaggerated truth. While this could be tailored for any target, there are thousands of websites designed purely to attract victims via search engines, with all manner of claims to extend life expectancy, help people lose weight, or predict the future. Many of these sites remain within the law by posting disclaimers that are either cleverly hidden, camouflaged, or minimized. Many sites appear to be based in the home country of its target audience but are actually hosted in countries with no laws to prevent their activity.

It's not just *what* the mark is told but *how* he is told it. Consider a counterfeit hundred-dollar bill, made of perfect paper and printed to the highest standards. It looks real and it feels exactly like other bills, but when compared with genuine c-notes, the fake can easily be spotted. But if the con artist controls how, when, and why the mark handles the counterfeit, then it can pass for the real thing. Perhaps I'd start by handing over the "funny-money," rushing them to put it in their wallet before handing over a real bill, thus avoiding a direct comparison. Similarly, I could start with twenty real hundreds and wait until they're in the mark's wallet before introducing the fakes. I could slip the counterfeit into the middle of a pile, then distract or force the mark to count quickly. I could even let the mark test a real bill, then switch it as they reach for their wallet (as per the "ticket scam"). I could be even more creative and plant a fake hundred behind the bar so the mark can compare the fake I give him to another one, apparently from the cash register.

A con man treats information the same way as he would a fake (or real) hundred-dollar bill, manipulating what you discover, and how and when you discover it. If the mark is particularly challenging, then a con artist might focus on what he can prove for a while; for a more gullible victim, the lie would be given greater prominence. In the case of my re-invented Spanish Prisoner scam for Uncle Barry, I kept him focused on what he could see and supported my entire story with a genuine US tax law and vague facts about moving money overseas. This was enough veracity for the average mark. An accountant would certainly need more proof, while a criminal might only need to smell the money to get involved. The line is a game played between hustlers and their intended victim with only two possible outcomes: the con men win or both parties lose.*

Inside the Bubble

A problem with longer cons is that the mark cannot be under constant supervision. He could stumble upon the truth or be

---

* In actual fact, the mark only thinks he loses an opportunity when, in fact, he probably just dodged a bullet.

talked out of the deal by a third party. Isolating the mark from influences outside of the hustlers' control is often essential. The easiest way to accomplish this is by building secrecy into the story. Victor Lustig used the threat of political scandal to keep his marks from talking to others and notorious con artist Yellow Kid Weil concocted many scenarios that were supposedly being kept secret from the public for one reason or another. Success of the con is often dependent on not sharing information that is completely false. If the mark does as instructed, he never has the opportunity to properly verify information. This tactic can also explain away conflicting facts, which is why "the secrets they don't want you to know" is a favorite phrase among questionable pitchmen.

Clearly, if the mark does as he's told, he does not seek advice outside the "con bubble" that the hustlers have created. It also helps to explain why certain facts cannot be verified: after all, they are secret knowledge that the con artist is sharing with the mark for their mutual benefit. For example, inside information that might influence someone to buy or sell shares could be easy to invent and difficult to verify.

Another approach is to anticipate conflicting information and address it *before* the mark can stumble upon it himself. This prepares the victim to dismiss anything that disproves the story. Additionally, a mark with a strong desire for the bait is easier to fool; if he really wants the prize, then the mark is already biased toward positive proof. A con man who preempts his doubts by preparing him to ignore contradictory information is likely to succeed.

All of these ploys serve another purpose: to isolate the mark. Inside the con artist's bubble, there is hope and opportunity and confidence; outside the bubble there is doubt and fear. Many con games succeed by making the bubble preferable to harsh realities and cold truths. Often, when a scam is over and the mark has been taken, the loss of that comfortable, hope-filled bubble hurts the mark as much as any betrayal of trust or loss of money. This is why it can be infuriatingly difficult to talk someone out of a scam once they are emotionally committed to it. In the right circumstances, if the con artists have done their job well, the bubble can only be burst from the inside and no amount of outside influence can help. How hustlers control both the elements of their story and how the mark perceives these elements are vitally important to the success of the line. In some cases, the entire scam depends on keeping the mark on that line, in order to slowly bleed them dry.

Believe

Of all the cons I've pulled on *The Real Hustle*, those that exposed phony psychics were, for me, the most difficult and personally damaging. We always took great care of our subjects on the show, carefully maneuvering them to the right locations under the best circumstances, blissfully unaware that they were about to be secretly filmed and scammed. After each con, a producer would approach the mark and gently explain that everything was going to be okay, that their friends or family were nearby and they hadn't really lost anything. For most of the scams, this was an easy process because sheer relief was a powerful factor, but when I pretended to have psychic powers, and hopes and dreams and fears and wonder were being manipulated, then talking someone down required much more care. In the end, the mark was always relieved and keen to take part, but emotions were usually high and I tried to stay out of the way until the mark calmed down. Personally, I was a complete mess afterward.

During these scams I would employ powerful techniques such as cold reading, using props to help prove my abilities. For one of our most effective cons, we injected red food dye into an egg and told the mark I could read her future by breaking eggs onto a plate. One egg was for health, another for relationships, and the third egg was for financial matters. I asked the mark which egg she wanted me to read first and she chose health. I cracked the egg and poured out the white and the yolk, commenting on how the yolk landed on the plate, its color and shape, and the thickness of the egg white. I analyzed the cracks created when breaking the egg and delivered a cold reading as if guided by these observations.

Cold reading is the art of telling people seemingly specific and accurate information that appears to relate to them personally. These readings are actually a cleverly constructed blend of general statements and universal truths tailored to the mark and accompanied by secretly obtained facts, easily deduced information, or guesses based on the experience of the cold reader. This can be a consciously learned skill that develops over time or a natural talent for so-called "shut-eyes" who genuinely believe in their own powers.

Whether the supposed clairvoyant sees the readings as a psychological tool, a deliberate deception, or a real psychic gift, the impact on the person receiving the reading can be devastating. As I read the patterns of fragmented shell and seemingly divined knowledge from the dissolving yolk, the mark leaned forward, absorbing every word and hoping for answers to her unspoken questions. Years earlier, magician, mentalist, and part-time medium Jules Lenier had taught me how to use every grain of information to read a "client." His chosen props were tarot cards or the client's palm, and he had a devilishly simple trick to determine what someone was really interested in before the reading even began. He would point out the lines on their hands, explain what each one represented, and then asked where they would like to begin. For the requested line he'd point out other aspects of the hand related to that line and again asked them where to start his reading. This simple process told Jules what the client was most interested in and where he should concentrate his efforts for a convincing reading. With the eggs I used the same ploy and knew immediately that there were matters of health that concerned our mark.

For me, this was useful for the opposite reason. I wanted to avoid anything that was too sensitive; I only needed to get the money while Jules's goal was entertainment. For many "psychic" scammers, such information helps them to hook their victim and keep them on the line indefinitely.

Demonstrating supposed psychic powers is playing with fire. Even when performed by expert magicians or mentalists in the context of a show, people often want to believe that what they're seeing is real. Max Maven is one of the greatest living exponents of mentalism and a highly respected thinker and performer in the magic community. After thousands of shows, he made the observation that even if the performer were wearing a bright red nose, someone would eventually approach him after the show and ask for a personal "reading." This "red nose theory of mentalism" is often discussed by entertainers eager to avoid misleading the public. I think that what happens on stage should stay there and that the audience is responsible for what they believe before and after the show. Others disagree and open their performances with a disclaimer, while some skew their powers toward psychological abilities that, while easier for a modern audience to accept, are just as fantastic as any supposed psychic abilities.

For me, this was especially difficult as there was no stage and no red nose. I was playing this for real; as I read imaginary signs in the first two eggs, it was little comfort to me that the truth was going to eventually be revealed. My reading was working all too well and I could feel the power it was having over the mark. Later I would reflect on how easy it would have been to abuse that power and heartlessly manipulate someone over time. The third egg, however, changed everything.

The mark had asked me to discuss health first, and I gave a solid, positive reading, telling her there was nothing ominous on the horizon. I wanted to move quickly past matters of health and give a more personal reading regarding relationships before breaking open the egg that would supposedly reveal her financial future. When I cracked the last egg and poured the dark, bloody innards onto the plate, the reaction was visceral. She gasped and I heard the breath become trapped in her throat as her eyes widened, reflecting genuine fear. I felt like a complete jerk, but the cameras were rolling and the end was near. I told her the blood only indicated a possible problem, but that she could easily resolve this. I wanted to explain how I could bless some of her money, that she could lock it away until the danger was passed and that if she did as I instructed, everything would be fine, but all she wanted to know was, "Are my kids going to be okay?" Suckered by a well-designed set and long-proven psychology, she was convinced enough to be genuinely concerned about the bright red omen I had just spilled onto a plate. Finances be damned, all this lady cared about was the welfare of her children.

It took several minutes to completely assure her that only her money was at risk. I gave her the pitch and asked her to bring as much cash as she could so that I could cleanse it. When she left to get the money, I took a few moments to gather my thoughts and prepare for the final phase of the scam, where Alex and I would switch her money for pieces of newspaper. While we waited for her to return I contemplated just how easy it would be to take horrible advantage of somebody with this kind of scam. Had I been a real con artist, I would certainly have used the mark's fear for her children as leverage. I would probably have isolated her from her family by insisting she keep our consultations secret and then bled her dry over time rather than going for quick cash. A genuine hustler couldn't care less about psychological damage, ethics, or decency. All that matters to them is GTFM: *Get The Fucking Money.*

The mark returned, we went through the motions of our invented ceremony to wash her money of negative energy, and switched it and locked the pieces of newspaper in a box, which was to be hidden under her bed for at least a year. Happy and grateful, she left to do as instructed. My producer and a camera crew greeted her outside.

Inside the store, I sat down and took a deep breath. I hated how this scam made me feel and was still reflecting on the lessons I'd learned when the mark threw open the door and charged back into the office. Her face was bright red and her eyes were on fire, but it wasn't just anger. She was hurt. Betrayed. It always takes time for people to calm down after I've conned them, but this type of scam was different, more intense. Worst of all, the producer and the camera crew, working on instinct, followed to film the confrontation.

"Why? Why would you do that? Why would you say something like that?" I remember her saying. She was hurt, perhaps scared, but at the same time, fearless. I talked softly, calmed her down, and the crew took her outside for her interview. Afterward, we sat down and I explained the techniques I'd used, from psychology to a syringe filled with blood. I explained how I had tried to avoid anything too sensitive or personal, but as she accurately observed, that was not in my control. It was up to her to connect anything I said to what she was thinking or feeling; I had no sway over how personal or sensitive that might be. My objective has always been to expose and demonstrate these scams, but clearly that had backfired.

Psychic scammers don't always hit and run. This particularly heinous type of con game grants the hustler so much power over their victims that the scam can sometimes continue indefinitely. Scams of this nature are all about the line and creating a constant flow of money from the mark. If the victim goes broke, wakes up to the con, or someone successfully intervenes, then the game is up and the hustlers move on.

Marilyn Baldwin, tireless anti-scam crusader and founder of Think Jessica, a well-organized publicity campaign to highlight the dangers of junk mail scams, lost her mother to hustlers who put her onto a "sucker list" when she replied to a piece of unsolicited mail. Over time the scammers told Jessica that her family didn't want her to have her own money, were jealous of her impending good fortune, and wouldn't let her make her own decisions. This played on her age, senility, and wavering feelings of self-worth. Soon, she was receiving several bags of junk mail per day. Worst of all, it gradually tainted the relationship between Jessica and her family, and the more Marilyn tried to reason with her mother, the more secretive and suspicious she became. After losing thousands to fake competitions and building a crippling commitment to fees for various scams, Jessica had started communicating with "clairvoyants" who demanded money to protect her from impending disaster or evil forces. These psychic crooks had a devastating effect on Jessica's relationship with her family until, by the end, she was sending away every penny she had. Inevitably, once the demands exceeded her resources, Jessica would panic, believing that she wasn't living up to her responsibilities.

Naïveté caused Jessica to become a victim, and once she was on the sucker list, the scammers were relentless. At one point, when Jessica could no longer afford to pay one of her clairvoyants, she received a letter saying that the medium could no longer protect her from dark forces and that something evil was hiding upstairs in Jessica's house. It's easy to dismiss Jessica and millions of victims like her because of age or gullibility, but she was clearly manipulated by her own honesty and determination to keep her word. Her last years were destroyed by hustlers, and she remained terrified to go upstairs until the day she died at the age of eighty-three.

There is no clearer example of a "con bubble" than scams that manipulate belief. Inside the bubble, real powers exist, life is more certain, and comfort is drawn from the seemingly spiritual or mystical. Con artists are able to grow and foster such beliefs with conjuring tricks, mind-reading stunts, and theatrical acts of legerdemain, but this is rarely necessary. Most victims already believe such things and are quickly drawn to someone who can validate and feed their convictions. This can build a relationship between the hustler and the mark that is too powerful for anyone to penetrate. The mark is easily isolated from those who "don't understand" or "refuse to believe" and, once under this kind of spell, people want it all to be true. After a certain point, it can be almost impossible for loved ones to drag the victim back to the cold reality of the world outside the bubble.

Though I'm not religious, I do respect the religious convictions of others as a matter of principle. Once anyone uses the beliefs of others as a means to control, direct, defraud, or mislead, they cross the line between honest and corrupt intent. How many times have you seen politicians cynically use religion to hustle votes? Con artists can use religion as a powerful weapon whether they are exploiting existing beliefs or inventing their own, but faith, as magnetic a force as it is, is not the most powerful weapon in the con man's arsenal.

Sex is a universal, natural motivation that has gotten more people into trouble than anything else in history. It might be the driving force behind all that's bad and all that's good in the world, but there's one thing for sure: we all want it at some time in our lives and if a con artist knows what you want . . .

The promise of sex (or the vulnerability of its aftermath) has been used by hustlers for centuries. All a beautiful girl has to do is walk into a sports bar to find someone interested in her; if she happens to be a con artist, then there's an endless supply of marks to be scammed. The most basic of these might be as simple as luring someone to an alley so they can be robbed or to a hotel room so they can be photographed and blackmailed.

On *The Real Hustle* we generally avoided scams that depended on manipulating people sexually. It's a dangerous game and there's almost no chance anyone would agree to be on the show afterward, but I did find a way to re-create a classic blackmail scam while keeping everyone fully dressed. Jess checked into a hotel in London, and we arranged for our mark to deliver a package to her room. When he arrived, Jess was dressed in a silk gown as if she was getting ready for the shower, and she asked the mark to help her with something on the balcony. Across from them, on the roof of another building, Alex and I took pictures as the mark helped Jess to remove an earring and Jess cleverly posed to create some damning pictures with the unknowing mark!

Later, the mark met Jess when she was apparently being threatened by two scumbag journalists (Alex and I were particularly good at this). The mark gave up his own money to buy the pictures to both protect Jess and avoid himself being splashed all over the front page of the tabloids. This was a strong facsimile, but a real hustler would genuinely seduce the mark, break into the hotel room at the most embarrassing moment, and take pictures that his mother should never see, let alone his wife. This blackmail scam depends on hooking the mark through a compromising situation, then making him pay to avoid embarrassment or ruination. Another scam plays on the same human needs but can have a much more powerful and devastating effect on the victim.

Whereas sexual blackmail scams begin with sex, romance scams also create the promise of love and friendship. These con games can be more damaging than any other type of scam because they depend on cultivating genuine feelings of love and attachment from the victim. Over time the mark is groomed to believe he is in a real relationship and these emotions are manipulated and directed toward the hustler's ultimate goal, which is usually money but—once someone is tangled in this type of web—can be almost anything. Today, victims don't even have to meet their dream partner personally. The Internet has allowed scammers to pull this con remotely, sometimes even pretending to be the opposite sex using Internet chat and photos of someone else as bait (a con called "catfishing").

The Russian Bride scam employs girls to run a con on multiple people around the world, using video conferencing, Internet chat, e-mail, and snail mail to keep the mark on the line. Along the way the victim is asked to pay for all sorts of "gifts" and help cover the cost of travel and visas so the girl can meet the mark in his home country. All of this money goes to the hustlers, while they continue to stall the mark with excuses of more bureaucracy, sick relatives who need medicine, legal problems, necessary bribes, and even ransom demands after the prospective bride has been supposedly kidnapped.

Romantic or sexual leverage is a powerful weapon that has been used for centuries by spies, foreign governments, politicians, kings, queens, organized crime, tabloid journalists, and anyone seeking to manipulate someone into a compromising situation. Whether these cons are large-scale professional operations or played by lone fraudsters, the effect on the victim is the same. Shame, regret, and genuine feelings of loss usually consume the mark and very few ever report being conned. Scams like these can last for months or even years before the mark either gives up or loses everything. The aftermath of this type of con game can be particularly damaging to the mark, who may never fully get over the experience.

The Hope Factor

With many con games, I have observed a strange and surprising thought process that allows the mark to buy a bogus story. I learned to use this logic against people in many of the most outlandish scams we pulled, but it also proved useful in more mundane swindles. If you've ever seen a TV show exposing con games or read other books that hope to protect the public, no doubt you have come across the following well-worn phrase: *If it seems too good to be true, it probably is.*

This is fantastic advice, and I have given it many times, but in the heat of the moment, when desire and hope are ignited, a more powerful logic works in the con artists' favor: *This is so crazy, it must be true!*

Hustlers have employed this angle for centuries, and it rarely fails to have a powerful effect. If the victim himself doesn't begin to think this way, it's relatively easy to introduce the idea. My experience has led me to believe that the more incredible the story, the greater the so-crazy-it-must-be-true logic. Remember, once someone is on the hook, he is searching for ways to believe. Even if a mark is negative and openly doubtful—even aggressive, the very fact he's talking to me proves that he's interested; and if he's interested then, somewhere inside, he hopes the story is true.

It's surprising to me that even the most difficult target can quickly become a victim to this form of confirmation bias. Anything which supports the mark's hopes is given greater weight and importance, and the more they want the scam to be real, the easier it is to influence them. In a classic scam like the Pigeon Drop, the whole idea might seem absurd from the outside. However, once someone is on the inside, and has a chance to take the money (and run), emotion can turn doubt into belief.

A Bigger Bait and Switch

Let's take a moment to consider another simple scam, similar to the ticket swindle, where we are offering something of value for a very low price. On *Scammed*, we re-enacted a clever version of this con by presenting our mark with a brand new iPad in a box as if it had just come from the Apple store. I arrived with two boxes, one of which was sealed, and let the victim examine the real device and pay for it. My fellow hustler, Robin, arrived to buy the other iPad and also examined the pre-opened tablet. The mark paid cash, which I placed in an envelope filled with *more money*. Robin then asked if she could take the opened tablet to show to her boyfriend who was waiting nearby in their car. I agreed to follow her, but as soon as she left I asked the mark if he would take care of the money while I took the opened tablet to show Robin's shy boyfriend. This would leave the mark with the still-sealed box and an envelope stuffed with cash. He agreed, comfortable that I would definitely return and happy because he still had the other iPad that he'd paid for. Once I left with the real iPad, all we had to do was wait and watch until, eventually, the poor mark opened the shrink-wrapped iPad box to find nothing more than a ceramic bathroom tile inside. And the money? I switched that for a duplicate envelope just as described in the ticket scam.

The hook and the sinker are the easy part of this scam. The iPad is a desirable object so there are plenty of people who'd want one, and the reason for walking away and the money switch are well-proven methods. However, in order to get the money, we needed a line that could be tested by the mark. Why am I selling iPads for almost half their value? How can this deal be legal or the iPad be real?

What would you say? What would you believe?

I had to say something believable but I had greater latitude here—thanks to the twisted logic of the hope factor. Even the most cautious buyer wants to score a cheap tablet—or else he wouldn't be there—but I can't take my story too far in either direction. If the story was too simple, then the mark might think I was hiding something, and thus walk away. If my story was too crazy, then the mark would resist because hope and belief can only be stretched so far. I needed something that made sense but was suitably out of the ordinary because, after all, iPads don't fall from the sky.

Here's the story I used for *Scammed*:

I work in marketing and we have meetings with clients all over the country. I'm in town to meet real estate developers and, as part of my company's hospitality package we give away iPads to potential clients. Five people didn't show up so I have five spare devices to sell before I fly back to New York.

Why sell them and why so cheaply?

If I take them back, I have to return them to Apple but if I sell them for the same price we pay—plus a little extra— then I don't have to carry them back and I don't have to tell my boss that five potential clients didn't show up.

I then talk about the economy, complaining that people don't invest like they used to. None of this matters to the mark, but it gives my story depth and buys me some time while the idea sinks in. The more the mark wants the iPad, the more my story makes sense to him.

Let's pull a little harder on that line and imagine the mark asks how a company can afford to give away expensive devices so easily. My comeback might go something like this:

iPads? That's nothing. If the deal is big enough I've given away Rolexes just to get fifteen minutes in the room with these people. Development deals are thin on the ground but the money for my firm is huge if they get the deal. In California I hear they're giving away Toyotas. Twenty iPads—a hundred iPads—is chicken feed.

This is all a fantasy, but it answers the question and allows me to give the mark some room to maneuver. If he comes back then I'm almost certain to get his money.

Look, I understand the question, I get it all the time but my flight is in a few hours. I have two other people interested and only two iPads left so don't worry if you're not comfortable buying it.

That's the get-out option. If the mark is starting to use common sense or worry is beginning to take over his desire, this is where he will jump ship. However, most people see this as further proof that my story is genuine and continue with the transaction. It's an "all-in" move, but if it's timed correctly, the mark rarely folds.

There are countless ways for a mark to rationalize an attractive proposition like cheap iPads. For some marks the suggestion that the item is stolen is enough; the seller sees any money as profit so its retail value doesn't matter. Then again, the criminality could scare off a mark as well. Or I could appear to be working a scam on my own company, and so long as the mark doesn't perceive any danger to himself, he'll bite. I might even claim to represent the manufacturer, or a competitor. Perhaps I found them on the street or picked up the wrong luggage at the airport that just happened to be filled with high-end merchandise. The reasons are endless so long as I can back it up with enough logic to give the mark confidence in the deal.

On *The Real Hustle* we once sold an Aston Martin for five thousand pounds (about $8,500) after convincing the mark that a scorned wife was getting revenge on her estranged husband by virtually giving away his nearly two-hundred-thousand-dollar car. A few convincing documents, some amateur dramatics, and a rented car were all we needed to take down several marks.

The Long Game

The line is often the journey between getting the mark hooked and taking their money, but it can also be the core of a great con when the story encourages the mark to invest, spend, or give money continuously. A clear example of this is the well-known Ponzi scheme, named after Charles Ponzi. Ponzi built upon a scam that was introduced in the United States by W. F. Miller, but while Miller made over a million dollars, Ponzi's scam took many times that amount because his story captured the imagination of the public, who mortgaged their own homes for a chance to invest.

Ponzi's idea was based on an imbalance between the value of return postage coupons that were bought overseas for small amounts but could be exchanged for postage stamps of a higher value in America. The purpose of these vouchers was to facilitate the return of documents sent from Europe, but the fact that a smaller amount spent in one location could be exchanged for a larger amount in another gave Ponzi a million-dollar idea. He used his story to attract investors, whom he quickly repaid along with the profits he had promised. Many immediately re-invested and word soon spread about the success of Ponzi's system. As new customers handed over their money, Ponzi used these funds to pay earlier investors. So long as new money kept coming in, old money could be rewarded; the scam grew so quickly that in a matter of months Charles Ponzi was a millionaire several times over.

Within a year, Ponzi's investment scam collapsed under its own weight when financial analyst Charles Barron noted that many millions of postal reply coupons would need to exist for Ponzi's claims to be true. In fact, fewer than thirty thousand coupons were in circulation, and once this news was made public, investors panicked, there was a run on Ponzi's "Security Exchange Company"—everyone asked for their money back at once—and the whole affair unraveled as a financial disaster for those involved.

This will all seem painfully familiar to victims of Bernie Madoff, who took *billions* of dollars from people. Madoff used new money to reward old investments until he could no longer attract enough fresh capital to meet his commitments. When

Madoff's version of the Ponzi scheme collapsed, investigators found a history of bogus trades that were used to explain how profits were being generated. Over the years, money was constantly being re-invested by victims, unaware that their rewards were nothing more than phantoms being generated by Madoff's staff. Whenever people cashed out, they were paid from billion-dollar accounts where their money had been sitting all along. Bernie Madoff succeeded in creating a scam where victims were inclined to keep their money invested and watch it appear to grow under his care. By banking almost everything he received, Madoff built an enormous fortune from which he managed his victims' expectations until suddenly, the wheels came off the bus.

The line is where the story can either fall apart or lock everything into place. If the story makes sense to the mark and doesn't raise unexpected questions, the chances are good that he will be satisfied. The Ponzi scam and Bernie Madoff's hugely successful variation illustrate just how powerful a story can be when playing a con. Ponzi's story simply couldn't stand up to scrutiny (which it quickly attracted), while Madoff's scam was built upon stronger foundations; he was able to run it for many years before it became impossible to maintain. In the end, when the house of cards falls down, the scam might seem obvious, but from inside the bubble, it's much harder to see past one's desire for the prize.

The principal objectives of the line are to satisfy the mark's concerns, feed him information, control his options, manipulate his perception, and overall, to give him confidence. The line is a relationship between con artist and victim that builds toward the moment of the sting or is skillfully abused to gradually extract money or resources; while on the line, the mark often becomes isolated from the influence of family, friends, or colleagues who might intervene. The simplest way to do this is to build the need for secrecy into a scam, but con artists also employ emotional leverage to cause the mark to ignore people around them.

When trying to con someone for television, time is short and what would normally be accomplished over weeks or months must somehow be squeezed into a matter of days or hours. The advantage is that risks to production become easier to manage, but it severely limits how much I can take from the mark. The more time a mark has to raise money, the more I can steal. A scam requires enough time for the mark to get involved, take a few risks, and perhaps accept something on faith, but not enough time to let the idea mature in his mind. Here the con artist must depend on the story to both distract and engage the mark quickly. In real-world scams, the more time a con artist has, the more money he can take. This can happen over an extended period of time, as illustrated by psychic and romance scams, or by carefully edging the mark toward a sting. Just as some scams are over as soon as the mark is hooked, some are all about keeping the mark on the line until the well runs dry. With scams like the one I tried to pull on Uncle Barry, the line builds toward a moment of commitment, where the con artist convinces his mark to drive over the cliff.

CHAPTER FIVE

THE SINKER

*U*ncle Barry had me on the ropes.

When he charged back into the office, the look in his eyes told me that I needed to be careful. While walking back to his hotel, Barry had been working out the numbers in his head and had a question that needed to be answered. As our hidden-camera experts quickly crawled behind the counter and producers scurried back to their hiding places, Uncle Barry and Randy were already walking through the door and I was suddenly back in character.

"How did you come up with that number?" Barry asked. "It doesn't make any sense. Twenty percent would be a huge profit on a deal like this but forty just seems like . . .where did that number come from?"

I smiled and nodded, feigning confidence, but my mind was racing for the right answer. With years of experience I had options that I could draw from other scams, but if I picked the wrong strategy, Barry would walk away. The truth is that 40 percent had been chosen to make the deal more attractive, but for a shrewd businessman, this number set off alarm bells. On the spot, I came up with a logical explanation. The entire scam hinged on what I would say next; I had to trust my instincts. Now, it was my turn to roll the dice.

"It's essential to show how much John and my other clients are paying at this end," I explained. "In this case, 40 percent is the minimum amount to avoid paying a higher percentage at the Euro end." I went on to explain that my system used loopholes in international law that protect investors from being "double-dipped" when moving large sums of money. If I could clearly prove that John was paying 40 percent in the United States, he would avoid losing 70 percent overseas. Had Uncle Barry known a little more about foreign investments or how money really moves between countries, we'd have been busted. Fortunately for us, he accepted my explanation.

We were back in business, but Barry needed to slow everything down. He explained that deals are built on relationships, and that even under the best of circumstances, it would be unwise for him to invest so quickly—even for such a modest amount. I smiled and agreed, apologized for my haste, and explained that I had reached for an opportunity without thinking. Barry accepted this and we agreed to meet for dinner. I now felt sure we were back on track. There was no doubt I could convince Barry to invest, but I needed to make him feel that his money was safe.

Had I been pulling this scam for real, I would have attracted as many marks as possible before skipping town, multiplying all those 20K investments into quite a score. Given time, I could have convinced people to invest a lot more than twenty grand, perhaps using Charles Ponzi's strategy of paying investors to attract a fresh supply of suckers. No matter Barry's personal wealth, he was not about to agree to put 20K into something until he was sure of it. During dinner, I cautiously suggested an idea that would put his money on the table without him having to fully commit to the deal.

"Meet me tomorrow and bring the money," I told him. "We'll walk it over to the bank and call your accountant from the manager's office so he can verify everything I've told you. I'll show you all of the transactions for the last six months and if you're still not sure, no problem. If you decide to wait, we'll still work together once you're completely comfortable."

Barry quickly agreed that this was a fair way to handle the situation. I took a small gamble by offering him another way out—but I was sure he wouldn't take it.

"If twenty thousand is too much, then I apologize if I misread the situation," I added.

When Barry quickly confirmed that he could easily obtain the money, I knew he was seriously considering my offer. At the end of the night, he guaranteed that he would come to my office the following day with the cash.

By the time Barry arrived with his breast pocket bulging, we were ready for the sting. All I had to do was separate Barry from his cash and switch it for paper. But first, I used a touch of theater to keep his confidence up. I turned my laptop around to show John, supposedly on a video call from New York. Appealing to Barry's ego, John said how happy he was that they'd be doing business together as Barry smiled and returned the compliment, never suspecting that John was actually upstairs, sitting in front of a backdrop. Next, I asked to see the money and watched Barry pull a thick envelope stuffed with hundred-dollar bills from inside his jacket.

"No need to check it now, the bank will do that when we get over there," I told him as my security guard approached with a heavy flight case. I opened the case and tipped it forward so our mark could see that it was filled with euros before adding his own money. As Barry dropped his envelope inside, the security guard asked to verify he wasn't carrying any weapons, a question designed to provoke a response. While Barry was joking with the guard, I smoothly placed the bag on the floor, passed it under the desk, and exchanged it for a duplicate case filled with pieces of newspaper.

Randy agreed to meet us later to celebrate, while Barry, the security guard, and I walked toward the bank down the street. The location of our fake office had been perfect. To take a car to the bank would have meant negotiating downtown Charleston's one-way street grid, and the beautiful weather and relative safety of the area made it natural to simply walk. Our bases were now loaded for the sting. All I had to do now was get away from the mark.

For the sake of the TV show, I wanted Barry to know that he'd been scammed right away, so once we left the office, our production team began clearing the room of all furniture, transforming it back to an empty shell. Meanwhile, I walked with

Barry and my security guard until, halfway down the street, I pretended that I'd left something important in my desk. Excusing myself, I quickly walked back to the office while Barry waited with the guard.

Minutes passed by before a car pulled up to the curb. Calmly, the guard walked to the car, got in, and drove away. Suddenly, Barry was alone on the street with what he still believed to be a bag full of money. Our mark was in the open and outside of our control. Across the street, cameras watched closely to see how he would react. We expected him to open the bag quickly and come back to the office, but none of us had predicted what Barry did next.

The sinker, where the mark is finally conned into handing over money or possessions, can either be contrived or unfold naturally. With many con games, hustlers must create an imperative that forces the mark to make a decision. The most common is time pressure, where some force or factor demands that the mark act quickly. Another strategy is to seemingly allow the victim to take over—he begins pushing for a deal to happen. In this scenario, a con artist can tease the mark, frustrating him until he's ready to jump at any opportunity. Saying no or withdrawing an offer can make people want it all the more.

Often the longer a mark is played, the easier it is to get him to commit. During the con, the mark commits time, money, and emotion until he becomes wrapped up in the lie, and desire often overtakes common sense in the early stages of a scam. Even with the most resistant of marks, there comes a point when he can almost taste the prize and believes that all he has to do is take one more step toward it.

"A fool and his money are soon parted," goes the adage. The con man's challenge in scams of this nature is to get the money and be able to walk away, to sink the mark without him knowing he has been sunk—until it's too late. How foolish a mark is in retrospect has little or no bearing on how sharp and attentive he was when his money was still in play. Every element of a con builds to a moment of commitment when the victim is determined to get serious. A mark might easily be *separated* from his money, but in most cases, *getting that money into play* is a con artist's biggest challenge.

Black Money

The Black Money scam is a perfect example of a con game that makes absolutely no sense to someone unless he has been roped by a gifted con artist. In essence, the story goes like this: The scammers have a container filled with pieces of black paper that, when treated with a special chemical, transform into genuine hundred-dollar bills. Convinced? Probably not. Presented like this, few people would think it's anything more than a joke, but versions of this scam have successfully fleeced suckers for centuries.

In a way, it relates to the idea of alchemy, where base metals can supposedly be transformed into precious gold or silver via some invented process and life-extending elixirs can seemingly be concocted via pseudo-magical means. As a con game, alchemy has endured for hundreds of years because the ideas are not only seductive, they somehow make sense to the public. Most important, they appeal to two of mankind's greatest desires: riches and immortality.

Alchemy was also the progenitor of modern chemistry thanks to seventeenth-century Irish philosopher and scientist Robert Boyle. I'm certain that early chemists found it easier to sell their skills as alchemic, which was more appealing to their medieval clients. More important, it kept the actual methodology secret, granting alchemists a power that was soaked in mystery. The notion of alchemy continues to endure because people still want what alchemists claim to deliver. Con men are smart enough to see that the idea of transforming lead into gold is still powerful, so why not give it a modern makeover?

Count Victor Lustig did just that in the 1920s when he retreated to America after successfully selling the Eiffel Tower *several times*. He had a cabinetmaker build a box with a slit in either end, a few fancy knobs, some buttons, and a crank on the side. Lustig would demonstrate how his Rumanian Box could accept a real hundred-dollar bill at one end and a blank piece of paper at the other. After a few twists and button-presses, he would tell the mark that the chemicals inside needed six hours to finish the process. Later, the count would turn the crank in the opposite direction and two perfectly identical bills came out of the box—even the serial numbers matched! Once a bank confirmed that both bills were real, the mark was all too eager to buy the box, and Lustig sold several for huge sums of money.

The black money scam is a modern variation of Lustig's Rumanian Box con game that uses a little alchemy to explain how it works and a backstory that hope-filled marks often accept without question. According to some versions of the scam, new money is printed on large machines that need to be tested extensively before the real cash is manufactured for the treasury. The money made while testing the machines is perfect and just as good as anything in circulation, but in order to accurately track how much is being made, the test sheets must be destroyed. The problem is that the incinerator is in a different state, so to avoid the chances of this test-printed money being stolen, it is painted with indelible black ink before being cut and packaged for transport. The result is boxes of seemingly worthless black paper that eventually gets burned unless someone happens to intercept the shipment and replaces the canceled bills with identical black paper.

This is the backstory that explains what the paper is and how it might somehow be turned into real cash. Just like Victor Lustig and his money machine, black money scammers use a powerful demonstration to convince the mark that their story is real. The victim is given a handful of black paper, cut to the size of real bills, and told to take it home and add it to a bathtub filled with water. They are also given a small supply of the "magic chemical" to add to the bathwater with strict instructions on how to soak the paper. The process, they are told, takes eight to ten hours! During that time, the scammers break into the victim's house while they are distracted (or asleep) and replace the worthless paper with real money before dropping colored dye into the water. On *The Real Hustle*, our marks, who were from out of town, booked into a hotel room and we simply had Jess dress as a housekeeper, gain access to their room, and replace the "money" that was soaking.

The process that accomplishes this transformation is similar to that of Count Lustig's. Instead of a mysterious box, a small quantity of chemicals added to a bathtub will dissolve the ink, leaving the original printed bill intact. Accompanied by some creative mumbo-jumbo about how the chemical bonds to the black ink and the backstory of a rogue chemist who developed the formula, this tall tale can easily connect with a mark who's eager to make a fast fortune. I've pulled versions of this scam several times for *The Real Hustle* and there are two questions the mark always asks: Why sell the paper at all? Why not just keep it and make your own fortune? These seem like challenging questions to answer, but they are a perfect motivator to sink the mark and get their money into play.

Many people might have great difficulty understanding how someone could be taken in by this kind of con game. Minus the story, the build-up, and the persuasive people involved, the very idea that someone would exchange real money for worthless paper is hard to comprehend.

Let's imagine you and I are pulling this scam together and that our victim has bought the story completely. How would you answer those questions? How could you use this challenge to actually bring down the mark? Think about it for a moment. What would it take to convince you, if you were the mark?

Why would the scammers share this amazing secret? The answer is that they wouldn't unless they *had to*.

Here's the story I would tell:

The problem with my method for cleaning black paper is that it's slow and, while it works for small quantities in small amounts of water, larger tanks simply don't disperse the chemical enough to guarantee cleaning all of the bills properly. In fact, all attempts to wash larger numbers of bills result in gray money that simply doesn't look right. The process works but only with small numbers of bills. Our problem is that we have a large supply of bills and plenty of chemicals but we simply don't have the time to clean them all.

This is where pressure for the mark to make a quick decision begins. The reason makes sense. It's logical and explains why we would offer the black paper to someone we'd never met. According to my version of this scam, it's essential that there's no direct connection between myself and the buyer. That way, we're both protected, and so long as the mark doesn't raise any suspicion by hanging their freshly washed money on the clothesline for all to see, there's no chance they will ever be found out. "Is this illegal?" I'd say "Technically, no, but I wouldn't put it on my resume, if you know what I mean."

Of course, this is all a lie, but it's staggering to me how easily that lie is accepted, even by the most challenging of marks. Once they've seen the process work, they want it to be true and this never fails to tip the balance. Once the process of "washing" and the reason for selling have been accepted, the con artist is able to apply pressure for the sting. All a good scammer needs to do is push the mark to take the deal or walk away, and if the mark has been played properly, it will be extremely difficult for them to let this opportunity go.

I might tell the mark that I need to leave the country imminently and can't abandon a garage or a storage container filled with black paper. If anything should happen like a fire or a flood, I'd lose everything. I'd offer the mark the chance to take as much paper and chemicals as they could afford before I sell it to someone else. Time is now against the mark, and pressure is easily added when another buyer calls to buy all of the paper.

By backing the mark into a corner this way, the con artist is gambling that he will quickly decide to go for the prize. An experienced hustler knows to play the mark carefully so that he doesn't actually feel too isolated or overly pressured, though in some cases a bullying, aggressive attitude might work with a mark who is wavering. My preferred approach is to avoid histrionics and appear not to care if the mark wants to buy. This subtle form of pressure is just as effective as being threatening. I think it's more powerful to reserve belligerence until it becomes a last resort.

Eventually, the mark is forced to decide quickly—commit or give up on the prize. (As the saying goes: shit or get off the pot.) Once time pressure has been applied, another powerful technique is to let the mark leave and consider their options. This is where a scam balances on the precipice between success and failure; the act of giving a mark space to breathe can be one more convincing layer to support a scammer's story.

The Double Down

With the black money scam, the mark stays convinced all the way to the bank and up to the first time they attempt to wash their money. On *The Real Hustle*, we had a storage unit filled with black paper, chemicals, and money drying on clotheslines. This is where we completed our transaction and the scene we constructed easily backed up our story. With a small twist on the scam, it could be used to hit the mark for even more money.

Let's say we've "weighed" the mark (estimated how much we can take) for fifty thousand dollars. We've told him the whole story and offered to sell him twenty thousand dollars worth of dyed, black hundred-dollar bills for just five thousand dollars. Shooting low like this has the advantage of creating an easier initial decision for the mark; there's a good chance he will volunteer to buy more after he's convinced. Depending on the personality of the mark, a con artist might let the mark think he is the one driving the deal or is the one applying pressure. The hustler might pretend to be uncertain about increasing the amount or claim he has another customer who wants the balance of the paper—this is all a ploy to secure commitment. As long as the mark is still chasing the prize, he will remain on the line. Give it to him too quickly and the blinders might come off too soon.

Once the mark sees dozens of boxes filled with money, ready to be washed, it doesn't take much of a push for him to try to buy more. This is a form of bait and switch that the mark *plays on himself*. He agrees to a deal for a small amount but is suddenly willing and eager to invest much more. Of course, if the mark doesn't suggest it, the con man will have no trouble introducing the idea with a more direct approach. The black money scam illustrates how a victim might be maneuvered into a position where he is ready to hand over his money. The double down shows how he can be manipulated into losing even more in the final stages of the deal.

Criminal minds are constantly searching for ways to exploit weaknesses like greed, naïveté, and belief. There are countless ways to apply pressure or groom a victim for the sting but, for the most part, it takes three simple steps:

1. Show the mark something he really wants
2. Convince him that it's real
3. Force him to decide

Con games are designed around human nature, and all a hustler has to do is learn what buttons to press and when to press them for a scam to work.

As we explore the various types of con games that have evolved over time, I'll further illustrate how the hook, line, and sinker principles are applied.

Forcing the Hand

The simplest and most common strategy con artists use is to create an *imperative* that forces a *commitment*. This might be a competing party to whom the mark might lose out, an opportunity that will expire, or a sudden, unexpected event that demands immediate action. It could simply be the destination in a carefully planned journey where the pressure is nearly invisible to the mark. If the line is about securing trust, the sinker is about securing commitment; one simply doesn't work without the other. The line builds to this moment, positioning the mark to be taken advantage of before letting him walk off a cliff.

This is the moment when the mark takes that leap of faith, and it is sometimes the point where he will later claim to "know" that something was wrong (though he goes ahead with the deal anyway). I've struggled to understand this feeling and to explain why people would continue if they genuinely felt this way. An answer might be found in the concept known as "social compliance."

As a rule, most of us function within certain limitations to fit into a society. We act in a way that keeps that society functioning and protects our place and position within it. Put simply: Most of the time, people don't like to rock the boat. Scammers abuse this tendency to comply by making it difficult or uncomfortable for a mark to raise an objection or change a course of action. This aversion to conflict is used in a con game to make the mark feel like he is being unreasonable or even dishonorable by raising any concerns.

A few years ago, a friend told me about a problem he had with his brand new washing machine. He decided to call a local repairman and found the name of someone online who quickly arrived to check his machine. According to the repairman, it was an inexpensive fix but he would need to take it to his workshop for repair. My friend paid him in advance and even helped him load the truck, all the while wondering if he was ever going to see that machine again. He didn't. I asked him why he didn't say anything or why he agreed to let him take it in the first place. "I didn't want to make a fuss," he told me. Of course, this is a very British attitude; I seriously doubt this scam would be quite so successful in New York City.

I've seen many scammers act insulted, hurt, betrayed, or disappointed when someone tries to stop and ask questions. With other members of the crew adding to this sense that the mark is somehow in the wrong, this kind of guilt is a powerful tactic. In essence, the method is to use the victim's honesty and good intentions against them, and I can think of no clearer illustration of just how shameless a grifter can be.

In the end, how a mark gets sunk is mostly a matter of allowing all that has preceded that moment to mature in his mind and to only apply pressure where and when it is needed. A ripe mark is like a fresh pumpkin seed; if you squeeze too tight, he's gone.

In Charleston, I knew that getting Uncle Barry to commit so quickly was going to be impossible so I switched to a different tactic: separate and switch. My new objective was to get Barry to bring his money, then steal it from right under his nose. Given time, I could get almost anyone to give me their money and agree to wait weeks or months for a return on their investment, but time was now running out. I created a scenario where our mark would feel safe and in control with the option to walk away if he wasn't completely confident.

Of course, I knew we would never even get to the bank, but Barry thought he was going to make his final decision there; bringing the money was simply a way to keep his options open. I knew that he might only be bringing the money for show. After all, I'd deliberately suggested that perhaps he wasn't as affluent or successful as the image he presented, essentially baiting him by suggesting he might not be able to afford to get involved. Uncle Barry was curious but not suspicious, so I designed a guaranteed way to let him find out more without having to commit. He later told me that he only wanted to know the whole story and had no intention of getting into bed on a first date. This is why, once the money was in my hands, I had no intention of giving it back. For his part, Barry was equally careful not to take his eyes off the bag, but I had constructed a natural diversion for the switch that didn't raise suspicion. Until he later saw the footage, Barry was convinced that the case full of money never left his sight.

On the street, once he was alone, we all expected Barry to rush back to confront me. Instead, he did the one thing I had been working very hard to avoid letting him do up to that moment. He stopped to think.

The Third Option

In the face of a surprising or shocking situation, the most common reactions are fight or flight; we were prepared for both. If

Barry made a run for it, we had people waiting to intercept him, but our bets were on him charging back to the office to confront me. Instead, Barry did the smartest thing anyone can do when they realize something is wrong: He considered his options.

It's easy to assume that I've been overly kind with my description of Barry as a savvy businessman who made our scam much more difficult than expected, but when we left him alone on the streets of Charleston with a bag full of worthless paper, he proved just how dangerous and unpredictable a sting can be. When planning the con, my fellow producers and I tried to anticipate the mark's actions in each scenario. This is very similar to how a gifted con artist prepares to engage his mark, playing out all foreseeable options and possibilities in his mind so that, in the heat of the moment, the best option has already been decided. When filming con games, I consider every possibility, then prepare for the unexpected. That afternoon, Barry did not immediately return to the office. Instead, he placed the flight case behind a large potted plant and sat down in front of the nearest store. Most people would just immediately react in this situation, but Barry wisely tried to assess his position before doing anything that might make things worse.

Was his money in the bag? Had he been ripped off? Is there more to this? What do they want me to do next? Sitting on a doorstep, these are the questions Barry asked himself as he searched the street for answers. He was certain that I wanted him to go back to the office with the bag so that was the one thing he was *not* going to do. Money be damned—he wanted to get as far away from that bag as possible. What Barry understood in that moment was just how in the dark he really was and he wasn't about to play further into my hands. Without enough information to make a clear decision, Barry waited to see what happened next.

Back in the office, confusion reigned as we all tried to decide the best course of action. In a way, Barry had turned the tables on us. Sure, we had his money, but we didn't yet have a TV show. Should I go and speak to him? Should we tell him the truth and have him "act surprised" for the benefit of our cameras? One thing I insist upon in my reality shows is actual reality, and I am convinced that the success of *The Real Hustle*, *Scammed*, and *The Takedown* depends on genuine moments that people simply cannot fake. Naturally, this wasn't terribly helpful when the crew was in a panic, but the producers were firmly on my side in this regard. So, we had only one option: send Barry's nephew, Randy, to bring back his uncle.

It took Randy over five minutes to convince Barry to return to the office. We had given him strict instructions not to explain anything and Barry was insistent about not walking blindly into any situation. After a lot of cajoling, Barry finally stood up and reluctantly followed Randy back to the office. There, he found an empty room with a phone sitting on a small table. When it rang, Barry answered and I told him about the events of the last two days. Barry was confused but cautiously interested in how it might play out. As I stepped back into the office, the look Barry gave me was a mixture of surprise and something more dangerous. Later, he confessed that he was seriously considering a right hook to my jaw, but thankfully, the camera crew was quick on my heels, followed by John, Robin, and the other characters who had been part of the scam.

Barry changed instantly. We hugged and laughed as I revealed exactly how we had taken him down. His interview was honest and insightful and fully illustrated how anyone can fall victim to a well-played con game.

Later, as we talked over dinner, I asked Barry if, had it all been for real, he would have reported the crime or told anyone what had happened. "I'm not sure. Probably not, to be honest . . ." he told me. "But I don't think I'd let it go, either. I sure wouldn't want to be in your shoes if me or my friends caught up with you." Barry flashed his trademark smile and I quietly wondered just what kind of friends he had back home in New Jersey.

THE COOL-OUT

"*You* ever trip up, on the street, you know? Stumble or hit your knee off a step? People turn to see, right? What do you do?"

Uncertain, I took a sip of my beer. HL glanced over at the bar and signaled for another pitcher before continuing the lesson.

"You make like it never happened, right? Or you act as if you meant to do it. Like when you get that nodding dog thing and start falling asleep in a warm room filled with people and act like you were just looking down at your crotch for inspiration or some shit. People don't like admitting that they're people. Get it?"

"People?" I asked.

"Human. Just human. Everyone thinks they're special and ego . . . ego is made of glass."

I struggled to make all the connections as a third pitcher arrived at our table. My head was already fuzzy, but while HL seemed completely lucid, his conversation was scattered and difficult to follow. I started to realize I was a little drunk. HL filled our glasses and continued.

"If they get a scraped knee, or a twisted ankle, people keep walking and act like it was nothing. The last thing they want is to show that they're weak and, if they're still walking, other people could give a shit. That's what I'm saying."

I nodded slowly, still confused.

"Blood or a broken leg, then people stop and help. And no matter how hard the mark tries to walk away, they're not going anywhere. They got to admit what just happened." HL poured another glass. "If you hit them too hard, they got to face up to it. Others will notice and they'll have to call for help. You don't want that. You want to hurt them enough to make it worth your while but not so much they can't just walk it off."

It was the late 1990s. HL was a stocky man with a passion for fried food and cheap beer, and was the kind of person you wouldn't look at twice. He was so ordinary it almost seemed studied, perhaps deliberate. He had a great deal of insight about short cons and claimed he had spent time working with a crew in the Midwest as a younger man. We had met several years before at Denny and Lee's magic shop in Baltimore. He was interested in conjuring, but after chatting for a while I found we shared a deeper interest in con games. That first day we spent many hours in a diner talking about different scams. HL's knowledge was particularly interesting because he seemed to have a greater appreciation for the details of a scam than most people who are interested in the subject.

This was many years before I would find myself pulling con games for real, so I was immediately drawn to HL's level of insight, and it was no surprise when he admitted that he had actually committed most of these scams himself. Over the years that I knew him, we would meet and catch up whenever I was on the East Coast. I would share new magic tricks in return for long discussions about the art of the con.

On this particular hot afternoon we were in a sports bar, just outside of Washington, DC. A football game was on a big TV in the corner, and HL was clearly invested in the result. I assumed he had bet on the outcome, but I later learned he was actually a small-time bookmaker. In between plays, I was trying to glean any knowledge he had about "cooling out" the victims of con games, to avoid them going to the police.

"You can put the squeeze on someone—at the end, maybe—or you can put them in the shit so all they want to do is get clean and wash off the stink of whatever they were buying into. But that's all bullshit, most of the time. You either don't hurt 'em too bad or you hit so hard they can't get back up."

He turned to me and refilled his glass. "The movies—when Paul Newman shoots Robert Redford to put the mark on his heels—that's show business. I'm not saying it doesn't happen, 'cause it definitely does. It's just not . . . not the usual way. Either you get them mixed up in something they'd never want to admit or you give 'em a way out that's better than saying they were a chump."

"What if they don't know they were conned?" I ask.

"That's some rare shit, right there. Happens, sure, but eventually, everyone has to wake up. I don't buy that people never know they were conned. Most of the time they know. Can't even admit it to themselves, maybe."

HL glances back to the TV.

He continues, "The best cool-out—the most satisfying—has got to be when they think it's all their fault. Like playing the tip. You know about that?"

I nodded.

"That's a great one," he said. "Nothing better than making them apologize after you took their money. Unless they thank you but, like I said, that's rare."

HL turned back to the television in time to see one of the teams score a touchdown. Across the bar, in the opposite corner, I noticed someone staring at HL, eyes filled with hate. Suddenly, I realized we were in trouble. Before I could get HL's attention, the big man was at our table, sitting down just as HL turned back. My friend's demeanor shifted immediately. He was frightened.

"Remember me?" The big man turned square onto HL, and under the table I heard a metallic click. "Remember me?" he said.

In the dark corner of the bar, I suddenly felt completely isolated, blocked in by this huge, imposing man who clearly had a problem with HL, who was feigning ignorance.

"I've never seen you before. What's the . . ."

"Six months ago. In Baltimore, you sold me that car. The one that wasn't yours. Remember me now?"

For some reason, I hadn't been able to figure out he was one of HL's marks until that moment; abruptly, I found myself in the middle of a genuinely dangerous situation. How much had HL taken from this guy? What was he about to do to HL, or to me? This was all beginning to sink in as the waitress approached.

"Hey fellas. I haven't see you two in a while," she said. "You guys doing okay? Need another pitcher?"

The waitress rested her hand on the stranger's shoulder and I suddenly realized she knew both him and HL very well. I sat back and took a deep breath as the waitress returned to the bar. HL looked at me, smiled, and shrugged as his friend closed the knife he had been using as a prop. It was a con and I was the mark. Had the waitress not intervened, I could easily have lost every penny I had at that moment.*

"Don't take it personally, Paul. Just trying to make a living!" he laughed.

We chatted for a while afterward but I couldn't tell you what we talked about. Inside, I was setting fire to myself, angry at being so stupid; to not have realized that, to HL, I was just another sucker. Since then, I've been able to figure out the scam. HL supposedly owed this guy money and was going to get cut if he didn't pay, and, no doubt, he would need me to front the cash while promising to pay me back later.

I assume this is what would've happened. I've never asked him, and since that afternoon, I've only seen him twice—the last time around 2005. Likely out of embarrassment, I've told this story exactly once. It's difficult to admit, even now, that I was so blind to the true nature of our "friendship" and was so easily convinced by the situation. For HL, talking about con games and being a con artist was just his "in" to scam another sucker—me.

---

* In fact, I was carrying a lot of cash at the time. While I had not shown this to HL, he was able to surmise that I might be carrying a large bankroll.

As I've already said, anyone can be a mark, and there's a scam out there to suit every type. This was mine. It wasn't the first, it probably won't be the last, but for reasons that took me a long time to fully understand, it has been extremely difficult to admit. Perhaps, in the long run, my reluctance to admit being so easily caught up in HL's flimflam has helped me to empathize with people who went all the way.

It's frustrating to me that so many scams go unreported. The majority of victims are too ashamed or upset to admit what they've done. They can't bring themselves to confront the reality of a lie they completely believed. Many people simply decide to walk away and hope to learn from the experience rather than prolong the pain by pursuing the people who conned them. There are many reasons for this that I will discuss in another chapter, but from the perspective of a con artist, this shame is the automatic "cool-out" that most scams rely upon to succeed.

It's not just about getting the money. In a con game, the objective is to *walk* away—never to run—and to continue playing the same con without fear of pursuit or recriminations. The sad truth is that when victims refuse to report these crimes, scammers remain free to prey on others until the law finally catches up with them.

Shame is a powerful emotion, and the smarter a mark is, or the higher their standing in society, the greater the chances that he won't tell a soul about being conned. This is one of the key advantages to successfully isolating the mark in the process of a scam. The fewer people who know what the victim has been doing, the easier it is for the mark to conceal what happened from friends, colleagues, and loved ones.

In general, scams depend on this self-imposed blow-off to let hustlers walk away scot-free. It's a numbers game that depends largely on how the mark has been selected and groomed. Whenever victims are drawn into a scam at random, the risk of someone reporting the crime or coming after the hustlers is increased; there has been no weeding-out of dangerous or troublesome marks. Scams like the jam auction need only to hide behind a convenient interpretation of the law and employ a healthy number of bouncers to dissuade anyone who might put up a fight. Other con games hit and run, leaving the sucker with nowhere to go once they realize they've been stung. But in cases when the prize warrants the effort or the mark presents a greater potential danger to the crew, a cool-out is tailored to the mark and built into the scam.

A constructed cool-out is almost a scam within a scam. It is a motivation for the mark to walk away from their losses and keep quiet about what happened. In the movie *The Sting*, Paul Newman's Henry Gondorff and his protegé, Robert Redford's Johnny Hooker, confront each other in front of their mark after Hooker has apparently ratted Gondorff out to the FBI. Gondorff shoots Hooker and is then gunned down by the Feds as the mark is dragged away. Despite losing a huge amount of money, Robert Shaw's mobster character can't risk getting mixed up with the FBI and the two people he'd go after are now both dead. Of course, it's all a big show to make sure Gondorff and Hooker can take the money without getting killed for it later. This is an excellent, if overly dramatic, example of a cool-out in action because it clearly illustrates why the mark would never come back for his money.

In the real world, hustlers rarely go to so much trouble, but it's not unheard of to drop the mark into a compromising situation so that all he wants to do is get out, regardless of how much he has lost. A simple way to do this is to "poison the well." Once the mark has committed and his money is secure, the nature of the proposition suddenly changes from being an honest opportunity into a criminal act.

On *The Real Hustle*, in an homage to *The Sting*, we convinced people to give large sums of money to my investment firm after seeing an impressive operation that gave my imaginary stockbrokers instant access to the latest financial data. Once their money was in our hands, the "police" suddenly burst in to arrest everyone for an insider trading scheme. This was all witnessed on closed-circuit cameras by our marks, who were then hustled out of the office and onto the street. They all got out of there as fast as their legs could carry them. From their perspective it looked like a seemingly legit operation was actually using illegal methods and that they were lucky not to get caught up in the whole affair.

This turn of events changes everything; all the victim wants is to get away and protect his freedom no matter how much he might lose.

A simple example of this is an investment scam where victims are told they can profit from a powerful new system that can predict the market with such accuracy that it's almost guaranteed to make a profit. Once the mark is hooked, he is convinced to buy into the company but soon learns that the "system" relies on insider information gathered illegally by a team of hackers. Now, money is no longer the mark's primary motivation. All he really wants is to get out before the police or the government moves in to arrest everyone. Another clever twist allows con artists to squeeze even more from their mark in order to walk away clean; a visit or a phone call from bogus investigators is sure to convince any mark to keep his head down.

Certain scams are designed to make the victim appear responsible for any losses; others create fake scenarios where an unforeseen event or disaster apparently ruins everything. These strategies are excellent for making the mark walk away without knowing he was conned. In fact, hustlers sometimes use them to take a second swing at their sucker. If the mark feels he was to blame, he might beg for another chance.

In the black money scam, there is a powerful cool-out that is sometimes used to back off a mark. During the scam, the hustler asks the mark to verify his story (that black paper can be changed into real money) for another potential customer, and the mark confirms what they genuinely believe at that time. Later, when they learn that they've been conned, the other "customer" confronts the mark and accuses him of being one of the scammers, perhaps threatening violence. This scenario can be so frightening that most people just want to get away.

This form of bait and switch is a powerful way to keep a victim quiet, but nothing is certain; people can be impossible to predict once someone has been conned. Throughout history, con artists have come to a violent end at the hands of their once-innocent victims. Whether hung by an angry mob, shot by a humiliated mark, arrested, or merely tarred and feathered, being a con man is a dangerous profession and almost everyone has to face the music at some point. The cool-out, constructed or automatic, is certainly one of the strongest weapons in the con man's arsenal, but it's always a gamble. There's always the chance that a victim is going to make a stand.

On *The Real Hustle*, we interviewed a former victim of the black money scam who was suspected of sending several con men to the hospital. After learning that he had bought nothing more than ordinary black paper, the mark told the scammers that he wanted to buy even more. They quickly agreed to meet the mark again only to find out he brought several friends and a collection of blunt-edged weapons.

Most con artists are remarkably brazen in their attitude. They just want to get the money, get out, and go after the next mark. It might seem satisfying to employ a few friends with baseball bats, but this is more likely to put the victim in jail than to recover any money or self-respect. Many are unfazed by victims who want to come after them, and previously charming and amiable con men quickly transform into hardened criminals when pursued. I would strongly urge anyone *not* to go after a grifter themselves—contact the police. More important, con artists are criminals and criminals tend to know many other bad people; always call the authorities and let them do their job.

My own experience with HL at that bar in Maryland taught me that not confronting the reality of a scam is preferable to admitting I was almost a sucker. Until writing this book, I had only shared this story with one close friend, afraid it might somehow taint my reputation or make me seem foolish or less qualified. I've come to realize the opposite: This experience was incredibly valuable. It taught me that con artists can never be trusted and that, to them, I'm just another mark, waiting to get clipped.

I often hear people say that "the best con game is where the mark doesn't even know he was conned." This is certainly true but, with a few exceptions (such as a well-run crooked card game), most marks soon realize that they were suckered somehow. The cool-out simply creates enough smoke for scammers to walk away, but that smoke eventually clears.

The vast majority of cons and scams go unreported because victims are naturally inclined not to admit or confront what has happened to them. In some cases, hustlers deliberately construct situations that force their victims to keep quiet. Eventually, someone will ring the bell, forcing the scammers to adapt or run. This cat and mouse game will continue to go in cycles. However, there are ways to fight back and to make the hustler's life more difficult.

INTERLUDE: TRUE AND FALSE—
HOLLYWOOD AND THE CON MAN

For me, it all started with *The Sting*.

George Roy Hill's 1973 film about a team of con artists trying to scam a Chicago mobster during the Great Depression remains one of my all-time favorite pictures. Paul Newman and Robert Redford were perfect as charismatic charlatans playing a long con surrounded by a cast of colorful characters—cartoons of real-life con men from that era.

It began my fascination with con games and introduced me to gambling sleight of hand as demonstrated by the hands of John Scarne during one unforgettable scene. I still remember watching it for the first time and the impact it had on me as a child, and have since seen it over a hundred times. It never fails to entertain or inspire, but as I've come to learn, it has very little to do with the world of real-life grifters.

In *The Sting*, con men are honorable thieves who willingly come together to avenge a murdered member of their fraternity. For Johnny Hooker, the fledgling con man played by Redford, revenge is the primary motivation; he even rejects his piece of the take once the con is complete. It's nothing more than an entertaining fantasy concocted from several sources to create a pitch-perfect Hollywood movie.

In reality, con artists can certainly be charismatic, sometimes even cool, but mostly, they are remorseless and cold as ice. To be a grifter, one needs to be willing to sink to any level when going after the money. There are no limits, no restrictions, and no rules. Most assuredly, there's rarely any honor among thieves.

Not all movies present con artists so kindly as *The Sting*. In *Nine Queens*, director Fabián Bielinsky introduces us to two con artists as they scam their way around Buenos Aires before stumbling upon the opportunity of a lifetime. The film begins by concentrating on how the two grifters con innocent people but quickly becomes a character-driven story that leads to a satisfying conclusion. In *Nine Queens*, the hustlers are not glamorized, but the story is told from their perspective. The film depends on the audience's natural fascination with the genre to draw them into the plot.

David O. Russell's excellent *American Hustle* draws from the notorious Abscam affair and creates a pair of hustlers who accurately reflect the kind of crooks who willfully prey upon people desperate for financial help. The film is a powerful portrayal of three people manipulating each other until the con artists find a way to escape their situation. However, the film bears little resemblance to the real events on which it is based. As the opening of the movie states, "some of this actually happened," but a great deal was added or embellished in the name of entertainment. In particular, the motivation that drives Christian Bale's con artist seems to shift as he feels remorse for bringing down Jeremy Renner's Carmine Polito, the mayor of Camden. I find this extremely unlikely. In reality, the real con man's only regret was probably that he wasn't making any money from the affair.

David Mamet's *House Of Games* conjures a dark fascinating world filled with intriguing personalities who easily seduce the interest of Lindsay Crouse's psychiatrist character. As we are taken deeper into Mamet's version of this world, we see past their fascinating methods to uncover a vicious, remorseless cabal of low-life hustlers. The con artists in Mamet's later film *The Spanish Prisoner* prove to be equally repugnant, even resorting to murder to accomplish their goals. Throughout the story the con men are charming, but their true colors are clearly shown when the mark needs to be "taken care of" at the end of the picture. It's hard to accuse Mamet of glorifying con men, though he certainly makes them interesting. He uses them to compose stories filled with intrigue without compromising their motivation as con artists.

Stephen Frears' *The Grifters*, based on a novel by Jim Thompson, introduces the audience to three hustlers: John Cusack's short-con operator, his girlfriend with a background in the long con (Annette Bening), and his mother, who is part of a large bookmaking organization (played perfectly by Anjelica Huston). This film illustrates not only con games in action, but the repercussions of living in that world. Violence, murder, theft, prostitution, and even incest affect and ultimately destroy the lives of the characters in this brilliant piece of drama.

The cons portrayed in these movies are usually dramatic variations on old con games. In *House Of Games*, the card-game scam is a variation on The Tip, a con game where the victim is asked to signal information but after making a mistake, either loses a lot of money or is forced to cover a debt. In *American Hustle*, the con artists turn the tables on the FBI with a variation on the original Spanish Prisoner scam while Mamet's movie (called *The Spanish Prisoner*) features a complex con that is actually an ingenious Separate and Lift scam where the titular con is used only as part of the distraction.

In reality, con games, cheating, or acts of deception depend on the circumstance in which they occur and the actions of those being conned. There is no surefire method or guaranteed system to hustle a mark, but a series of objectives that contribute to the success of a sting. Con games can therefore provide writers and filmmakers with a never-ending source of stories, and while they might mostly be fictional, they can serve to expose or educate people about the possibilities that exist.

There is a natural attraction to con games because people are drawn to anything that seems clever or skillful. Con artists who manipulate people and cheaters who perform feats of incredible dexterity are fascinating to audiences and a handful of performers capitalize on this.

The master of this genre is Ricky Jay, who is both a highly accomplished magician and an authority on con artists and their methods. Jay brings this world to life through his shows and his written work, and I have no doubt that his friendship and professional relationship with David Mamet has been mutually rewarding since Mamet's insight into the nature of con artists seems to be in tune with Jay's.

Ricky Jay is also one of the finest sleight of hand experts I've ever seen. His live shows feature staggering demonstrations of skill as he easily locates the four aces and deals cards from any part of the deck to dazzle his audience. But, as Jay points out, there's a big difference between sleight of hand for entertainment and making moves at a card table. Whereas a royal flush dealt from a shuffled deck might result in a standing ovation for Ricky Jay, it might send a genuine "mechanic" to the morgue. In reality, a professional card shark would need only a tiny fraction of Ricky's skill, using just one or two moves to get the money without attracting attention. Jay is an expert showman in every sense of the word, but what he demonstrates is not reality but a fantastic compilation of show-stopping sleight of hand that would be mostly unnecessary, if not dangerous, in a real game. He's an entertainer who builds his shows around classic effects while sharing fascinating stories filled with colorful characters, incredible anecdotes, and unforgettable demonstrations.

Drama, pathos, action, and comedy make for great entertainment, but real-life con games are usually banal by comparison. In a scam, nothing dramatic really happens because in order to make something seem real, it should appear almost ordinary. On reflection, a con might be dissected into phases or elements, but even with the most outlandish scams, the victim is assured by a sense of normalcy.

This depends a great deal on the hustler's personality, but I have found that, even in the most extreme scenarios, a sense of calm certainty on my part helps to give the mark confidence and keep him on track until the sting. Melodrama can be useful, but it needs to serve a purpose, and the mark needs something or someone to anchor or guide him. I've threatened my TV marks with arrest, intimidated them physically, and orchestrated arguments or events to force a desired reaction, but most of the time this is just an ingredient or a convincer. It is in the calmer moments that I can convince the mark to move toward what he wants or needs.

It's possible to entertain and inform at the same time. In *The Takedown*, *Scammed*, and *The Real Hustle*, I had to film each con or heist quickly, which meant having to squeeze all of the elements together without much time to let the mark think. This created many challenges, but the cons are more exciting this way and it makes for better television, which is why our show ran for eleven seasons.

The Hollywood version of con men can vary from funny or charming raconteurs to cunning thieves who would stop at nothing to get what they want. It might seem that anyone could turn their hand to the art of deception if they knew a trick or two. In reality, though con artists come in all shapes and sizes, their raison d'etre remains the same: *to take whatever they can by any means necessary.* Without being able to detach from the repercussions of one's actions, it would be impossible to succeed as a con artist. Hustlers ruin lives without remorse, often blaming their victims for believing their lies. It takes a specific type of personality to show empathy, build conviction, and foster a relationship before betraying someone's trust without suffering an ounce of guilt.

In *The Sting*, the marks are all criminals who deserve what happens to them; in reality, hustlers prey on anyone worth taking down, and honest, hard-working people often make the easiest targets. I often hear the old phrase "you can't cheat an honest man." In my experience, that's bullshit.

Part Two
INNER SECRETS
OF THE CON GAME

*N*ot every hustler is a master con man. Most are just common criminals employing proven methods to prey on the unwary. A crooked genius might develop a new con or a clever twist on an old scam, but once it has proven successful, it can spread like a virus to less sophisticated grifters.

Online scammers quickly pick up on new ways to steal money. The Internet offers less risk and greater anonymity, so any variation or new idea quickly spreads to a swarm of digital deceivers. This ability to hide online allows almost any scam to be attempted there; but, in the real world, con artists are much more careful about adopting new ideas. Con games begin to grow once all the kinks have been worked out and information starts to circulate. A really great method for a scam might be kept secret for years in order to stop it from "getting out" and becoming overplayed, but eventually they are all shared or traded until the ideas reach the common herd.

In my experience, most hustlers care only about the potential score and take little to no interest in how or why their scams work. Occasionally, I've met individuals (such as HL) who may know a lot of cons, but ultimately care only about making money and looking for new ways to steal. While intelligence and cunning are common in con games, these qualities are often found more in the scam than the scammer. In real-life con games, played directly on a live mark, it's more likely that the con artist is smart enough to play the part and adapt to most circumstances; but online scams don't require much of a brain or personality to pull off.

It's important to note that not all con artists are experts in the art of deception. Many are simply street-smart crooks willing to do or say anything to take a buck; but the methods they employ are often the product of much more talented minds. Con games are built upon strategies that have proven to be very effective over time and become powerful tools in the hands of anyone willing to apply them. There's only one Shakespeare, but there are plenty of actors who try to re-enact the product of his genius. It is therefore in the best interest of the public to share these methods as widely as possible and to keep them high in the public consciousness.

The Internet has proven to be a powerful tool for scammers, but it can also severely limit the lifespan of an effective con. A good idea is quickly overused as the Internet becomes saturated with similar attempts to trick victims into giving up secure and personal information or get involved in the latest variation of the Spanish Prisoner or Pigeon Drop. News agencies and social media soon spread the word about the latest scams, but since most of us are now bombarded with information on a daily basis, the regeneration cycle for ideas (crooked or otherwise) has become shorter. New versions of old scams quickly reappear.

What remains constant are the underlying principles of hook, line, and sinker; almost universally, scams depend on the victim's circumstance and state of mind. Almost all con games are simply old wine in new bottles. By keeping the public engaged and interested in all varieties of confidence tricks, I genuinely believe it will become much more difficult to design and pull off effective scams. Why shouldn't ordinary people be armed with the same (or superior) information as those who might prey upon them?

In the coming chapters, we will explore many different types of scams to learn how the elements of "hook, line, and sinker" are employed to get the money. The principles remain the same and can be easily identified if you stop, think, and reassess any scenario. Always remember that con games are much easier to identify from the outside but surprisingly easy to fall for from the inside. The art of the con is in making an ordinarily transparent lie appear completely real to the mark. And, as in all seduction, the target is often blind to everything but his own desire.

CARNIVAL OF CONS

There was a tidal wave at Coney Island, when I was a child, ripped up the boardwalk and did about a million dollars worth of damage, houses and everything. The only thing left standing was those little milk bottles.

—Woody Allen

The box was about three feet square and six inches deep, filled with shallow holes along the base that were numbered, seemingly at random, from one to six. The leather cup standing inside the box held eight marbles, each the perfect size to rest in the holes. On the counter was a printed game card that would turn these simple props into one of the most powerful con games of all time.

We set up our stall near the English seaside town of Bournemouth, close to the promenade and pier. Nearby, other stalls hosted honest games promising toys of all sizes to lucky players. Our prizes were considerably more attractive. Xboxes, flat-screen TVs, watches, and every kind of home appliance we could fit onto the back wall. Getting people involved was going to be easy. I had spent years trying to convince the network and my producers that this scam was worth using for an episode of *The Real Hustle*. In the end, it was simply added to the schedule for convenience, a filler between more interesting, sexier scams. I was the only one with any enthusiasm for it and expectations were low. But I had seen this little game before and had spent years working on the secret. This was more than just another item to me. I knew it might be the greatest little scam of all time.

Our first mark walked up and was soon hooked by our wall of merchandise and, as was traditional, I offered him a free throw to illustrate the rules of the game. Tossed from the cup into the box, the marbles rolled and bounced until all eight rested in random holes. I then picked up each of them, adding the numbers of the holes they resided in until I had a total. This random number was then compared to a game chart, similar to a monthly calendar, which was on display around the stall. The chart featured possible totals from an eight-ball roll, some of which would give the player points, while others rewarded him with a house prize (marked "HP" on the chart) or nothing at all. The objective of the game was to collect ten points, rewarded by winning totals, in order to claim one of the prizes behind me. If the player's roll added to twenty-nine, an extra prize was added but the cost of each roll was then *doubled*.

This seemed like a lot to take in for the player, but his first roll made everything clear. I counted his total to be forty-four and, checking the chart, this gave the player five points, taking him halfway to a winning score. I moved a little brass slider along the rail to indicate his points and told him that he could keep that score if he wanted to continue playing. Without hesitation, he reached for his wallet and we were on our way.

His first couple of rolls resulted in no more points, but eventually he rolled a twenty-nine. This, I told him, meant he could select a second prize to play for, but it also meant he had to double the stakes, each roll now costing double the original amount. On his next roll he got lucky and hit a fifteen, and another one and a half points were added to his score.

So it continued until he had stumbled onto twenty-nine several times, increasing his prizes but forcing him to spend more money to stay in the game. Occasionally he scored another half point until, finally, he was just one point away from winning a home filled with video game consoles and televisions. After just six rolls of twenty-nine, each roll was now costing thirty-two pounds and another twenty-nine would bring it up to sixty-four pounds! I watched as he pulled the last of the cash from his wallet and counted. He had enough for one last roll. If he scored one point, it would all have been worthwhile. He up-ended the cup and watched the marbles tumble and bounce until they settled in their holes. I counted each one and checked the chart. I moved the slider to nine and a half.

The mark pulled open his wallet, as if expecting more money to magically appear. He was three hundred pounds in the hole and the game appeared to be over. His friend had already loaned all of his money; all seemed lost until I stepped in and pointed out his ATM cards. "I'm not supposed to do this," I lied, "but if you're back here in two minutes I'll hold that score."

He looked at me, then at the wall of prizes. His inner voice was counting how much he'd already lost and he was pulling back from the brink. But thirty seconds later he was running to the cash machine to get all the money his bank would allow.

One of my favorite jokes is about a guy who meets a beautiful girl in Coney Island. One thing leads to another and she invites him home to spend the night. Entering her bedroom, he sees that the walls are filled from floor to ceiling with shelves containing soft toys of every description, from enormous teddy bears to tiny, stuffed cartoon bunny rabbits, hundreds of them on every wall. Ignoring the toys, he undresses and jumps into bed. Later, as they lie together, the man asks, "How was I?" and the girl turns to him, looks deep into his eyes and says, "You can have any toy from the bottom two shelves."

For a child in 1970s Scotland, the closest thing to New York's Coney Island was Burntisland, a tiny town north of Edinburgh in the Kingdom of Fife. Every year I would go to the annual fair that stayed throughout the summer, with gut-wrenching rides, greasy food, and carnival games. The ground was always torn up and this grimy "Fun Fair" was as unpleasant as any I've seen since, but the lights and painted trucks somehow distracted me from muddy shoes, rotten candy apples, and poorly maintained machinery. I was regularly dragged away from rocket ships filled with screaming passengers and whirling "Waltzers" orbited by trails of partly digested hot dogs. To keep my grandmother sane, I spent all my pocket money on the game stalls.

I loved the games, but I rarely went home with more than a handful of candy. I could hook a rubber duck with my eyes closed, but I couldn't throw at all, and almost any game that required hand and eye coordination was safe from me. The only exceptions were that I could shoot pretty well (I later rated as a marksman in the British Army), and I could cover a large painted spot with metal coasters on my second or third try. Yet, no matter how many shots hit the target or spots were covered, I never seemed to win more than a small toy or plastic gizmo.

One such "prize" was a bright green frog with a silver spring attached to a rubber suction cup. Pushing the spring against the plastic base of the frog caused it to stick until the spring forced the base and sucker apart, throwing the frog into the air. I loved it. One day I walked into the post office near my grandparents' house and saw a display box filled with the same plastic frogs, each one costing a fraction of a single game in Burntisland. That was it; I never played the stalls again. Just like the guy in the joke, I knew I'd been screwed.

My position on carnival games has softened over the years as the pissed-off ten-year-old inside of me gradually conceded that the games were never about winning prizes. The atmosphere, the sights, the sounds, and the smell of the fair were what really attracted me; winning was never the point.

The games are there to make money, and the prizes reward the few who get lucky. It is possible to win many of these games, and I recommend you take your best shot. The beatable games are not the problem, even when the odds of winning are stacked against you. It's the games that have been designed solely to fleece suckers and force them to lose serious money that you need to be aware of, even if you never set foot on carny ground again. These games are miniature, ingenious versions of much bigger scams, and understanding how they work will help develop your newfound grift sense.

Fair or Foul

Carnival games, in all countries, are played in accordance with the honesty and good intentions of the stall operator. Almost any game can be manipulated against the player, but a fairground where no one wins will soon be deserted as word spreads. It's a game of give and take, and the carny's job is to ensure he takes more than he gives in order to make a profit.

Going to the fair and playing the games should be fun, and I hope you win a prize or two, but if you dream of emptying the shelves to impress your friends, then prepare to be disappointed. The operator's job is not just to run the game but to stay on top of how much stock they "throw" (allow people to win). Twenty percent of every dollar might be returned to the players, but the number of winners is then determined by the cost of the prizes, which are called "plush." Good-looking plush attracts more players but costs more to fill the stall. If a soft toy costs the carny two dollars and the game is played for one dollar, then the stall can only afford for one in ten players to win when throwing 20 percent.

Stall owners also vary how much they throw back depending on factors like weather and how long the carnival has been in town. It's not unusual for them to pepper the crowd with more prizes at the start of a run and then pull back, throwing a much smaller percentage toward the end, when most of the easy money has dried up. How these losses are controlled is the uncertain ground between a fair game and a crooked one, but, for the most part, it's no different than playing a slot machine without knowing the exact odds against you; most people sitting on stools in Las Vegas have no idea what the return is on the machine they're feeding.

Games can break down into types. Skill-based games appear to be much easier than they actually are, so profit depends on players needing to buy several attempts before they either win or earn a small consolation prize. Group games, where several players take part at once, are easy money as the players are competing against each other to win one prize. The size of that prize is determined by the size of the group, so it's easy to stay on margin. Physical games, where the player's strength or athletic prowess is seemingly tested, are fair but the chances of winning are still against you. Percentage games grind out a healthy profit over time, and, like all joints, are easily manipulated since the operator decides how to apply the "rules" depending on how much plush is taking a walk.

Practice Imperfect

If you've ever hoped to win a giant teddy bear for your sweetheart, then you should know by now that it involves more than luck and skills. Some games can be beaten if you are willing to make up your own props and spend time to learn the basics before putting money down. Many games are homemade by the stall operators, so the weight and size of what you'll be playing with may vary, but in games of skill, the principle is what matters. A little muscle memory and knowledge of the best strategy can be a great advantage.

Cover the Spot is my game of choice. I have several sets at home and occasionally I spend some time practicing the drop, where the first disc must land exactly or the game is already lost. Whenever I find a stall running this game, it usually takes me a couple of tries to get the drop right with their props, but I almost always walk away with a modest prize. Even though I own my own rig (actually several) and take the time to practice, I'm no real danger to the stall operators unless I get it 100 percent right every single time. In that case I might walk away with a giant piece of plush, but that's a rare occurrence on any game.

Even when the games are honest tests of skill, the chances that anyone would make their own rig and spend time to earn their chops are so small that most carnys don't care. They control the outcome and they've had a lot more practice running a game than anyone has had playing it. Many stalls sport a sign that says "One Prize Per Player Per Night," an easy way to filter out the wise guys who know how to play. As soon as the operator spots someone who's in the know, he throws him a cheap tchotchke, points at the sign, and sends him on his way. Others control the game by referring to the rules with varying degrees of honesty. Bucket games, where a ball is tossed over a rail or shelf and into an angled basket or plastic tub, depend on the ball to bounce out most of the time. If someone starts to perfect their throw and get the ball to stay inside, then the operator tells them they stepped on the red line, or leaned too far over the rail. These stalls are run by "alibi agents" who use a litany of excuses to dismiss successful players. Alibi joints vary in strength from difficult games like the basket toss to easier games where the alibi (excuse) is used constantly.

Even if you've developed a knack for the basket toss, the ball is more likely to bounce out from the angle you're throwing it from. Operators demonstrate by throwing from a different angle, using the side to deaden the ball so it doesn't jump right back out and then throw from the rail, leaving that first ball in the tub, which cushions the next two balls. I've even seen stalls where the operator has a special ball that looks identical to the others but is heavier and less inclined to bounce. To win, you need to throw the ball so it enters the tilted basket almost vertically, but some stalls forbid such throws, leaving you with nothing but luck to depend upon.

A completely gaffed version of the basket toss is the infamous Scissor Bucket where players must throw a ball against the base of a solid wooden bucket so that the ball falls down, through a hole, and into a pouch. These gaffed units can be lined up and used to scam as many people as the operator can afford buckets. The secret is a dampening block that is moved forward until flush with the rear of the base. With the block in this position, the force of the ball knocks it away, dampening the ball's forward motion enough for it to fall into the hole. Without this block in place, the backboard would bounce any ball straight out of the bucket. As the block is hidden behind the backboard and inside the unit, it's impossible to tell the difference other than to know that, if the ball goes into the hole, the block must have been in place to kill it.

There are many gaffed games that allow dishonest operators to control almost every outcome while appearing to offer a fair game. Catalogs from gambling supply houses list everything needed to operate games fairly *or* dishonestly. These are now considered collectibles, but modern reprints can be found filled with all sorts of fanciful devices designed to cheat or steal. Among them are many carnival games built solely to make money without the operator needing to take any risk whatsoever. Modern-day carnival supply companies sell prizes and all the props needed to operate modern games, from plastic tubs with the right kind of balls to specially made basketball hoops, narrower than the real thing and oval in shape so even Michael Jordan would have trouble making a shot.

There's an angle for every game on the midway. To beat the plate game, where coins are thrown onto ceramic plates, players must throw the coin lightly toward the far wide rim of the plate in the hope that it bounces back into the middle of the dish. Carnys have been known to bake these plates in a kiln until the outer diameter sags slightly, considerably reducing the chances of a winning throw. Throwing lightweight plastic rings into an enormous box crammed with empty soda bottles seems like an easy proposition when the objective is to land just one ring over the neck of any bottle. The odds are about 700 to 1; I've actually read that hundreds of rings have been dropped simultaneously without a single ring ending up as a winner. In hundreds of tests, investigators found that every winner resulted from a ring bouncing randomly and that the only effective strategy would be to throw two rings together so if they happen to drop onto a neck, the bottom ring will be deadened by the ring above it and stay in place as the upper ring flies off to find its own fate. Not surprisingly, most stalls insist that you throw one ring at a time!

Tin can or bottle games are easily gaffed and can be set to win or lose. If one of the cans is heavier than the rest, then setting it back slightly on the bottom row will mean the ball will lose all of its energy, knocking the lighter cans off the shelf. Putting the heavier can on top of the pyramid makes a winning throw possible and is used when the operator demonstrates or needs to lose a few games to avoid playing his joint too strong. The heavy can is not the only way to fix these games. With two glass bottles at the end of a wooden runway, it seems there can be no gaff but there is: simply edging one forward by a hair is enough to kill forward motion of the lightweight ball and keep one bottle standing. In games where bottles, cans, or "cats," need to be knocked off a shelf, the space between the shelf and the back wall determines how fair the game really is. The more space there is for the object to topple over, the fairer the game.

These rigged games are not limited to the midway. The Tip Up invites players to push up on the neck of a bottle that begins lying on its side, until it stands. If the bottle stays upright, the player wins; if it falls back over, he loses. This is a simple but ingenious game that takes advantage of the fact that almost all bottles are off-balance and slightly heavier on one side. The game operator determines which side is heavy and sets that half on top to guarantee a loser. The additional weight, though slight, is enough to carry the bottle past the standing position so it always falls over. If the bottle is set with the weight on the bottom, then it's possible for the bottle to settle on the base.

I once made up a version of this game to demonstrate how much money a con man could make in an hour. Starting with nothing, I gathered the necessary props, had the bartender loan me a bottle (that I'd already tested), and got a crowd of people to play. By manipulating who could win and when, I made over five hundred theoretical dollars before convincing one unlucky chump to let it ride and try for three stands in a row. The first two were easy but, thanks to the way I set the third, he didn't stand a chance.

Some people take a dim view of any game with a "gaff" designed to make it seem a lot easier than it actually is. Newspaper reports and television exposes take basketball champions to the midway who find they can't shoot a single basket or special forces snipers who can't shoot out a red star that's six feet down-range. Reporters go on to reveal that the baskets are not regulation size, the balls are overinflated, or the fairground guns aren't properly calibrated. Why on earth would a carnival game observe NBA regulations or provide properly sighted weapons? In my opinion, they're looking at the wrong games. These stall owners are offering entertainment, and while I agree that there's a deception in the way they present themselves, trickery should be accepted in this world. It comes with the territory.

The Flat Joint

While the midway offers games with little chance of success, it may also feature a particular breed of game that's designed purely to steal money. A "flat joint" or "flat store" is a game where there's no real chance of winning. Many legitimate carnys dislike having these games around as they generate a bad feeling, public distrust, and, all too often, police attention. They can still be found in carnivals, but they are just as likely to appear anywhere that offers a fresh supply of unwary victims. Some games can be reworked on the fly, starting as a percentage or skill-based affair but becoming an outright scam when the operator offers to change the structure of the game.

The Work-Up

Once the carny convinces a sucker to play toward some kind of agreed outcome or score, then the prizes become much more attractive. This approach allows a crooked carny to pick and choose his targets while presenting his stall as a typical, honest game until a mark agrees to play the "work-up," and it is no longer a game. Then it becomes more akin to a robbery.

The Queen's Cut

To help you understand how this type of scam works, it would be useful to invent our own game. I'll shuffle a deck of cards and offer you the chance to cut to any card. In this game, if you cut to a queen, you win a dollar, but every cut costs you a dollar, so I either keep your dollar or give you one of mine whenever you find a queen. This isn't really fair since, with four queens in a fifty-two-card deck, the odds are against you. But you should have a one in thirteen chance of cutting to a queen, which is much better odds than some that you'll find at the fair.

Let's also imagine that this turns out to be your idea of a great time, so you're happy to play and no one gets hurt until I offer you the chance to work your way up to a much bigger prize. Since you love this game so much, I generously offer to play for more money. This time, you get to cut the deck one hundred times. If you happen to cut to all four queens, then I will pay you five hundred dollars, but you still have to pay one dollar every time you cut the deck. That means you might have to pay me as much as one hundred dollars, but you're pretty sure that, with a hundred chances, you can cut to all four queens so you agree to play.

Sound fair? There's a catch.

Every time you cut to a heart, I'm going to add a hundred dollars to the prize, but you also have to pay double each time you cut. After cutting to five hearts, the prize fund would double to a thousand bucks—but you'd be paying thirty-two dollars for every round. Three more hearts create a prize fund of thirteen hundred bucks, but now you're paying $256 per cut! What you don't know is that I've secretly trimmed the queens so they're slightly narrower and shorter than the other cards and, because of the way you must cut and show the face of the upper half, the chances of cutting to a queen at all are slim to none. Cutting to all four queens would take an act of God, especially since I've palmed-out one of the queens!

Clearly, this is not a game at all, but rather a complete con. From the player's point of view, it might appear to be a reasonable proposition. Once he's doubled his stake a few times, the odds against him should be clear, but I can keep the player involved by offering to also double the prize money whenever he cuts to a heart. Now there seems to be a real chance to make some money, but by the time he's cut to ten hearts, each turn will cost more than a thousand dollars and most people would go broke long before that.

This imaginary game clearly illustrates how trying to work your way up to a prize, where the price to keep playing constantly increases, is a sure way to lose a lot of money; when the game is fixed or the odds are heavily stacked against you, it's just a matter of time before you're cleaned out. The important thing to remember is that real games of this nature are designed to seem beatable, that's the point. But in actuality, they continue to take the player's money until there's no more to take.

Getting Hooped

A Hoopla game features a table filled with tall and short blocks of wood. On top of these are prizes that can be won if a wooden or plastic hoop is successfully thrown over one of the blocks and lands flat on the table, and is not hooked on the block in any way. Getting a hoop over any block is difficult, though achievable with a flat-topped cylindrical block, but other shapes can make a legitimate throw almost impossible. The game of hoopla is an excellent example of a flat store that can operate a legitimate skill-based game until the right sucker walks up with deep-enough pockets to reach into.

First of all, the cheap prizes (the ones that are actually winnable) are moved away and the operator introduces more attractive prizes, including Rolex watches and bottles of expensive champagne. The only catch is that every ring costs a couple of dollars more. After the first round, the player has lost more money than he intended but has been frustratingly close to winning several times. Of course, it's designed this way. The operator offers more rings for more money in return for removing some of the blocks. This makes it much easier to concentrate on prizes the player really wants, so he accepts and loses another fistful of dollars. Before the mark can back away, the hustler now moves the remaining blocks closer, offering more rings for more money. Now it seems entirely likely that the player will win, but despite hooking the rings around the edge of the blocks several times, none fall completely over their target.

Looks easy, doesn't it?

The hustler moves the block even closer and demonstrates several times that he can throw the rings over the block. Having come this far, the sucker buys a handful of rings for even *more* money, certain that this time he couldn't possibly fail. He loses again, and the game continues until the mark either walks away or runs out of money, usually the latter.

Hoopla is a brilliant little scam because it seems so easy, yet is almost impossible to win from the player's position. The wooden blocks are flat on the bottom but their top is cut at a steep angle, which makes it fantastically difficult to throw a ring over, unless you are throwing toward the highest side of the block. If the lower side of the angled cut is toward you, then you might as well throw your money into a drain. The operator is naturally on the tall side of the blocks and can easily throw hoops from there. In fact, the blocks can be incredibly close to the player without improving his chances unless he reaches forward and drops the hoop straight down, which would be a foul throw, naturally.

The hustler's ability to appear to make the game easier and improve the mark's chances while taking more money each time are the hallmarks of a work-up scam or "trap game." The mark is moved gradually toward the prize until it seems like he can't possibly fail; then the true odds (which are enormous) do the rest. In Blackpool, a popular seaside town on England's west coast, hoopla stalls have been known to set up along the sea front, drawing people in with free throws and friendly banter until someone takes the bait and plays for bigger prizes. People regularly lose hundreds, even thousands at these grubby, ugly little stalls playing for expensive bottles of booze, jewelry, and fancy watches. This is why they are called "trap games" because, once a player has lost so much, it's very difficult to walk away. They just end up following their losses even deeper into the hole.

Speaking to friends "in the know" I was told that several people had been mugged after refusing to play and that rumors of drug dealing from these stalls were rife. I once walked up to one of these games and was quickly recognized from *The Real Hustle* and threatened. Smiling, I backed away, but it was clear that these guys meant business.

Despite claims that hoopla was merely a game of skill, Blackpool police finally managed to close the stalls down after passing the blocks to a statistician for analysis. He quickly proved that the odds were unreasonable and the operator was then charged and taken to court. Personally, I was disappointed that it took so long, especially since the FBI had performed similar tests on the same props decades earlier. When breaking down the operation, police even discovered that the prize Rolex watches were cheap knock-offs and the bottles of booze were all empty!

Mark Mason, a dear friend and now a dealer in magicians' props, was once one of the biggest game operators in Blackpool. His joints varied from mini jam auctions and trap games like the Razz to the ticket scam, where players would pick sealed paper tickets from a large basket hoping to find the name of a winning football team. Everything in the basket was a loser; Mark would secretly hide a winner in his palm and add it to their pile of chosen tickets. The objective was to pick out ten tickets, and if they could find three winning teams, they'd win a prize. By adding the winners with a little sleight of hand, Mark was in complete control of how many winners they found and could use this to keep them playing for that last golden ticket.*

Once someone has lost a lot of money to this kind of game, it might seem easy for him to walk away, but in the heat of the moment, the player is convinced that he is *so* close that he is certain to win eventually. The con is *designed* to lure the mark into believing that winning would easily compensate for the money he has already lost. This is why prizes in a trap game must be bigger and more attractive. If the victim has lost three hundred dollars but is playing for a two-thousand-dollar prize, then he will keep playing until either he runs out of money or it no longer seems worth playing. Hoopla is a powerful trap that succeeds because it looks like a simple game that's entirely possible to win.

The king of these games comes in many different guises, is known by countless names from Lucky Numbers and Thunderball to Cuban Bingo, but most famously it's known as The Razzle Dazzle.

Razzle

I'm often asked to name my favorite scam and, like trying to decide a preferred film or book, this question is impossible to answer truthfully. The term "favorite" isn't really appropriate since we're talking about a criminal act, but the question is a

---

* Mark gave up that life decades ago and is now a passionate advocate of informing and protecting the public.

natural one. I've pulled over five hundred different con games, so surely there's one that stands out? There are many con games that I find fascinating or ingenious to varying degrees (many are described in this book), but if you put a gun to my head and forced me to name just one scam that embodies everything that interests me, the Razz would be it. If fate or misfortune threw me onto the street and I had to resort to larceny, the razzle dazzle would be my game of choice.

It took several seasons of *The Real Hustle* to convince production that the razz was worth filming, because it was incredibly difficult to describe in words. Game charts with points for certain scores, a box with numbered holes, and a cup filled with marbles hardly sound like great television; but, when we finally built the props and filmed the scam, the result was everything I'd hoped for. The razzle proved to be a perfect example of how and why scams work, and after the first mark walked away penniless, my producer leapt out of hiding and ran over to the stall shouting "that was fucking fantastic!"

My interest in this particular game began with a conversation in Las Vegas. A friend told me a funny story about a hustler who was arrested for playing the razzle when the victim's wife became convinced he was either drugged or mesmerized. Later, I did a little research to learn more about the game but found that there was very little information available to me. I had trouble understanding why this particular swindle was so strong or how it could make so much money with such a simple secret.

The razzle depends on the operator to miscount quickly and without hesitation. The hustler in my friend's story had worked the razz for so long that when he was hired as a blackjack dealer, the pit boss had to constantly stop him from accidentally busting out his own hand when his mind naturally reverted to old habits. In a razzle joint, it is *when* the miscount is used that makes it such a perfect little scam. Rolled fairly, the odds of scoring any points are astronomical, but once a victim starts to play, the operator uses the miscount to give him points and keep him in the game. Put simply, you only cheat *in the mark's favor!* Over time, the player's score can creep closer and closer to the prize without any real hope of winning.

Once I got my head around this simple secret and why it was so powerful, I needed to know more. To practice, I built a simple little joint with a game chart from an old gambler's supply catalog, eight tiny dice, and a large leather cup. Quickly, I learned how unfair the game really was when played honestly. I then began to experiment with ways to fake the count.

Jeff McBride, a fellow magician, had worked a razzle joint one summer when he was a teenager. I called him long-distance to discuss how his version of the game was played. Jeff tipped me to a simple secret that made the miscount almost impossible to detect and looked every bit as fair as an honest count. Once I'd mastered this, I started practicing on my kids and in a few weeks I was ready to do it for real, but it took two more years before razzle became part of *The Real Hustle*. During this time I learned more about the game and that it had been banned many times because it was just too strong.

Mark Mason told me that he always went for the money and is now quite open about his attitude in those days. "There

A classic Razzle set. Just add suckers.

were some guys who would always leave them a few bucks. Me? No . . . If it was to be got, I took everything I could get. I'd actually try to see inside their wallet . . ." In Blackpool, variations on the classic razzle joint ripped off so many tourists that after hundreds were left penniless, the town council stepped in and banned all numbers games, which made way for the hoopla stalls to take over. In order to demonstrate the razzle dazzle for TV, I needed to show just how powerful it could be and how much money it could make.

The game works like this: Once someone approaches the stall, I engage them in a little chat, talking about the prizes and making sure they understand what they might win. If the mark is interested, then I sell him a couple of rolls to get him started. After each roll, I pick up the marbles one at a time and toss them back into the cup, adding up each number to create their total for that roll. As I pick them up, the total increases so I'm never calling out the numbers that the marbles are sitting in, just the sum of these numbers as it increases. "Two, six, twelve, eighteen, nineteen, twenty-four, twenty-nine, thirty-five!" Counted this way it's very hard to follow and correlate the numbers for each ball and the total. Using the counting trick I'd learned from Jeff, I could easily manipulate the total until the last two or three marbles brought me to a winning number. Within the first couple of rolls, I'd miscount to forty-four, which gives five points to the player. *That* takes him halfway toward a prize so long as he keeps playing. Now I slow down and let the odds take over, counting fairly until the player hits a roll of twenty-nine (the most common number, rolled fairly), which is marked on the chart as "ADD." This number forces him to play for more money, sometimes even doubling the price per roll. After a couple of twenty-nines, I miscount again to throw him another point or two and continue feeding the player points as the price to play steadily increases.

The prizes can also be increased during the game, and on many game charts, certain numbers are labeled "HP," which can mean whatever the operator chooses! Most often, "HP" is translated as a "House Prize," where either a piece of plush is given to the mark to keep him happy or another big prize is added to the mark's ultimate goal. I've heard of some hustlers who use

"HP" as "Half Points" in order to reduce the player's score! Initially, this seemed unnecessary to me. Then I understood that it allowed the con artist to continue awarding points so the player is always scoring while occasionally being forced back. Also, each time the player's points were halved, another prize could be added. The result is that the player gets a lot more action (winning and losing) and the game operator eventually offers to ignore the "HP" rolls (and stop reducing his score) as further leverage to keep him playing. Psychologically, this gives the mark the impression of progress, when of course, there has been none.

It's not an easy game to follow unless you're actually playing, but it should be clear that the operator is in complete control of the outcome. The only thing getting played in the razzle dazzle

Game charts and coupons for a "free roll." There are many versions of "The Razz"—all are a scam.

is the mark. One of the most powerful aspects of the razz is its ability to put the victim on "the send"—to a cash machine. Once they've lost everything they have, there is a built-in angle that hustlers use to keep them playing if they can get more money, which is what sent my mark running toward the ATM on the show.

By the time the player is out of money, his score could be as much as nine and a half points—painfully close to the ten points needed to win. This is where the operator leans into his sucker to offer him a deal he can't refuse. Claiming that he's never seen such bad luck and that he feels sorry for the player, the hustler offers to hold the score for five minutes if the player can get more money. He then sweetens the deal by offering his mark twenty rolls to make that last half point, and shows all the money the player's lost so far and adds it to his potential prize! The catch is that the player has to come back with whatever amount the hustler demands to continue playing. In one devastating move, the con artist has upped the stakes, offered an irresistible deal, *and* restricted how much time the victim has to act, making this a perfect example of a con game in action. It relies a great deal on the "sunk-cost fallacy" that keeps gamblers chasing their losses with more money. As the gambler's prayer says: "Please God, let me break even. I need the money!"

For my first mark on *The Real Hustle*, offering to hold the score until he came back with more money was a powerful hook. His common sense began to wake up and I could feel him resisting; then he saw all of the money he'd lost, which I folded and placed under one of the prizes. I then said "If you can get another three hundred, I'll hold the score and I'll let you win back your money. I can't say fairer than that." That was all I needed to say. Five minutes later he returned with more cash and I gave him twenty rolls to make half a point. This time I counted every roll fairly and let him follow along until the last roll sent him home, broke.

We repeated the scam four times and in every case, if they could go and get more money, they did so. I calculated that, based on the daily maximum withdrawal from an ATM and the amount of cash most people would carry, making a thousand pounds an hour would be easy. In a holiday destination such as Blackpool, where people tend to bring more cash, the potential hourly score could be much higher and the damage to the mark much more severe. How many victims have lost all of their savings at the beginning of their vacation and had to take their family home early? Luckily for our victims in Bournemouth, I gave back all of their money!

I adore this scam because it's powerful, it's clever, and it's one of the most effective illustrations of how easily people can get sucked into a con game, but it also reminds me of just how badly people can be affected by this sort of crime. The razzle doesn't merely steal your money, it convinces you that you were unlucky and irresponsible at the same time. Walking away, most suckers have no idea how they were able to lose so much, so quickly. They feel oh so close and just so unlucky, when it was all designed to make them feel that way. Luck had nothing to do with it.

On the midway, in the middle of the fair, there's a lot of fun to be had, but wherever you find them, con games like hoopla and the razzle dazzle succeed because they appear to be just as harmless. Never forget that these are textbook scams designed to trap their victims and squeeze them for every penny. Next time a carny offers you the chance to play for bigger stakes, stick to the soft toys. Pay to play, not to win.

STREET GOT GAME

His hands were deep inside the pockets of his five-hundred-dollar blue jeans, and I could see through the overpriced denim that his right hand was tightly holding onto his wallet. He leaned forward, chin down, eyes watching every move—he was clearly ready to pop. The sweat on his brow meant it was only a matter of time before he jumped into the game.

I was in Las Vegas and had spent several weeks studying various casino games, learning ways to beat them from grifters and advantage players. The game I was watching was not inside a casino, it was on the street, right outside Caesar's Palace on the corner of Las Vegas Boulevard and Flamingo. It was run by a man in his fifties, throwing three playing cards onto a pile of cardboard boxes. The idea was to follow the queen of hearts and try to pick it out after the cards were mixed. The "dealer" was surrounded by people, some of whom pushed and shoved to take part, even throwing money at the cards if they could find the lady.

My hand was holding onto my own wallet but for a different reason. I knew that this game was nothing more than an operatic scam, and if I didn't bet, I might just as soon have my pocket picked clean by someone in the crowd. I was in the front line, watching every move. Across from me, I saw the sucker was lit up like a Christmas tree, ready to jump in at any moment; the heat was on as the hustler pressed me to join the game or get lost. Someone threw a fifty-dollar bill onto the queen and a hundred dollars was quickly passed to the "winner" by the dealer. Again, the cards were shown and thrown; the sucker finally pulled out a twenty-dollar bill. He bet on a card but the previous player had bet his hundred dollars on the same card. "I gotta take the bigger man!" the dealer shouted as he showed the queen and paid the other guy.

I started to feel the squeeze as people on either side blocked me from moving back while the dealer upped the pressure on me to play. I realized that, to this cardsharp, I must have looked just as ripe as the other guy, who was starting to turn red under the shifting neon streetlights. Finally, the dealer accidentally dropped a card, and as he bent over to pick it up, someone in the crowd reached for the queen and bit down on the corner with a mouth full of yellow teeth. The crippled card was replaced on top of the boxes before the dealer returned and continued to play without noticing the sharp bend that had appeared on his money card. Once the cards were mixed, the dealer called for bets and the sucker saw his big chance. A thick, folded wad of cash was placed on the bent card. "Fourteen hundred!" he shouted, triumphantly. "That's fourteen hundred fucking dollars!"

The dealer didn't miss a beat. He told the sucker to turn over the card and, as soon as we all saw that the bent card was *not* the queen, the cash was gone. Someone in the crowd shouted "Cops!" and suddenly, the sucker and I were alone on the streetcorner, staring at a crimped card that had cost him a small fortune.

There is no such thing as an actual street *game.* That fact should be enough to keep people away from Three-Card Monte, the Shell and Pea, the Razzle, and the Endless Chain, but experience tells me otherwise. A hustler once told me that "you don't need to be a dummy to play but it sure does help!" I'd argue that, no matter how intelligent you might be, walking up to a game on the street is nothing but a dumb move with expensive consequences.

Magicians are fascinated by street games. There are many books, pamphlets, and instructional videos dedicated to the genre. A few companies sell the required props, which are often much better than those used by professional hustlers. The shell and pea has become a very popular performance piece with artists like Bob Sheets creating entertaining, funny, and magical presentations. Some performers use injection-molded shells, balanced perfectly to avoid accidentally flipping over; others use beautifully painted shells in the shape of scarab beetles. On the street, a few bottle caps and a rolled up piece of tape are enough to get the money.

When I speak to conjurors about these scams, they reveal a wealth of ideas and techniques designed to steal the pea, move a card, or manipulate an outcome, but they rarely consider the psychological trickery that manipulates a mark; after all, it is of little use when there's no money on the table. Without any skin in the game, the audience is passive and interested only in the movement of objects, so the magician's job is to make this as entertaining as possible.

Watching Bob Sheets perform his signature routine is a lesson in legerdemain. Bob's repertoire of sleights and subtleties is far greater than your average hustler because, on the street, one simple move can steal thousands of dollars. Conversations with Bob, Whit Haydn, and other experts have always been revealing, but as they will tell you, the simplicity of the street game is one of its greatest strengths, and most hustlers have a limited but effective repertoire.

First, let's establish that it's not a "game." The objective of the hustler is not to offer odds or to pay winners under any circumstances. There are only two possible outcomes, depending on your ability to resist peer pressure and temptation: Either you'll lose money or you won't. Street games are theatrical muggings designed to fool people into thinking they have the upper hand, using techniques that have been successfully ripping off suckers for centuries. Many victims are well aware that these games are crooked, but, armed with a little information, they walk up to a game thinking they might be able to "spot the move." A few minutes later they're broke and wondering what the hell just happened.

There's a lot we can learn from street games like three-card monte or the shell and pea. Many writers point to sleight of hand and clever gotchas as the secret to these scams. These are important elements and fascinating to be sure, but swapping out a bent card only works if the mark makes a bet in the first place. And getting the mark to bet enough to make the scam worth someone's while is determined by other, more powerful factors. Like many scams, the size of the prize is determined during the build-up to the steal. It's a game of foreplay where the final outcome is a product of psychological and physical dexterity. The hook is the game itself, the line is the journey to the big bet (when the mark thinks they have the upper hand), and the sinker is a clever twist that keeps the hustler one step ahead of the crowd.

Going straight for the sucker's money is clumsy and less profitable than manipulating the mark into betting everything he has on the turn of a card or the location of a pea. Here is where the real con game happens. Any idiot can trick someone into losing a single bet, but it takes hustle to get the mark to bet everything he has.

In 2006 I was in Stockholm for a conference and spent my spare time walking around the city. At that time there were several shell mobs working the streets, starting games on the edge of popular thoroughfares while spotters kept an eye out for the police. I spent a day following two of these gangs as they scammed their way from one street to the next, making a couple of hundred euros with every setup. Both mobs played an identical scam, and at the end of the day I saw them meet in a nearby restaurant with what I assume to be a third group. Twelve people making three to five thousand euros per hour is a healthy profit, and I have no doubt they're still playing today. They played on a piece of carpet that was dropped onto the ground and used matchbox drawers and a piece of makeup sponge that was wrapped in white masking tape (they dropped one as they walked away from a group of baffled German tourists and I was quick to grab my souvenir). The operator, who ran the game, leaned down to mix the boxes as the crowd tried to guess where the ball was hiding. An attractive girl watched the crowd as the operator pitched the game until their shills were surrounded by potential victims.

The job of a shill is to play the game according to a predetermined plan, but also to follow instructions from the operator as he tries to work someone into the game. The common assumption is that the shills win money to attract suckers and prove the game can be won, but they serve a more important purpose. Once a victim has been identified, the operator uses the shills to stall him until he's ready to lose everything. The mob (a team who operate street games) might take a few bucks from someone to see if they've got gamble, but if that causes them to walk away, taking twenty dollars might cost them the chance to steal hundreds.

In Sweden, the shell mob had a simple way of determining how much their victims had to lose and manipulated them into betting it all at once. The girl was a professional roper with an eye for the right face in a crowd. Once she spotted someone with the desired look, she moved in and pushed her way to the sucker's side. Meanwhile, the operator traded money with the shills or took the occasional bet from members of the crowd as the roper sank her claws into their real target. "It's in the first one, over there," she'd tell them, accurately predicting the winning box every time. Slowly, she'd move closer, pointing out the location of the ball as the shills seemed to always bet on the wrong boxes. In a few short minutes, the mark was listening to every word with wallet in hand, and as soon as he went for the money, the same scenario was played out every time.

With the roper now holding onto his arm, the mark would take out a bill in order to make a bet and the girl would peek into the wallet to see how much he had. She'd point out one of the boxes and the sucker would hold out his cash, but one of the shills would jump in to bet more money on a losing box. The operator took the bigger bet but showed that the sucker had made the right choice. By now, the girl was breathing into his ear, whispering that he should bet everything on the next round. The ball was tossed under one of the boxes and they were quickly mixed, but this time the winning box was accidentally tipped up slightly at the front end, revealing the ball underneath. The mark would immediately pull out his money as the roper encouraged him to place it all on the winning box. I even saw a girl pull more cash from one guy's wallet to make sure they got it all! The mark was then invited to lean down and look under the box himself. The ball was gone, and by the time he stood up, the girl was too. Before the bewildered victim knew it, he was alone and penniless.

I was fascinated by this simple operation and found the use of a pretty girl to be a clever addition to the traditional scam. Typically, most monte mobs depend on an operator to run the game, some shills to follow instructions, and a couple of spotters to act as lookouts for the police. The operator usually does all of the work and decides how best to work each mark up to a big bet. The Swedish mob employed their roper to devastating effect, and each time I watched them play, she never failed to manipulate the mark. I even saw the same approach used on a married man as the shills pushed between him and his wife so the roper could step in and work her magic. When that game was over, I suspect that losing money was the least of his problems. This variation is not new, in fact it's mentioned in many books on the subject, where shills would tip off other players until they had enough confidence to place a bet. In modern versions, the closest I'd seen was a rough hustler badgering members of the crowd for "not having the balls to bet." This was a subtler and more powerful approach that played on more than the mark's desire to win money; it worked on his ego, too.

That night I discussed my observations with a performer who specialized in the three-shell game and had performed thousands of shows talking about "how they get you" before raising the roof with his magical version of the game. Surprisingly, he wasn't interested in seeing the Swedish mob work. "They're all Russians. Amateurs. A real mob has an Englishman, a French girl. . . ." And so he went on to describe his perfect "mob." For him, it was a performance piece and unless they fit his theatrical ideals, or used a move he hadn't seen before, my

Russian gang in Stockholm was of little interest. Personally, I understand his point of view. He's an artist and for him it's all a show. Other performers have made the mistake of thinking that hustlers share the same interests and have tried to engage monte mobs to discuss methods. This is like Robert De Niro trying to do mix it up with real mobsters just because he once played Vito Corleone in *The Godfather: Part II*! It's understandable that magicians care more about technical details because they are the tools to building an act, but when the same methods are revealed to the public in an effort to expose street games, the natural inclination to focus on sleight of hand distracts people from the real danger.

Even if you are completely familiar with "the hype," "the steal," "the lay down," or "the bent corner," there's no chance of winning. If you step up looking to be a smart ass, the chances are you're mixing it up with people who are much more dangerous than you, and I mean physically, and it's never a good idea to get between hyenas and their supper. If you think you can outplay a street mob, you're just as juicy a mark as all the other suckers waiting to play. Operators know when someone is wise to the standard methods and many are able to exploit a player's knowledge with a well-placed double-bluff. In these circumstances, the build-up is ultimately the same while the final switch can be changed, or the gang simply waits until a know-it-all throws down his cash, then runs away with it!

When watching a street game, we see classic scams at work, manipulating emotions and building expectation while focusing the mark on a perceived advantage until they're ready to burst.

The sleight of hand used is fascinating, but without the mechanics of a good con game it wouldn't be worth the hustler's time to learn. It would remain nothing more than an entertaining conjuror's trick.

The Work

Monte relies on several moves to change the expected order of three objects before or after they are mixed. With playing cards, there is often a heavy downward bend placed along the middle of each card so that the center of each card is raised above the playing surface. I've seen a couple of variations on this where the cards are roughly bent with a sharp v-shaped fold running along the card so that the center is raised but the rest of the card lies flat. I've also seen it played on pieces of thick carpet with no bend in the cards.

Variations are played with round black rubber discs and a piece of white paper stuck to one or with cardboard beer mats and even square pieces of wood with a clear grain running in one direction. In the last ten years, the discs have been more common on the street than cards, but to more easily understand how the game works, I'll describe the classic version of Find The Lady.

The Hype

The most important sleight is "the hype," where two cards are openly picked up at once, one over the other, maintaining a tiny gap between the two but aligned along one edge. The lowermost face is then shown with a rotation of the wrist before being turned down and tossed to the table. There is a fair hype and a crooked hype, and the success of this move depends on them looking identical. With a fair hype, the lower card that was just shown drops to the table with a downward swing that hinges at the wrist as the thumb and fingers release pressure on the outer and inner edges of that card. The fake hype mimics these actions exactly, showing the face card of a pair but throwing the uppermost card in an identical wrist turn. The illusion can be perfect when performed well.

The fair hype is clearly demonstrated several times before any money is wagered, but when the operator spots an easy mark, the fake hype is used to switch the winner for a loser so the crowd is following the wrong card from the outset. I've only seen the hype used this way to grab a few bucks from curious marks or to find a suitable victim for the build-up. Many people walk away as soon as they lose but when someone stays, there's a chance he might be rich pickings if he takes the bait. Action might come from anyone in the crowd, so there are strategies to deal with anyone who bets randomly or can follow the hype. If money is forced onto the correct card, there are several sleights that can switch out that card for a loser.

The "Mexican Turnover" uses a card held by the operator to flip over another card on the table, switching these cards in the process. The card that began on the table ends up in the operator's hand, while the card that started face down in his hand is now face up on the table. I've seen magicians do this move for decades and it almost always looks terrible, but on the street, it is performed without hesitation in a fluid, continuous action that's impossible to follow with the naked eye. In a street game, the winning card is switched out and immediately switched in as the other face down card is flipped over. In action, someone picks the money-card, then the operator picks up a loser and uses it to flip the winner face up, switching it so the winner is now in his hand. The winner is then used to flip over the other face down card on the table and the switch is repeated so the winner turns up at that position. Now the losing card that's in the operator's hand is shown and the sequence complete.

Another way to switch cards is a more blatant method that somehow fools the eye and is used in other versions of monte with rubber or leather discs. In this method, a losing card is held in the hand and the winner picked up under that card, then immediately flipped forward, revolving face up onto the table. This can be performed fairly or used to switch the lower card for the one already in the hand by releasing the uppermost card in the flipping action and retaining the card that was just picked up. Both versions can look identical but only fool people when done quickly and in rhythm with the game.

The Shell Game

The three-shell game works in a similar manner to the monte, allowing the mob complete control over the location of a pea or small ball that's being followed by the crowd. Using a sponge or rubber peas combined with soft surfaces like pieces of carpet or rubber-backed pads, the operator is able to steal these with an imperceptible sleight as the shells are being moved around. So clean is this move that magicians often cover a shell (that has the pea underneath) with a glass and can still steal the pea right under the noses of an eagle-eyed audience.

Bottle caps and matchbox drawers are just as effective, but the latter allows for a powerful "accidental peek" where the near end of the box is tapped so the end nearest the crowd lifts up, permitting them to see the ball underneath, which is then immediately stolen out! With traditional shells or bottle caps, the operator may let the crowd see the ball roll from one cap to another, where it is quickly—and invisibly—moved to the third shell. I've seen illogical versions where a shell is clearly shown empty to concentrate the sucker on the remaining two, but the pea ends in the previously empty shell, just like a magic trick. Incredibly, this still gets the money and that's all that matters on the street.

Clearly, if the cards or the pea can be switched before, during, or after they are mixed on the table, it's impossible to win. Remember this when you see a street game; the purpose of these scams is to make people not only think they can beat the game but that they have an advantage over the operator. To this end, the mob works together to create a trap that sinks their mark every time. In essence, these scams all convince the victim that they can't lose, and while some suckers will jump in without thinking, most people need a good push in the form of the build-up.

The Build-Up

There are two key forms of build-up used to manipulate the mark; these can either be applied directly, as with the Russian girl who openly talks the mark into betting it all, or subtly, by stalling the mark until he is convinced he can beat the game and eager to do so. The former builds excitement while the latter frustrates the victim as he tries to make a bet but is held off until he reaches for his entire bankroll. In both cases, the sequence of events is similar.

In London, modern street game teams are often Eastern-European families, and it's comically easy to spot the shills in the crowd since everyone looks similar and closely related. The shills are an important element in a monte mob, and I often look to them to determine how experienced or effective the mob might be. Some operators travel and hire local characters to fill in the crowd, giving them basic instructions and limited responsibilities. I see this from time to time when the operator is trying to do too much and is sometimes openly shouting instructions to his rookie crew members as he tries to fleece his marks. With more experienced mobs, the shills work more efficiently and follow the game operator's lead almost instinctively.

It is well known that shills in a crowd are there to bet and win money as part of the show, but they are most effective when they are used to *hold off* a potential sucker until he's ready to pop. It's a simple procedure: the shills start losing! As the crowd watches, members of the mob begin throwing bets toward the wrong cards or shells or matchboxes. The people around them can follow the winner easily, but instead of questioning why the shills are losing, the most common response is to believe that they are somehow much better at this than the losers. The natural conclusion is that if they were to bet, they'd win.

Eventually, this begins to pay off as outside money is brought into the game. In some cases the operator takes these bets and either switches or steals out the winner, or sees that real money is coming in; he then hypes, steals, or switches during the mixing procedure before taking bets. Either way, if real money lands on the winner, it can easily be replaced with a loser to steal that cash. But there's a more powerful strategy that keeps the mark playing and encourages him to throw down more money: the over bet. Here, a mark, or even several, might bet on the winner, but a shill, holding out a larger amount, bets on one of the losers. The operator claims he has to take the bigger bet and rejects the marks' money while showing that the shill has lost. The marks then see that they would have won, and if they stay in the game, chances are good that they'll pull out more money, especially when they fall for the big steal.

The Big Steal

The big steal is where the mark is convinced that he can't lose, and there are always new ways to manipulate people into thinking they're on top of the game. It's not necessarily a subtle ploy, but it is devastatingly effective if the mark is ready to throw down. The bent corner, for example, is the most powerful, and least subtle, part of the monte scam. Just as I saw on the street outside Caesar's Palace, this clever ploy makes suckers out of almost anyone once they are emotionally committed to the game. Eager to bet and sure they have the upper hand, all a good mark needs is a push to make the big bet and the bent corner almost always gets their money.

The bent-corner scam almost always "gets the money."

It works like this: The mob orchestrates a reason for the operator to turn away or pick something up, and when this happens, one of the shills reaches for the winning card and openly bends one corner for all to see. The operator returns to the game, seemingly unaware that his money card has been marked. The cards are shown and mixed, exactly as before, except the winner is now obvious; the marks see their chance and make their move. The bent card, however, is no longer the winner because, during the mixing procedure, the operator is able to bend another card, switch it for the winner, and then remove the original bent corner. This can be done so quickly and deceptively that magicians regularly employ this move at the conclusion of their monte demonstration. Ricky Jay has used it to devastating effect on talk shows by employing friends and fellow guests as shills to bend the corner to the delight of the audience. Even under the unblinking eye of the television camera, the bent corner switch is invisible.

In the three-shell game, the tip-up of matchbox drawers has a similar effect. I've also seen operators encourage victims to place their foot on the shell they think holds the pea. A flash of the pea convinces the mark he has the right one and placing his foot (or hand) on it convinces him that it can't be switched out. The operator then acts as if he thought the mark wanted a different shell and plays out a scene where he's trying to call off the bet, further convincing the mark that he's made the right choice. In Stockholm, this strategy was even stronger thanks to the pretty girl pushing the mark to "go for it."

The lipstick swindle is a relatively novel twist that we employed on *The Real Hustle*. It combined the Swedish strategy of using a pretty girl to lead the mark and a simple idea for marking the wrong card. We played it in a crowded bar, near the windows so our camera crew could see everything. Jess was chatting to our potential victims as I approached. After a few minutes of chat and couple of card tricks, I offered to play a game for money. Alex stepped in to serve as my shill while Jess proved to the marks that she could always pick out the winning card, and while she whispered poison into their ears, Alex would pick the wrong cards and lose.

Once the marks were convinced, Jess held up a finger, and as I dealt with Alex, she openly drew her finger across her painted lips, transferring red lipstick to her fingertip. She then used this to mark the middle face down card on the table. When I threw all three cards face up, the middle card was indeed the winner, but I had secretly switched the cards as I turned them over. Jess had marked a loser, but I had switched the winner into the same position as the cards were turned face up. This convinced everyone that Jess had successfully marked the money card.

I repeated the switch as I turned everything face down, mixed the cards, and called for bets. Sure enough, the mark came over the top with all the money he had and was shocked when he lost. When he complained, I noticed the marked card and turned the tables on him, calling *him* a cheat! This gave me the chance to walk away and let Jess cool them out. Jess was quick to follow us when the sucker threatened her, proving that, pretty girl or not, when someone loses, it's best to get the hell out of there.

Another strategy is to have a shill act as a big bettor in the final round of play, with the operator concentrating his attention on his secret assistant. In this example, the "hype" is used to switch the winning card or rubber disc so that the crowd thinks it's in the center when it is actually on their left. The shill steps in and asks how much he can bet on the rightmost option, which everyone knows is a loser, and the operator agrees to take all comers. Just like the bent corner scam, the operator drops something and turns to retrieve it as the shill switches the right option for the one in the middle, where the crowd mistakenly believes the real winner was all along. This is a powerful strategy because it causes the onlookers to believe that the operator is the victim of the shill and, most important, that they can capitalize on the situation and join the bet. For people who have already lost a few times, this is a powerful motivator to win back their losses and many people jump at the chance.

Naturally, they all lose, the winner is shown on the left, and the game suddenly breaks down or the crowd is allowed to walk. From time to time, an honest voice in the crowd will warn the operator of the apparent attempt to cheat him but this is easily ignored; I've heard that on one occasion, an eager mark punched someone out for doing this!

A clever variation on this approach is the newspaper feint, where the winner ends in the middle of the row of three but the onlookers are convinced that it's on the left or right. Here the newspaper on which the game is being played (on top of boxes or a small table) is spun 180 degrees, apparently sending the winner to the other end of the row. This is played as a secret move that the crowd "catches." My friend Lee Asher once saw a monte player pick up the newspaper as a tray and return it after turning it slowly. In both examples, the onlookers believe they have seen something they weren't supposed to see when the opposite is true; since the winner had already been secretly switched to the middle, it never actually moves. Clearly, the purpose of the feint is to make the crowd believe that they have caught out the operator, which motivates them to jump at their chance to beat him.

These moves, sleights, and strategies are designed to manipulate people, and it is a common mistake to focus on how they manipulate the objects in play. It is fascinating that cards, shells, boxes, or discs can be switched or that tiny balls can vanish or appear at will, but knowledge of exactly how this is done won't help you if you make the critical error of getting involved in the first place. Monte mobs are prepared for people who know their techniques, and it's an easy matter to use other, lesser-known methods, or, simpler yet, to just throw or mix the objects honestly while pretending to cheat! With the bent corner, all the operator has to do is leave the bend in place and not switch it at all, while a shill pretends to fall for the original ploy so that a know-it-all mark can jump in and bet on another card, certain that he has the upper hand. If I were to do this, I'd even flash one of the unbent cards so that the mark is convinced that the other unbent card is the winner. A little knowledge can be a dangerous thing and these gangs are nobody's fool. They can spot a wised-up mark from fifty feet and have no problem letting him play.

In the end, it's all about building the victim's confidence and creating an irresistible opportunity. Just like all con games, it's more about what's happening inside the mark's head, knowing how people react to engineered scenarios, and taking advantage of human nature.

LIFE IS SHORT

"*D*o another one!" demanded the bartender as the applause faded.

I put my cards away and shook my head, smiling as the crowd joined in. I had been performing for about ten minutes—small miracles and "betchas" for an audience that had grown considerably in that time. I had successfully won a few drinks and performed the seemingly impossible. Nearby, the owner of the bar watched with interest but kept his distance as I agreed to one last trick.

"What's the biggest bill you have in the cash register?" I asked.

The bartender turned, opened the register, and pulled out a one-hundred-dollar bill.

"Okay, that'll work," I said, removing a pen from my pocket. "Here's the bet. You sign this bill—any way you like—and I will wrap it up in this paper napkin. Then, I'm going to make it vanish and reappear—with your signature—inside the register!"

Everyone looked at the cash register behind the bar, behind the bartender, and against the back wall. It seemed impossible for me to gain access without being seen, but I continued, "If

I can do it, I keep the hundred. If not, I give you another hundred-dollar bill. Fair?"

It took a few minutes for him to agree. He verified all of the conditions several times until, egged on by the crowd, he finally conceded to the bet. Using my pen, he signed the bill and watched carefully as I folded it, taking great care not to do anything suspicious. I then placed it under the napkin and pinched the top to hold it in place. No one blinked as I did this; they were all eager to catch me out if I made a single false move. To verify that the hundred-dollar bill was inside, I let the barman reach under the napkin and feel it. A few other people did the same until everyone was certain of where the signed bill really was.

With a dozen pairs of eyes watching closely, I folded and rolled the napkin into a tight ball, then set fire to it! The bartender panicked but I assured him that it was all part of the act and that there was nothing to worry about. I took another hundred from my pocket and slid it under a glass to reassure him. Meanwhile, everyone continued to watch as the napkin burned and slowly turned to ash.

When the flames died, I reached into the ashes and rubbed them between my fingers before looking up at the bartender, saying "It's gone!" Everyone laughed, but I wasn't kidding. I looked the bartender in the eye and told him that the signed bill was now inside the cash register.

Turning, he slowly walked to the machine, perhaps expecting me to try something at the last moment. He knew that there was no way the signed c-note could be inside, but he'd already seen me perform miracles with pocket change and was clearly nervous. His hand trembling, he hit a button and the drawer popped out to reveal the signed hundred-dollar bill in its original compartment. Shocked, he showed the bill to the crowd. Everyone checked the signature, utterly baffled. I quickly reminded him of the bet and he grudgingly handed over the money.

As I left I reminded the audience to tip my victim generously before walking over to my friend, the owner, who was laughing his ass off. Seeing this, the bartender realized he'd been set up; but he still had no idea how the trick was done or how much I had *actually* stolen from the register.

The term "short con" refers to a confidence trick played for fast money—whatever the mark has in his wallet or can obtain quickly. They are usually hit-and-run ruses that target all walks of life, from small businesses and stores to unwary tourists. Simple scams such as short-changing, dine and dash, or thefts by distraction can be regarded as short cons. Some swindles can be more complex, as in the magic bar bet I just described. Most of the time, they happen quickly, often in a single interaction designed to trick people into giving and losing their money or possessions.

Short cons tend to rely on predictable behavior, where a grifter simply takes advantage of a situation in order to steal from his or her victim. The hook or the line might be small or even nonexistent as these scams are all about getting the money quickly. Once caught in the middle of a short con, the mark can only escape by breaking social conventions and walking away or by confronting the hustlers directly. But short con artists are not easily dissuaded. Once they have someone in their sights, they will keep going after the money, trying any tactic to bring down their mark.

Like hyenas, they can be relentless. One of the clearest illustrations of this was a piece of video footage I saw several years ago from an airport parking lot. A couple had arrived with several suitcases and were carefully protecting their bags in the waiting area when a group of distraction thieves approached them. The gang attempted several tactics to get the couple to take their hands and eyes off of their luggage. They asked for directions, they dropped change, and offered to help carry the bags. Each time, the couple politely refused but the thieves were relentless, continually circling their targets, looking for an opportunity. The couple did a great job of protecting their property—until their friend arrived to pick them up. The man and woman both embraced their driver and, in that instant, the gang simply grabbed the bags and ran. I wouldn't call these thieves con artists, but it clearly shows how determined and shameless a criminal can be when they think something is worth taking.

There can be a cleverness to more sophisticated distraction scams. On *The Real Hustle*, we had Jess enter a cafe with a bag from a nearby clothing store. She placed the bag on a chair and asked a businessman who was sitting nearby if he would mind watching it while she went to the bathroom. Who could say no to Jess? Nearby, I watched the mark follow Jess with his eyes, and when the moment was right, I walked by, picked up Jess's bag, and pretended to go after another woman who was leaving the cafe. Supposedly, I thought the bag had been left behind by the woman who was leaving, and as I chased her outside, the mark followed quickly and took the bag from me. I apologized, explained my mistake, and walked away as the mark returned to find that while he had been chasing after me, Alex had stolen his jacket and briefcase.

This illustrates how hustlers can construct a scenario that depends on their victim to *act as anticipated*. There's no traditional hook in a con like this, just a situation that creates a trap for a victim to fall into. In a sense, instinctive reactions and typical behavior *are* the hook because the victim simply acts in a way that is natural to him. Theft by distraction might not be a scam in the strictest sense, but it can reveal something about the way these criminals think and interpret the world around them. Once a common reaction or behavior has been identified, hustlers might see a way to exploit that situation.

The simplest distractions depend on predictable actions that are often instinctive to most people. Approaching a cafe, I once knocked on a window to get the attention of someone inside while tapping my wrist and miming "What time is it?" The mark responded by showing her watch and holding it closer to the window. I waved thanks and walked away as Jess left the cafe with the mark's bag, which had been hanging on the back of her chair. Had she not leaned forward to show me her watch, Jess would not have been able to take the bag. It took the victim twenty minutes to notice her bag was gone; no one else in the cafe had seen or suspected a thing.

Pickpockets also depend on the predictable behavior of crowds. On the street, they know where people tend to gather in large numbers or are forced into close contact with each other: places like crosswalks while waiting for the light, busy escalators, or crowded markets. These situations allow thieves to get close to people and make a steal without raising suspicion. Getting close enough to pick a pocket or dip into a bag is the first step; what they steal or how they steal it is then a matter of skill. Some "dips" are incredibly gifted and can deftly remove items held in seemingly impossible to reach places but, for the most part, pickpockets tend to go for the easy money. Some will simply cut into a bag or outer pocket with a sharp knife and catch what falls out, while others will blatantly open someone's bag to look for anything worth taking. Around the world, many tourists have turned around to find someone with both hands buried in their backpack.

Years ago, while working a pitch in a Glasgow shopping mall, I regularly saw an old man walking around, watching people closely. He was clearly up to something, and a few days later, he was arrested by security. Several people had reported losing wallets and small purses and the old man was their prime suspect, but after searching him, they found no evidence and were forced to let him go.

Upon hearing this, I asked security if they had searched his umbrella, which he was always carrying. He was later observed picking pockets with the hand that held the umbrella, then immediately dropping the wallet into the folds of the umbrella! I've seen the same ruse in London, with a clever twist. After it had been raining, the pickpocket would get too close to their mark, soaking the victim's leg with the wet umbrella. This gave the thief a good reason to step back and apologize, extracting a difficult to reach wallet in the process.

In Spain's beautiful capital, Madrid, I have watched dozens of pickpockets work in the crowded cloisters of the Plaza Major, in busy Internet cafes, and in the city's busy Metro during rush hour. Most working pickpockets are more audacious than skilled and simply learn the daily patterns of movement that allow them to get close enough to take anything within reach. Many work in teams with each member willing to go for a victim's belongings while other members of the gang do the distracting.

One of the simplest strategies I've seen was used in the Metro where some ticket turnstiles have a short enclosure leading to a retracting wall that opens and closes as tickets are inserted into the slot. Two thieves time their approach to the barrier so that a potential victim with a backpack or shoulder bag becomes sandwiched between them. The pickpocket is behind the victim as his partner inserts an expired ticket into the slot, which is rejected, stopping him from going through. In a busy station, people naturally follow closely behind one another, but when a barrier refuses to open, two or three people are suddenly pushed together and need to back out of the enclosure to allow the person in front to get out. This situation is engineered so that the victim doesn't react to the person behind being so close, and while everyone is backing out, the pickpocket can easily grab something of value.

I spend a lot of time in Spain. It is my favorite country to visit, and Madrid is one of my favorite places on Earth. Though they are there, I can say it is by no means the worst place for pickpockets and opportunist thieves. In truth, almost any place where there are a lot of tourists or people out of their element will attract those willing to steal. The most effective methods tend to be those that adapt to each location.

Around 2004, a doctor from Kazakhstan told me about an ingenious method for stealing wallets. The thieves would use children to loiter in shops or markets, looking for anyone taking a wallet from their back pocket. When they saw a suitable target, the child would stand behind the victim, waiting for the mark to replace his wallet into the same pocket while they held a short length of soft string or wool in front of that pocket. When the billfold was pushed down it caught the middle of the string, leaving two ends dangling from the top of the pocket. As the mark walked away, an adult would spot the "tail" and easily steal the wallet by pulling upwards on the string and catching it! This is an ingenious idea that requires a knack to set the string properly, but once done, picking the pocket is almost automatic.

My friend Apollo Robbins is, in my opinion, the greatest living theatrical pickpocket. He has developed a level of skill so high that he is able to steal almost anything from anywhere. I've watched him pull wallets from tight hip pockets, watches from wrists, and even rings from fingers. Watching Apollo work is a lesson in the art of distraction as he manipulates members of his audience into doing exactly what he wants in order to steal their belongings. Putting Apollo on the street would be like sending an astronaut to fix a washing machine. His incredible degree of skill in this field teaches us an important lesson: *anything* can be taken if the conditions are just right. In the context of a show, Apollo is able to dictate those conditions, take whatever he wants, and make the audience love him for it. In truth, you're more likely to be targeted by pickpockets with a fraction of Apollo's skill, but watching him work can be a sobering lesson about just how vulnerable we really are.

Many scams are built on common misconceptions, presumptions, and automatic reactions. Pickpockets and distraction thieves teach us that predictable behavior is well, *predictable* by others, and thus can easily be used against us. Like the ticket turnstile scam, more complex confidence tricks manipulate people into situations where their choices are preordained and their actions are easily anticipated.

Assume Nothing

One of the simplest short cons I ever pulled was also one of the most profitable.

In Las Vegas, while filming *The Real Hustle*, Alex and I dressed in simple, generic outfits that resembled those worn by valets around the city. Outside an expensive off-Strip restaurant, Jess distracted the real valet driver as Alex and I took his place and waited for the first two cars—a Porsche and a Hummer. Jackpot! The car owners took our homemade tickets without question, gave us their keys, then walked into the restaurant. By the time the real valet returned, we were long gone with half a million dollars worth of automobiles. Two hours later, the owners learned the truth and reacted accordingly. It took our producer a long time to calm them down. He was probably lucky that one of our marks had left his handgun under the seat of his stolen Hummer.

Scams that prey on supposition are among the easiest to pull off. In the UK, simply by wearing a bright, luminous-yellow "high-viz" jacket, people assume the wearer to be in a position of authority. These jackets are so common and well known that whenever we wore them for a scam, people would approach us to ask for help or directions. In one simple con, I placed a crude sign over a ticket machine in a parking lot that told people it was out of order and that they should pay "the attendant." For thirty minutes, I took people's money and gave them bogus parking receipts before walking away with hundreds of pounds— all thanks to that ugly yellow jacket. Many years earlier, Frank Abagnale Jr., whose life story was the basis for the movie *Catch Me If You Can*, used the same principle when he dressed as a security guard, told bank customers that the overnight deposit was out of order, and invited them to drop their money into a temporary safe-box. Dozens of people read the sign and handed over their cash and shop takings without asking any questions. When we pulled the same scam on *Real Hustle*, we barely had to say anything—the uniform and the sign did all the work.

Presenting marks with recognizable scenarios and depending on their predicted responses is a common strategy. Across Europe, hustlers wear simple suits and carry counterfeit credentials to impersonate the local police, stopping tourists on the street to ask questions as a means to steal wallets and passports. We used the same ruse in London to stop a man who was carrying a bag of expensive items from an electronics store. We suggested that he might have stolen these items and asked to check his receipt. As expected, he was so keen to prove his innocence, it was an easy matter for me to keep his belongings while Alex walked him back to the shop. Inside the store, Alex simply walked away, supposedly to find the manager, as our angry mark waited with receipt in hand. Eventually, the mark learned the truth and realized that he had just given away thousands of dollars thanks to a cheap suit and a replica ID.

When confronted with authority, most people usually comply, but even if they resist, the threat of further problems usually forces them to tow the line. In these cases, the situation tends to dictate the victim's reaction. We're so used to behaving in a certain way that it's not difficult for a con artist to predict what we'll do. In all of these scams, a simple question or two might be enough to expose the deception, but even against a gifted grifter, it's possible to smell a rat if you are able to stop and think.

Counterswitch Bills

Common crooks occasionally develop clever methods to pull off simple crimes. Passing counterfeit money would seem to be one of the easiest rackets, but getting caught with fakes can mean serious consequences. One of the cleverest ways to "clean" small amounts of counterfeit cash—trade it for real money—is to buy something inexpensive with a genuine fifty-dollar bill. The cashier will hand over two twenties and some change. These two genuine bills are then handed back to the cashier while asking for four tens instead. The twenty-dollar bills are easily switched as other change is being counted, and if the clerk notices anything wrong with the bills, the hustler wouldn't immediately be suspected because the money apparently came from the clerk's own register.

In practice, when returning the two twenties, salespeople don't bother to check *unless* they suspect a switch, which is exactly what happened while filming an episode of *The Real Hustle*.

The show had started inviting celebrity guests to take part in the scams, and the model Caprice was tasked with switching two twenty-pound notes underneath a cheap DVD during a simple transaction. But when she tried to pull it off, the cashier saw the whole thing and started yelling for her manager. Jess, who had accompanied Caprice, made for the door, leaving our celebrity guest alone with the angry staff; thinking fast, Alex and I walked over from our secret production base wearing suits. We entered the shop and claimed to be the police, flashing our wallets and asking what just happened. The staff immediately accepted our story, and moments later, we walked out with Caprice and a large amount of cash from the register for "evidence"!

This situation shows how a con artist can adapt to seize an opportunity, but what I find truly fascinating is that despite seeing the switch, the same eagle-eyed cashier didn't notice that all I flashed her was the inside of an ordinary wallet with a picture of my kids. It's not just what a hustler says or does: when, where, and the way in which it is said can be just as important.

As it turns out, this particular scam is extremely rare because, while it offers the benefit of plausible deniability and reduces suspicion during the act, it requires the hustler to present himself in a certain way (in terms of image and dress) to avoid suspicion and to engage the cashier directly when asking for change. Most crooks just want to get the money and get out, and the direct approach works so often that adding steps to the process doesn't seem worth the effort. Most criminals prefer the easiest method, which is natural; if they were willing to do a little more work, they might have chosen a different career!

Though there is a cleverness to confidence tricks, most crooks tend to prefer the path of least resistance. Their rule is to get in, get out, and get away. Scams only spread when they are simpler and more effective than the alternative.

A few years ago, I consulted for Scotland Yard (headquarters of London's Metropolitan Police) and gave a lecture on the art of deception. Afterward, one of the senior officers mentioned a small scam that had baffled the police under his command. Local shops were reporting losses from their cash registers, but in most cases, there was no way the money could have been removed without someone being seen. The only common factor was a group of people who had all come into the shop and had asked the clerk to exchange ten-pound notes for twenty-pound notes. Each time, the clerk checked the ten-pound notes, then counted the correct number of twenty-pound notes into the grifter's hand. The answer struck me right away, and I quickly explained how a hustler might be able to steal extra money during such a simple transaction.

As it turns out, I was right on the money.

The secret was simple but ingenious. Whenever scammers entered the shop, they were preceded by confederates, who bought small items using crisp, new twenty-pound notes. The con artists would then buy something with a larger denomination (or ask for change) so the employee would count money from the drawer containing the same twenty-pound notes used by their cohorts. The money was real but coated with a thin layer of dry rubber cement so that when the hustlers received change from that drawer, the treated bills would stick together and be easily counted as one. The gang was arrested a few weeks later attempting the same scam in a different county.

The Evolution of a Free Lunch

Short cons rely a lot less on baiting a hook than more complex con games do. Instead, they use the line and the sinker to create or adapt to common—and seemingly innocent—scenarios. While distraction theft and pickpocketing are among the most basic scams, creative crooks continue to develop clever ways to steal. Even with a basic scam like the dine and dash, where crooks try to avoid paying a large restaurant bill, there are dozens of devious methods to "walk the check."

The most obvious way to escape paying for dinner is to just get up and leave, but waiters are not shy about chasing down delinquent customers, especially when some owners will hold their staff responsible for an unpaid meal. A cleverer method would be to arrive with several shopping bags and leave those at the table while stepping outside to smoke or make a phone call. The bags might be filled with old newspapers, but they would automatically convince many waiters that the customer is coming back until he is long gone.

Switching checks is another clever way to steal a meal. Two hustlers enter a restaurant and sit separately. One orders an enormous steak dinner, while the other has nothing more than coffee and an appetizer. After both hustlers receive their checks, one walks to the bathroom, secretly exchanging the paper slips as he passes his partner's table. The first grifter then pays for the smaller check and leaves. A few minutes later, the other con artist complains that he only had coffee and a small salad but his check is for much more. The waiter will usually write it off as a simple mistake on his part and blame the first customer for not saying anything about getting the wrong check. This scam is often attempted as waiters change shifts, when it is easier to get things mixed up.

The dine and dash can become even more sophisticated when scammers force an innocent diner to pay for their meal. Years ago, my friend BH explained a con that he used as a poor student to score several free meals. After eating, BH would stand up to leave and pretend to notice something under someone's chair. Reaching down he would produce a wallet and ask the person sitting there if it belonged to him. Since the wallet belonged to BH, they would always say "no," so BH told them he would hand it to the staff on his way out. Just as he was about to leave, BH asked the mark's name and if they would mind waving so he could show the waitress where he found the wallet. The mark would then watch BH walk across the restaurant, talk to a member of staff, and indicate where he found the wallet. The mark would then wave and smile before returning to their meal.

What the mark didn't realize is that, when BH approached the waitress, he told her an entirely different story. He'd say, "My uncle is here and insists on buying my dinner. There he is . . ." and would wave at the mark who kindly confirmed his story by returning the gesture. Later, when the mark asked for his check he'd find BH's meal added to the bill, which he had unwittingly permitted with his wave.

I've pulled this scam several times for television. On *Scammed*, where I was able to adapt and re-invent the cons we pulled,* I added another layer by dropping my wallet and waiting for the mark to notice. This time, as I left, I offered to send

---

* *The Real Hustle* was only permitted (by the BBC) to re-enact *existing* scams, but on *Scammed*, I was challenged to invent my own versions.

them all a bottle of wine for finding my wallet and asked their names so that, when talking to the waitress, I could call over and confirm if they wanted red or white wine. What I told the waitress was that my friend Luke wanted to pay and also wanted another bottle of wine. When Luke confirmed this, my story was quickly accepted.

This is a great example of two different perspectives being used to conceal what's really going on, but when both sides compare their versions of events, it can take a while before the truth is pieced together.

Short cons become more sophisticated as scammers learn how to manipulate people into performing actions based on their normal routine. The art of "change raising" is a perfect example of this.

Change Raising

Despite what many of us believe, human beings aren't very good at performing several tasks at the same time or analyzing multiple pieces of information at once. Without the opportunity (or inclination) to separate actions and give them the proper attention, people naturally estimate and make assumptions. Being able to predict or manipulate these actions is one of the hustler's most powerful tools.

Change Raising is an old-school scam played on small businesses, bars, or stores where cash is exchanged in return for goods or services. The hustler makes a small purchase, and when he gets his change, he then engages in a series of interactions with the cashier meant to distract him from giving the correct change. During this transaction, the cashier unwittingly hands over more money than intended. This is a difficult scam to explain in print as it is supposed to be confusing! Performed live, it looks like a magic trick and can be extremely difficult to reconstruct.

I'm going to describe exactly how I would pull this scam, from my perspective as the hustler:

In a small casino, just off the Nevada freeway, I walk to the cashier's cage with two fifty-dollar bills in my pocket. I take out one fifty and ask the cashier to break it into ten five-dollar bills. She takes my money and deals out ten fives, which I take to my pocket, but as she's about to put my fifty into the drawer, I stop her and ask, "do your slot machines accept fifty-dollar bills?"

"Sure they do," she says.

"Then I've made a mistake. I don't want to feed all of these into the machine one at a time!"

I pass her the stack of five-dollar bills and take back the fifty, but when she counts the fives, there's a problem.

"You've given me too much. This is ninety-five dollars!"

Sure enough, I've given her nine five-dollar bills and the fifty that was in my pocket, leaving one five-dollar bill in the same pocket.

I now take the stray five-dollar bill from my pocket and say, "Do the machines accept hundreds?"

"Yes, of course." She replies.

"If I give you this five, how much is that in total?"

Ninety-five plus five is obviously one hundred. When she confirms this, I say, "in that case, just give me a hundred-dollar bill. Sorry to waste your time!"

She hands me a hundred in return for the cash in front of her, counting to make sure she hasn't made a mistake. She has, but unless she's familiar with this scam, has been properly trained, or immediately counts all of the cash in her drawer, the truth won't become apparent until the end of her shift when she will be fifty dollars light.

Put simply, I walked up with two fifty-dollar bills and left with a fifty and a hundred.

Confused? You should be. Change raisers are experts at keeping their mark focused on the wrong thing at the wrong time. I've even seen footage of a scammer repeating this con several times with the *same* clerk, until his cash drawer is hundreds of dollars light.

Here's how it works:

I have two fifty-dollar bills and receive ten fives in exchange for one of my fifties, but before my original fifty-dollar bill goes to the drawer, I change my mind and apparently trade the stack of five-dollar bills back again, taking my original fifty from the clerk and pocketing it.

The money I just handed to her is actually too much because I've secretly exchanged one five for my other fifty-dollar bill, so that when the cashier counts, she tells me I've given her too much.

The correct way to resolve this would be to give me back the fifty in exchange for the stray five-dollar bill, but instead, I let her keep that fifty and *add* the remaining five so that the cashier is holding one hundred dollars.

The correct course has not changed, she should still only give me fifty dollars, but it now seems logical to give me a hundred-dollar bill in exchange for the hundred dollars she is holding.

The cashier doesn't realize that she's already given me fifty dollars in exchange for that cash, which I quickly removed to my pocket, and that she only needs to give fifty dollars more to make it right.

Performing one transaction at a time protects the cashier and her employer from this con. By keeping the cashier focused on the money in her hand, the hustler cons her into giving an additional fifty dollars. The fifty-dollar bill I put into my pocket after handing back the ten bills should have stayed on the counter and have been included in the cashier's calculations. Instead, I removed it and allowed her to forget about it. Essentially, fifty dollars is stolen in the middle of the con; even if the cashier realizes this, it's easy to pass it off as a mistake. Unless she already knows the con and calls security.

A hustler once told me how a cashier took back the bills, handed over the first fifty, and then counted them as just fifty dollars. She deliberately kept the added fifty for herself, smiled at him, and said, "thanks." She knew exactly what he was trying to pull and ended up robbing him from the safety of her cage.

Major Las Vegas resorts train their staff how to spot this type of con. Large companies have implemented strict procedures that staff will not break, no matter how hard someone tries to make them. Change raising, in all its forms, relies on distracting the victim with a procedure that encourages them to perform two transactions at the same time. The hustler interrupts the first transaction before it is completed, then introduces a second transaction. In the case above, the cashier should have put my original fifty-dollar bill into the drawer and finished that exchange before taking back the ten bills and counting them. This way that original fifty would not remain in play and could not be spirited into my pocket while she counted the other bills. Put simply, she should have just counted my money and given me change, but this scam works because it makes the mark count, give, give, count and then give again!

Tricks and Traps

Entire books could be written (and have been) to record all the short cons that exist. In essence, they are well-constructed tricks designed to trap people into losing something through seemingly normal, everyday actions. Unlike a con game, where bait is used to attract and focus the mark, a good short con is most effective when it appears to be invisible, ordinary, or accidental and does not arouse suspicion until it's too late.

Short cons where the hustler hooks the mark and draws him into a trap are rare, but they certainly exist. One of my favorite examples is the old Put and Take spinning top, a tiny plastic spindle with several sides with either the letter "P" or "T" over a small number or the letter "A." The game is simple—it's based on the dreidel game played by Jews on Hanukkah—and can be played by any number of suckers. Everyone begins by dropping a dollar into the pot, then each take turns to spin the top, which decides whether they *put* more money into the pot (P) or *take* money from it (T). If "P3" comes up, three dollars must be added and if

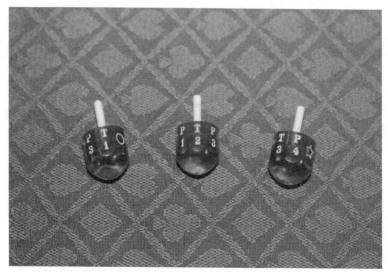

A "gaffed" set of Put and Take spinning tops (the mark only ever sees one).

"T3" appears then three dollars are removed by that player. "PA" is an unlucky roll since the player must now match everything in the pot, doubling its value. "TA" would win the pot outright and the game would begin again with a fresh round of dollar bills.

This type of con depends on a gaffed top that looks entirely normal but has been specially molded to land on certain sides depending on the direction that the top is spun. This means that a spin in one direction wins most of the time and a spin in the other direction loses most of the time. Since most people spin the top clockwise, the hustler simply needs to spin counterclockwise in order to win.

Such a simple swindle needs only a few people to generate more than enough action to make it worthwhile. These tops usually sell for hundreds of dollars and come with an honest top and a gaffed duplicate that appears identical to the untrained eye. Professionals would often buy dozens of honest tops so they could apparently leave the one they'd been playing with behind so the suckers would still be playing long after the hustler was gone.

This is an old scam and extremely rare today, but I know a few people who make professional cheating devices, and they're still selling the occasional set of tops to non-collectors who are almost certainly using them to steal. As a short con, I regard this as something of a classic. The grifter enters a bar, and after a little flimflam, gets enough action to start a game before leaving with all the money. This is the simplest version of the game, but there's a devilish twist that turns this scam into a double-whammy.

After the first game, the hustler waits until everyone leaves and then confesses to the owner of the bar that the top is gaffed. Apparently drunk, the con man convinces his mark to buy the top so he can win back what he lost and make a lot more besides. A few days later, another grifter enters the same bar and acts like a chump until the owner offers to play the put and take game for money. The owner then gets cleaned out *again* in an apparent run of bad luck, completely unaware that his spinning top has been switched for one that works in the opposite direction!

Short cons catch the victim out when they least expect it, sometimes (though rarely) after a contrived setup, and in the put and take scam, one con creates the perfect conditions for another.

In the magic bar scam described at the beginning of this chapter—where I lit the c-note on fire—a few betchas and a couple of conjuring tricks was enough to create the perfect opportunity for a bizarre proposition. With a crowd of people demanding to see more magic, it was a lot easier to convince the bartender to agree to such a large bet and to honor it after I won; however, even if he refused to pay up, I would have come out ahead. After giving me the hundred, the register was actually short almost two hundred dollars.

I first learned of this scam from the Eddie Fields book *A Life Among Secrets*, but I'm assured that the idea is an old one. Fields himself was a successful short con artist, a pool hustler, and a gifted magician who dabbled in psychic readings. He had also been a successful pitchman, and I have no doubt he was able to easily build a crowd in any situation. The secret to this scam is a confederate in the crowd who is the last person to reach under the napkin and confirm that the signed hundred-dollar bill is still there. He secretly palms the bill after reaching under the napkin while I continue on and pretend as if the bill is still inside. As I go through the motions of rolling up the napkin and burning it, all attention is focused on me and the ashtray as my partner quietly walks to the other end of the bar and buys a drink from the other bartender using the signed hundred dollar bill!

While everyone was watching the napkin burn, the *other* bartender unwittingly did the dirty work for me by replacing the signed bill in the register before giving my confederate over ninety dollars in change! Assuming that the first bartender honored our agreement, we could actually have walked away with $190!

This was all for the benefit of the bar owner, who is a dear friend and asked me to pull this scam on his own staff to prove to them how, even under the most impossible of conditions, anyone can be scammed.

There are an enormous variety of short cons, and they are extremely hard to spot until it's too late. Unlike a street game or a confidence trick, short cons like distraction steals, change raising, or the dine and dash take advantage of everyday situations and natural reactions. More involved short cons like the magic bar bet or the put and take game are hit-and-run scams that happen so quickly, the mark can barely remember what happened or even how he got caught up in the action.

I firmly believe that the more we can expose these scams, the more difficult they will become for hustlers to pull off. Training staff to follow procedures is an effective way to defeat change-raisers, but there's more than one way to "make a take." A little time demonstrating these scams to all employees who handle cash would give them enough experience to recognize almost any variation.

Sadly, most people who have enough knowledge to suspect a short con learned the hard way, having fallen victim to a scam in the past. When I pulled the BH wallet scam for *The Real Hustle* in London, the waitress came running after me once she discovered the ruse. Even after seeing my hidden microphone, she refused to go back to the restaurant without me.

As she said to me afterward, "I've been cheated before and wasn't going to let you go without a fight!"

FEEL THE HUSTLE

The guy just wouldn't shut up. This was his local pool hall, he was a well-known character, and our cameras were in the open, supposedly to watch a hustler in action. He incorrectly thought that *he* was the hustler; in fact, he was playing the part so well I could barely get a word in. As he barked his way around the table, I glanced over to my "girlfriend" Melissa, who was racking balls at a nearby table. My friend Jason England stood nearby, loving every minute as the mark mocked my attempts to play while the camera crew watched every poorly aimed shot I attempted at the table. Finally, after another defeat, the loudmouth threw down a challenge. He'd play for money but would give me enough weight to make it a fair game.

This meant that I could play with a starting advantage that would even out our obvious skill difference, but I remained uncertain despite the mark's attempts to bully me into betting. Finally, as I walked back to Melissa, the mark spat the words I'd been waiting for: "I'll even play your girlfriend, if you're too scared!"

"You'd give her the same weight?" I asked, and the mark stopped in his tracks. This hustler had spent so much time and energy bad-mouthing me for the benefit of his peanut gallery, he'd paid no attention to the girl at the next table. As soon as the mark hesitated, it was my turn to drive the train. "Seriously? You don't want to play a girl?" The onlookers laughed and the "hustler" regained his composure. After a few minutes of backchat, he agreed to give Melissa a starting advantage. Not as much weight as he'd offered me, but it was more than we needed. When Melissa stepped up to the table, I could see that our mark already knew he'd been taken.

For twenty minutes I had let him showboat for the cameras and his buddies, while Melissa quietly waited in the shadows. As soon as she leaned forward for the break, it was clear Melissa knew what she was doing and the mark recognized her instantly. He had just given points away to Melissa Herndon, known on the professional pool circuit as "The Dragon Lady."

Our hustler had been hustled and was forced to bring his A game, which turned out to be considerable; even with an advantage, Melissa barely won the game. Handing over his money, the mark suggested another round, this time starting even. Melissa agreed, and we racked the balls and stood back to watch the show. Melissa had been deliberately holding back her skills— "sandbagging"—to con the mark into a second game, but as it turned out, so had he. With the stakes now much higher, both players fought to the finish when Melissa pulled off a perfect winning shot as the mark chewed his teeth in disgust. "One more?" he asked, but I shook my head. I was pretty certain he had more in reserve and we'd already won enough to call it a day. But as we left the pool hall, Melissa was disappointed. "Why did we stop playing? We could have skimmed that guy all day," she said. Turns out she had still been sandbagging our mark and was just getting started.

Not everyone spends enough time in pool halls to fall victim to a hustler, but you can find yourself being pressured by similar strategies in many walks of life. From a car salesroom to unwanted calls from boiler-room investment firms, the tactic used is commonplace: Someone tries to secure a commitment by making you focus on the supposedly positive aspects of a deal, without revealing (or misdirecting you from) its negative aspects.

It's worth learning how to recognize situations where one side might have an unfair (but legal) edge over the other; in the gambling world, there's a particular breed of player who can make a great deal of money identifying flaws in the system.

The short man in the peaked hat moved around the table, taking shots without hesitation, each finding its mark with disturbing accuracy. Like a cat prowling for mice in the shadows, "Moves" leaned and turned until he had the perfect line, then quickly fired at the cue ball.

"I just want to know if they've got gamble," he told me, "otherwise I'm wasting everyone's time, you know?"

I sat on a stool nearby as he easily cleared the table, examining a pair of flip-flops that looked perfectly ordinary on top but when turned over, revealed a remarkable contraption. Its purpose was to allow a hustler to control the flip of a coin with 100 percent accuracy.

This cheap-looking plastic footwear allowed Moves to slide a switch to either the right or left, releasing a quarter onto the floor from underneath his feet. The device was inlaid into a well he had cut into the sole with another cut-out, which was filled with sticky wax. With a flick of his wrist and a snap of his fingers, Moves would spin a coin on the floor, and while it was still spinning, he would stamp his foot onto the coin, trapping it underneath. "If they're going to bet on a coin toss, they'll bet on a game," he explained, and depending on their answer, Moves could reveal the coin to be either heads-up or tails-up since the original coin was now stuck to the sticky wax and the toe switch could dictate which coin was released before lifting his foot. Whichever side of the coin Moves revealed depended on much more than whether the sucker called heads or tails. This was not just a trick to win easy money, it was the opening gambit in a game of hustle.

Moves is a fascinating character, smart as a whip, charming, funny, and accustomed to making people feel comfortable around him. His personality and demeanor is so disarming that it's easy to assume you could beat him at anything. The first time I saw him play, I thought that maybe he was all talk and had very little skill at the table. Of course, that was his intention. Anyone can hold back or conceal their real skill, but the hustle is all about making people believe what they're seeing. The slightest suspicion that a player is sandbagging will send a sucker to the door. As I got to know him better, he started to open up, to reveal more about his approach to the game and to show just how much skill he really had.

For Moves and other hustlers like him, it's not about who has the most skill at the table; it's about who has the most *game*. His coin-toss device was a fascinating piece of work, but how he used it was of more interest to me. One-on-one, he might score a one-off bet, depending on how much the sucker threw down. In other situations he might bookie the bet for a large group and use the device to make sure he came out with a healthy profit. If more people bet on heads, he'd release tails, and so on.

The interesting part was how he would use it to hook someone into playing for money at the pool table. If the mark wants to bet, Moves would push him to see how much he was willing to risk. This told him everything he needed to know about the person as a potential mark and if there was money to be made, Moves would use his tricked-out shoe to *lose* the bet! Then he would suggest a few games for the same amount as the coin toss and the real hustle would begin. Once his foot was on the coin, some bettors have tried to bully him into a huge wager, but he was prepared for that and ready to take on any amount, since he was certain to win.

Hustling is all about keeping the mark in the game, generating false hope, manipulating expectations, and twisting the victim's perspective about the situation they're in. A one-off bet or proposition might make any amount of money, but a smart operator keeps his mark engaged so he comes back for more. Gamblers are addicted to action; some argue that whether they win or lose is irrelevant, but the *prospect* of winning is what keeps most people playing; this is the bait that a good con artist needs to keep their mark chasing. It's a mistake to believe that hustling, whether it be at pool, golf, or even tennis, is based entirely on skill. Expert grifters can turn players with much greater skill into suckers with empty pockets. Hustling is about finding the right angle and developing the optimum strategy to beat the mark and keep them coming back for more.

My friend Dean Dill is one of the kindest and most generous people I know. From his charming barbershop in Glendale, California, he runs a small business supplying props to magicians while ministering to fellow Christians and occasionally cutting hair. His shop is a hangout for hundreds of people, many of whom travel thousands of miles to meet one of the nicest guys in the magic community. At one time, Dean included Johnny Carson among his friends and magic students and was even a guest on *The Tonight Show*. But in another life, Dean was a talented tennis hustler.

Dean's proposition was to offer to play anyone without using a racket, catching the ball and throwing it with the same hand. To regular players, even pros, this sounded like a tough challenge and a good bet, but Dean had a simple advantage. Once he caught the ball he could throw it anywhere he liked—always to the most difficult place for the sucker to reach. He could throw it low and fast to the other side of the court or lob it gently so it just cleared the edge of the net. Catching it was the hard part, but Dean already played a decent game of straight tennis and was used to getting to the ball in time. According to Dean, getting to the ball and catching it was easier than returning it with a decent swing. After a few minutes, the sucker would be exhausted, having run all over the court to return the ball.

Dean taught me a similar scam for golf, where the hustler plays with only a putter and must throw the ball from the tee until it gets to the green. This immediately puts the sucker at an advantage since most golfers can hit a ball much farther than it can be thrown. The scam is in how much of a handicap the hustler can negotiate. Personally, I'd play for three free throws per hole, but one is probably enough to get the money if you have a decent arm (I don't). The secret is in developing strong putting skills on the green and reasonable accuracy when throwing a ball hard, but the most important skill is in the hustler's "short game." The objective is to get the ball as close to the green as possible without touching the velvet. This means that the hustler gets to throw the ball from very close to the pin and ensure it lands within an easy putting distance to the hole. The bunkers are a huge help because all I need to do is aim for those and I'm assured that the ball won't accidentally roll onto the green.

After learning this hustle, I bought about a hundred buckets of balls at my local driving range and practiced on weekdays, when the place was empty. I walked my local course to see how well I could play, and my score was much better than it would be when played normally! Best of all, I attracted enough attention at the range to get a game going until another player pointed out that I was the guy from TV. After that, all bets were off.

If you can bet on a game, you can hustle it—even chess players offer opponents all sorts of starting advantages to entice them into a wager. The principle of handicapping is supposedly to level the playing field for players of varying degrees of skill, but when one player is lying about his true ability, the balance can easily be shifted in the hustler's direction. Over the years I've collected a lot of methods to hustle various games and they are all based on giving the mark a perceived advantage or making a proposition that seems so unlikely (or downright impossible) that it seduces a sucker to bet.

Proposition bets are a personal favorite of mine. There are thousands of them in existence, from simple bar bets and physical stunts to cunning setups or feats of skill. Many books have been written on the subject, often collated from old texts, or in many cases, simply pulled from a couple of Google searches. Get online now and you will find a never-ending supply of betchas, but there's a lot more to a prop bet than just the secret.

The all-time king of the proposition bet might have been Clarence Alvin Thomas, aka Titanic Thompson, a legendary gambler, and possibly the greatest hustler of all time. From an early age, Thompson had a knack for perfecting unusual skills that often involved throwing objects with unerring accuracy.

From rocks to horseshoes, he practiced until he could not only beat a game but use the same skills in other situations. According to legend, Thompson could throw a hotel room key down a long hall and straight into the lock. He could throw a clothespin straight up and into the high ceiling of a hotel lobby (skewering a fly in the process), and he could take any walnut and throw it over a building, while others could barely get it past the first floor window. In his later years, Titanic Thompson would hang out at a local pool hall, waiting for other sharks to swim by. Despite his expertise in other areas, Thompson was an average pool player, but he used his lack of skill to attract gamblers to his table, where he would begin working them toward a lucrative side bet.

After losing a few games for small beer (low amounts that barely scratched his bankroll), the old man would point out an open window at the other end of the hall and comment that he once threw a playing card straight out that window from the far wall. This often got someone's attention, and before the marks knew what hit them, they had hundreds of dollars riding on a single playing card, hoping that this old-timer couldn't even get close to the window. With a sharp sweep of his arm and a snap of the wrist, Thompson sent a card sailing over a dozen pool tables and out the window into the cold night air.

And he wasn't finished. With his suckers still feeling the sting, Thompson would offer to do it again, to prove it wasn't just luck; this was usually turned down until Thompson yelled for someone to close the window halfway. Now the marks were back in the game, and sure enough, Titanic did it again. All of this was just an appetizer. Thompson was about to take his pigeons for everything they had, with a proposition that sounded so crazy it almost never failed to get the money.

With his marks still sore from two large losses, Thompson would have the window lowered again, until there was no more than a ten-inch gap at the bottom. Even with such a small opening, people weren't interested until, seemingly without thinking, Thompson claimed he could make the card fly back and stick to the outside of the window. Seizing on this comment, Titanic Thompson's victims were suddenly keen to win back all their money and more. Thompson was ready to cover any size of bet and, by now, the whole pool hall was watching as thousands of dollars were laid out. Despite the seemingly impossible nature of the bet, Thompson threw his last card out of the tiny gap and the crowd gasped as they saw the same card catch the wind and fly back onto the outside of the window, where it stayed.

Thompson's career is filled with stories of how he secured an unbeatable advantage for these bets. He once hired a dwarf with huge feet to sleep in a long tent on the beach, with his feet sticking out. Thompson would walk by with a few fellow gamblers and offer to bet on the height of the man in the tent. Based on the size of those feet, most would guess over six feet and all Thompson had to do was bet just under the lowest estimate and he was sure to win. He moved road signs several miles closer to a destination so he could gamble on how long it would take to get there. He would propose bets on how many watermelons were in the back of a truck, which he had already paid to unload and count the day before. As a child, he bet that his dog could jump into a muddy river and collect a marked rock that had been thrown there minutes before. His victim had no idea that this kid had spent a whole week marking every rock on the river bed (at that location) with the same "X."

Titanic Thompson was a successful gambler, but his real skill was in these proposition bets that were easy to make around people with large amounts of money and a willingness to bet on anything. While some of his feats were genuine, the best stories feature cunning tricks that were used to guarantee a win. He hired a kid to climb a ladder and pin a fly to the ceiling of his hotel. That kid was a seventeen-year-old Moves, who spent several years learning from the elderly Thompson. The pin bet worked because the ceiling was so high you had to climb a ladder to even see if one was stuck there. Thompson would wander around the lobby, followed by a crowd as he tossed pins skyward while people ducked to avoid the falling pins. With ten chances, Thompson simply had to take only nine pins and merely pretend to throw one of them. When nothing came back down after that throw, Ty would indicate a tiny black speck on the ceiling. Climbing a ladder, his mark would have to confirm that a fly was indeed pinned there.

Moves also helped Thompson win a simple golf bet. Titanic was an exceptional golfer and once commented that he could never be a professional because he couldn't accept the pay cut. He played left-handed but spent years developing a decent right-handed game so he could beat people as a righty, then offer to play left-handed for much higher stakes. Afterward, Thompson would take the losers out for dinner and bet that he could hit a forty-foot putt on the eighteenth green, and once the bets were in, he'd meet his marks early the next morning, drop his ball far from the pin, then make a miracle shot that curved along the green and straight into the hole! This was partly thanks to Thompson's skill as a golfer but mostly due to the garden hose, filled with water, that Moves had laid on the green overnight to create an invisible track that led straight to victory. All Thompson had to do was get the speed and direction right and the ball would follow the track and sink every time.

For a great proposition bet, the hook is baited with a challenge that seems to put the odds in the victim's favor, but there is usually an unknown factor, whether it be skill, a secret, or overnight preparation. For a few drinks or to decide who picks up the check in a restaurant, these bets are mostly harmless, but in the company of serious gamblers, an expert hustler can score thousands of dollars. As stunts, prop bets are little more than interesting tricks, but when there's real money on the line, they can be devastating. More money might be won and lost on a post-game betcha than was ever risked on a poker hand or game of pool.

How did a seventy-year-old Titanic Thompson make a card fly out of a window, then back again to stick on the outside? Thompson could throw cards much farther and with even greater accuracy and could close the window until the gap was just a couple of inches wide, but this doesn't explain how he could guarantee the card would return and stick to the glass. That was up to Moves, who sprayed the window with a clear, sticky substance and waited outside with a huge fan aimed right at the window! As soon as the card flew out, the air from the fan caught it, sent it straight back, and the spray-on glue did the rest.

The hustle is not in the way Thompson tricked his way to success. It's in how he worked his marks into a corner and forced them to think they had the upper hand.

Listen Up

In a classic hustle, stakes can be raised as the conditions appear to improve in the mark's favor. The victim then becomes so focused on these conditions that he can be more easily manipulated.

A simple betcha that illustrates how easy it is to be fooled this way is the Ben's Mother puzzle. To begin, I take a penny, a nickel, and a dime and I pass them one at a time into someone's hand, giving each of the first two coins a name. Then I ask my victim to name the last coin correctly. With the proper timing and inflection, this can turn into a baffling and frustrating guessing game where the stakes can keep going up to create more pressure.

Here's the wording:

"Ben's mother has three children."

I hold up the penny. "Penny."

I pass the penny to their hand and hold up the nickel. "Nicky."

I pass them the nickel and hold up the dime. "And . . . ?"

Almost no one gets this the first time.

"You owe me a drink," I say. "Let's do it again."

Now I repeat the above sequence and, again, they don't get it.

I repeat several times, each costing the mark a drink. Now I say, "Okay, I'll tell you the answer for ten dollars or we can keep going, but if you think I've cheated you in any way, or if after I tell you, you think the answer wasn't completely fair, you don't have to buy me anything. Agreed?"

No one ever wants to buy their way out, so we continue.

They lose again and again, and the more they lose and the more they owe, the harder it becomes for them to hear the answer. Without the pressure of the situation or the visual distraction of the coins and with no money on the line, it's very easy to figure this out. Ben's mother has three children—Penny, Nicky, and *Ben*.

This bet will either fail in the first couple of rounds or will keep going until the victim has had enough. It clearly illustrates how the conditions of the bet and the amount being risked distract a mark from the solution while misdirecting their attention with the procedure.

While this is little more than a gag, it could be a profitable one if I really took people's money (I don't). But it clearly illustrates how a good hustler operates. It's all about keeping your mind on the challenge while concealing the solution. Hustling is about maximizing the victim's losses, and while a quick hit can be profitable, the real art is in keeping the mark at the table. Personally, I'm a lousy pool player, but I have a passion for prop bets that can be built up or repeated. There's one feat I spent several years mastering that builds to an unforgettable and profitable conclusion, and it's a perfect example of how a simple stunt can become a profitable hustle.

The Snatch

In my shows and seminars, I invite someone to hold a coin in their outstretched hand, with their palm open and flat.* I stand a couple of feet away, with one hand raised like a chubby cobra, and propose to reach down and grab the coin before they can close their hand. The mark can only close their fingers as quickly as possible and is not allowed to move their hand down or away. If you've ever seen the old TV show *Kung Fu* starring David Carradine, you'll remember a similar challenge from the opening of every show.

Coin snatching is a simple, genuine physical proposition—either I get the coin or I don't. I could use this to win a couple of drinks, but to make this into a hustle, I need to work the mark and the crowd to a point where they believe they have the upper hand and want to take my money. To do this I need to gradually build to a point where I appear to have gone too far and made the challenge too impossible, so that it attracts more suckers into the action.

---

* I learned this from Kip Pascal's excellent self-published book, *Coin Snatching*.

Let's start with my limitations. I can do this from a considerable distance, especially if I pick the right person to work with. My experience is that players of certain sports, like basketball and squash, can be a lot more difficult because they have developed a much faster physical response than most. I've developed an eye for people I can beat easily and have much greater latitude with the proposition. The slower an opponent's reaction time, the farther away I can be and still reach the coin.

To some extent, distance actually helps, and I can play all sorts of tricks to make it seem like I'm too far to reach. An effective ruse is to reach forward, then step back so that my hand is apparently too far to get the coin but my shoulders are actually square-onto the mark and by simply rotating my upper torso very slightly, my reach is greatly extended. This move is covered as I tell them to make sure I don't move my feet. When they look down, my shoulders turn but my arm retracts to compensate, so that when they look back, my hand occupies the same point in space but is now more than capable of getting to the coin.

Once I'm at the maximum distance and they've already lost once, it's relatively easy to convince the mark to try again. This time I wait until I'm ready and remind the mark to keep his hand flat. As soon as I see them respond to this, I go for the coin and success is all but guaranteed.

The secret to this game is easily illustrated with another simple bar bet. Ask someone to hand you a crisp, flat ten-dollar bill. Have him extend his hand, closed into a fist, then extend his first finger and thumb, ready to pinch the bill, which you hold from above by one of the short ends. The challenge is for your opponent to catch the bill after you release it, but this is almost impossible because, once he sees the bill fall, the message from the brain to the finger and thumb arrives too late to catch it. Begin with his fingers about halfway down the bill, ready to close. You can later repeat this and raise the bill so there's more time for them to react once it's released, but be careful because eventually, your opponent will become attuned and more focused (depending on how many drinks they've had) or will get lucky and try to anticipate when you are going to release the bill, rather than waiting for you to actually drop it.

This problem with reaction time is the secret to the coin snatch, so I always make it very clear to my victim that any attempt to move their hand away from the target zone or close their fingers before I move is counted as a loss. This covers all bases, but it also adds greater pressure.

To effectively hustle people with this stunt, I need to gradually work my way up to the maximum distance, where the suckers will perceive my chances as being almost impossible, when I am actually just as comfortable snatching the coin under those conditions. Starting close, I might bet for a dollar a time but I would let them win a couple so that I don't come on too strong.

Once we've played a few times, I suggest taking a step back, but only if we increase the bet. I lose the first one and win the next two. I start on a fourth but as tension builds, I take another step back and ask if he wants to play for even more money. Since he has already won a couple of rounds, he feels confident enough to accept the bet, but I go on to win twice. Now I step back again, this time until my hand is apparently too far away and tell him to make sure I don't step forward, increasing the amount being bet one more time.

Following this structure I can keep offering more rounds, holding back my true level of skill until the mark reaches his betting limit, but there's still one more proposition that can not only squeeze the mark for more money but rope in the crowd too.

If you place a coin into your hand (a quarter is perfect), laying it on the outstretched fingers rather than on your palm, and close your hand tightly, you will feel the coin inside your hand. The tighter you squeeze, the more you can feel that coin. Now remove the coin and close your hand again—can you still feel the coin? You should be able to. This phantom coin is the basis of my final proposition, which never fails to get the money and attract other people into the game. Here's what happens:

I have the mark hold the coin tightly inside his fist, then remove it and close his hand again to confirm he still feels a coin inside. Now I have him hold out his hand, palm up and flat, as before. I repeat the snatch, but this time we both keep our hands closed and raise them for all to see. Now I offer the bet to the crowd: Who thinks I have the coin and who thinks the sucker has it? The crowd goes one way or the other, but the mark begins to believe he really has the coin in his hand, so I offer him the chance to play double or nothing for everything he's lost so far. More often than not they take the bet, but I still don't let him open his hand until the crowd decides which way to bet (by round of applause). Now that the mark is convinced he has the coin, the crowd tends to bet on him, but that turns out to be a big mistake. When my opponent opens his hand he *is* holding a coin, but not the one we've been playing for! Instead of the quarter, he finds a copper coin of similar size. Somehow I not only managed to snatch the coin, I also switched it in the process! The winning quarter is revealed inside my fist before I give my mark (and the audience) a free pass.

You can see how this simple stunt has been broken down and reconstructed to escalate toward the big finish, each phase increasing the mark's losses but keeping him in the game as the conditions become seemingly more difficult for me while appearing easier for him. This principle of gradually increasing the stakes transforms a trick into a series of traps where the sucker's interest in the proposition and the hustler's ability to manipulate determines how much is ultimately being played for.

Concealed or unusual skill is often the basis of a good hustle, but secret information and trickery are also employed to get the money. Some, like the loud-mouthed hustler who lost his shirt to the "Dragon Lady," use an aggressive, taunting approach to badger their marks into submission. Others, like Moves, are charming and friendly, establishing trust before taking their victims to the cleaners. Almost all play on a person's inflated sense of self-worth and an overly optimistic faith in his own abilities. Whether conscious of it or not, even if someone publicly proclaims a lack of ability in any pursuit, somewhere inside, his ego is telling him the opposite. A good hustler makes the mark listen to *that* voice and ignore the other side of himself that should be yelling at him to walk away.

In truth, most people don't gamble very often and might never be faced with a proposition bet for big money. That being said, let me remind you of the advice given to Sky Masterson, Marlon Brando's character in the film adaptation of *Guys and Dolls*. Masterson's father warned him that one day, someone would walk up and claim they could make the jack of spades fly out of a brand new deck of cards, hop onto his shoulder, and squirt cider in his ear. "But son," his father told him, "do not accept this bet, because as sure as you stand there, you're going to wind up with an ear full of cider." This has become a well-known story and I bring it up not only because it aptly illustrates why you should walk away from any proposition bet (no matter how crazy it sounds), but because it applies in an interesting way to my friend Moves.

He too has a deck of cards and also proposes to make the jack of spades rise up and squirt cider, but to him it's just a gag—a special device he made in his workshop that pushes open the box and then causes a brass, enamel-painted jack to extend and then squirt liquid as LED lights flash in the jack's eyes. When I first saw it, I was amused but doubtful that it had any value to a hustler, and I asked Moves if it ever made money.

"A few bucks, maybe, but that's not what it's for," he told me.

And that was that.

You learn, when dealing with guys like Moves, who make a living from their secrets, not to ask too many questions, especially if the answer isn't forthcoming. In the months since he showed me that particular contraption, I've tried to understand its true purpose. Here's a guy who can clear a pool table and has a hidden compartment in his trunk filled with devices like his coin-toss flip-flops that are all designed to win money by any means necessary. Why would he have such a goofy device? I've come to realize that this gag has nothing to do with winning money and everything to do with another important element of the hustle: softening up the mark. The coin toss might tell him if the mark is worth his time; his "jack in the box" is merely a way to break the ice or release the tension after Moves starts to win.

Moves likes to play pool for money, and he likes to have the edge on his opponent. Winning money with prop bets is a way to make some cash, but it's really about figuring out who has "got gamble" and who has the deepest pockets to play into. A cider-squirting jack and a mechanical flip-flop are just means to an end—to put a sucker at the table.

TRICKS, BABY

"*I* don't want you to pay me anything right now," I said. "All we need to know is that you are able to afford the deposit and one month's rent. If after that, you are successful, then we will proceed."

The mark and her friend walked around the flat, still unable to believe that a place in such a prime location was available at such a low price. I had already anticipated this and was waiting for the inevitable question: why so cheap?

"There are two reasons," I told them. "First, the client needs to rent the space immediately so it is priced to attract tenants quickly. Second, the lease is for only three months at a time, as the owner might return home within a year or two. In my experience, it's more likely they will be gone for much longer. The weather in California is so much nicer than it is here!"

The mark accepted this as I pretended to take a phone call with bad news about another potential tenant who was apparently having trouble raising the necessary security deposit. I returned and confided to the mark that she had a real opportunity to secure the apartment if she was willing to act quickly and was genuinely able to afford the flat. To prove this, she would need to wire the necessary amount to a friend or relative and then show me proof of the transaction. This would confirm that she had the funds without having to give me any money until the deal was complete. I explained that this was necessary when trying to rent a property so quickly as many people claim they have enough money but soon fall through before a deal can be completed.

"You have to understand," I told her, "once we agree to manage a property, it's essential that we have a real tenant or it might cost my company a lot of money. Time wasters are all too common and very expensive."

Of course, this was all a complete lie. The flat did not belong to us in any way. Had we been real con artists, it would simply have been a matter of breaking into someone's property while on vacation and renting it to several marks before the owner returned. Lack of time can be an issue in these circumstances since most apartment rentals are not arranged in one afternoon, but our scam was able to steal two months worth of rent in just a couple of hours.

"How do I send the money? I don't understand why that's necessary. Why don't I just send it to you?" the mark asked.

"It's just a matter of proving you have the means. You don't pay us anything until you receive the keys but, under the circumstances, I can assure you that, if you're willing to act quickly the apartment is yours."

I could see the story was working; she was close to committing and all she needed was a gentle nudge. "It's perfectly safe. You simply go to the bank, take out the money and send it by wire transfer to someone you know and trust. Fax me a copy of the receipt and I'll be satisfied you are able to rent this property. I'll see to it that you have first refusal on Monday morning. We do it this way so that you don't have to give us any money until you take the apartment. You have to be careful these days—there are a lot of con men out there who just want your money."

The mark quickly filled out the rental forms before heading to the bank, and while I gave the same story to another potential victim, she did as instructed and wired over two thousand pounds (almost five thousand dollars) to a friend, then faxed us the receipt. According to my story, the mark could then simply cancel the wire and take back the money, but as soon as she sent that fax, her cash was as good as gone.

Con games evolve over time. Con artists are always looking for fresh ways to trick people and new methods are often incorporated into old scams, which have been around for centuries. Selling or renting a property that belongs to someone else is nothing new. If a hustler can convince a mark that his story is true, he can easily take the money and run. A simple flaw in the money transfer system (at that time, around 2009) allowed scammers to con people into thinking their money was safe when they were actually being manipulated into giving it away.

What our victims didn't realize was that the transfer service we asked them to use only required a proof of ID and the number of the transfer receipt for someone to collect the money that was being sent. It was true that they could have canceled the transfer and retrieved the money and that their trusted friend could pick it up instead, but once they shared the paperwork with me, Alex was able to make up a fake ID (a library card) and quickly collect the cash. The real estate scam was just a way to hook the mark. The line was simple and the means by which the mark's money was stolen had been adapted to the time and place.

There are hundreds of classic con games but almost all rely on the same principles. Victims become wrapped up in a story while focused on a prize and are eventually convinced to commit (and lose) their money. It's easy to see these elements from a distance, but a con game often reflects the hopes and desires of each mark, and for most, the experience is personal, even traumatic. Cons like these happen quickly, over hours or days. Their objective is to take a lot of money in a short period of time, but while there is enormous variety in the stories being told, most are just window dressing for age-old scams.

Bait and Switch

In London, in the 1950s, Dick Chevelle was a well-known magic dealer whose family owned a fur coat shop in the city center, which had an ingenious scam to attract people into the store. In their window was a beautiful fur coat on a mannequin with an incredibly attractive low price. Every year, hundreds of women came in to try on that coat but it refused to fit any of them. The shoulder on one side was a little loose or the sleeves were too short; there was always some detail that meant the coat wasn't quite right. Naturally another coat would appear, and then another until the customer found one that fit perfectly. By this time, the price had escalated with each new garment until it was more than double the price of the coat in the window.

The scam was in how the coat was tailored and the wooden mannequin specially made to display it. There was too much room in one shoulder, one sleeve was a slightly different length, the other was a little narrower at one end, and the length of the coat was different on each side, but when hung on the mannequin—which had been made to compensate for all of these flaws—it looked beautiful. Once placed on a potential customer, the coat would never fit until, one day, an old lady walked in with a walking stick and a hunched back. For her, the coat was a perfect fit, and she insisted on buying it for the price advertised in the window.

Bait and switch has become such a well-known strategy because it is now a common (questionable) business tactic used to lure customers with an attractive offer before upselling to a more expensive alternative. You've no doubt seen many examples of this, from simple psychological ploys and cleverly worded advertising to outright lies that are difficult to disprove.

Con games like the iPad scam, where a mark is left holding a cheap floor tile or White Van scams, where electronics are offered to people under the pretense of being excess or stolen stock, are much more blatant. Once the victim has examined a device, it is secretly switched. People return home to find they've bought a box filled with potatoes or cheap bottles of water instead of a Blu-Ray player or camcorder.

The Gold Brick game is a classic bait and switch scam where something is presented as being of much greater value than it actually is. The term refers to scams where a mark was convinced to buy a bar of gold from someone who either needed to sell it quickly or had no idea of its true value. In some versions, one con artist would play the part of the seller while another would "partner-up" with the mark to buy the gold cheaply. In essence, the mark thought he was scamming some yokel until he took the gold to be assayed and the truth dawned. This scam was usually accomplished with one real gold bar and a few gold-plated duplicates, but modern variations rarely need to switch the merchandise, relying instead on spurious proof of value that's easily accepted by a mark.

In a variation on this ploy, scammers would "salt" a mine by scattering tiny gold nuggets or rough gems for their victim to find before agreeing to buy a worthless hole in the ground. In the Thai Gem Scam, tourists are lured to bogus stores to buy supposedly expensive stones at bargain prices. Planted evidence or sham experts can be more effective than trying to make a switch or passing off a duplicate, but the principle is the same: prove by means of deception something is real and worth more than the mark is asked to pay. Whether you switch the genuine article out, employ a confederate to give a false variation, or invest in a few tiny stones or nuggets up front, the mark is ultimately fooled into buying something that proves to be worthless.

One of the most ingenious variations on this scam allowed the mark to bring his own expert, to test everything, and to keep his hands on the merchandise at all times.

In a hotel room in New Jersey, a jeweler and his associate met someone they believed to be a gold dealer who was about to return to Europe with a briefcase full of gold chains. The gold dealer was, in truth, an expert con artist who had roped the jeweler with a story about not wanting to take his gold chains back to Amsterdam after an unsuccessful business trip. He was willing to sell the chains at a very attractive price, if the jeweler was able to pay cash right away. Naturally, the mark wanted to test the gold and the dealer agreed for him to bring someone along for that purpose; but, before he would let him start the test, the con man demanded to see the money. The jeweler showed him the cash, the test continued, and every gold chain the jeweler tested proved to be solid, eighteen-karat gold. After a brief negotiation, they agreed on a price. The jeweler then took the whole case and returned to New York, while the fake dealer went in search of another victim.

The chains that the jeweler bought were solid gold, but worth only two-thirds of what he paid—but the chains were never switched. How the mark was tricked was ingenious. Just before the jeweler had his employee test the chains, the con artist demanded to see the money, and while the marks were misdirected, switched the tiny bottle of acid that was used to test the gold. The results were now determined by the scammer's chemical, which was designed to react to fourteen-karat gold as would be expected for eighteen-karat gold! This is an excellent example of a deceptive mind at work. Why try to switch a large briefcase full of chains, when you can switch a tiny plastic bottle instead?

On *The Real Hustle* we reconstructed another ingenious con game that was originally played on wealthy homeowners around London in the 1960s. Posing as an antiques dealer, a con artist would offer to value a mark's collection of artifacts, paintings, and objets d'art. During this valuation, the hustler would spot a vase or small statue and ask if the owner had a complete pair, since this would be worth many times more than just one. The mark admitted that he didn't, and the charade would continue until, a few days later, the con artist would return and excitedly tell the mark that he had found a matching vase and that, if the mark bought it, he could make a huge profit at auction.

Accompanying the con artist to see the other piece, the mark would buy it for a large sum, believing he was about to make much more when selling his new pair, but upon returning home, the victim found that his original item was missing. It had been stolen by the con artist before leaving the house, then sold back to him as a supposed duplicate. In this variation, the bait is switched-in and sold to the person who *already owns it.*

Separate and Lift

Certain con games are designed to isolate the victim's property so it can be easily taken. These scams can be as basic as the "watch my bag" distraction scam, or as complex as the scenario I devised for Uncle Barry in Charleston. Like the bait and switch, variations can come in all shapes and sizes but the principle remains the same: create a reason for the mark to be separated from his money or property, then take it. Making someone believe the story is the hard part.

The real estate/money transfer scam is a good example. In this case, the mark is convinced to place his money into seemingly safe hands but is conned into giving the hustlers everything they need to collect it. The separation happens when the victim places his cash into the transfer system and the steal comes once he shares the paperwork.

A similar scam used a flaw in the international check clearance system used by banks to process funds from overseas. Con artists would pay for goods and services but when their check arrived, it would be for too much money. A four-hundred-dollar invoice might be paid for with a four-thousand-dollar check. The scammer would ask the victim to simply cash the check and wait for it to clear, then send back the balance minus two hundred dollars more for their trouble. This seems perfectly reasonable and once the four thousand dollars appeared in the mark's account, he is happy to comply. Unfortunately, even though an international check could clear in ten days, it actually takes *longer*, sometimes weeks, for the banks to work out that the original check was from an empty account. At that point, the four thousand dollars would be removed from the victim's account while his own money, which he sent to the scammers, was long gone.

In the Murphy Game, which is a twist on the white van scam, victims are shown an expensive item that's apparently being sold to someone in a bar. When people become interested, they are offered the chance to buy the same merchandise but need to go to a second location to collect it. Assured by the person originally buying the item, the suckers quickly agree, but both the buyer and seller are working together. On the TV show, I played the part of someone buying an Xbox from Alex who supposedly worked in a nearby electronics store. As soon as our victims saw the Xbox packaging, they all wanted one, so Alex took us to the back of "his" store, collected the money, and asked me to come inside to help carry out the boxes while everyone waited for us to return. In a real con, we would have just walked straight through the store and into a waiting car, but we watched them for about thirty minutes until someone decided to look at the Xbox I had left with them. Inside was nothing more than a heavy ream of printer paper.

For a mark to let someone walk away with their money—or to leave it where it might easily be taken—requires a careful balance between trust and expectation. The simplest separation scam might be an "exchange of trust," where a mark is asked to keep an eye on someone's laptop in a busy cafe while they step outside to smoke or make a phone call. Later, when the mark goes to the bathroom, he is inclined to ask that person to return the favor, and as soon as they're out of sight, the hustler packs up both devices and heads for the door.

A similar scam, for a much bigger score, was known as "van dragging" in the UK, where hustlers would pose as warehouse workers to redirect delivery vans to a second location where the goods would be off-loaded and whisked away. The most common reason given for sending trucks elsewhere was "broken loading bay doors." Thanks in part to the lack of concern shown by many truck drivers for their load, this story proved to be extremely effective. Once the scam became well known, it soon died off until, several years later, a clever variation appeared.

Drivers would arrive to find a sign explaining that there was a problem with the loading area and instructing them to call a phone number when they arrived. This went straight to the hustlers, who would appear dressed in a similar manner to staff from that store. They would convince the driver to offload in front of the loading bay, and once the truck was gone, the scammer would bring in his own vehicle, load it quickly, and be gone in a matter of minutes. All of this happened at the back of a busy store and several managers have opened their loading bays to find their new stock being loaded into someone else's truck. The sign with a phone number was a clever convincer, but more brazen hustlers also approached delivery drivers in the days or weeks leading up to the theft, dressed appropriately and acting like they worked in the store.

"Seeding a mark" is the process of convincing someone slowly by building a sense of familiarity. Walking into a loading bay and chatting with drivers, perhaps even bringing them a coffee or a snack, can pay dividends when asking them to later break their routine. In pulling the classic Jamaican Switch scam—made famous by George Roy Hill's film *The Sting*—I used this technique to build trust with my intended mark. Over two weeks I regularly visited a local restaurant, chatted with the staff, and gradually created the image of a local businessman with a new store opening nearby. Each visit, I would sit at the bar and engage the manager with light conversation, so that by the time I was ready for the scam, I was well known to several members of the staff.

The Jamaican Switch is a simple ruse where the mark is convinced to take a sum of money from the con artist and place it together with his own money. The actual switch varies but the principle remains the same: have the victim place all of his money and the hustler's in the same package, then switch that package for a duplicate filled with paper. In the past, female grifters would tell victims that an ex-boyfriend was waiting outside a local bank to stop them from depositing money. The sucker would then agree to take the money to the bank and she would convince the mark to keep all their money in one package, illustrating where to hide it on his person. During this demonstration, the grifter would switch the bundle and the mark would later leave with nothing but newspaper.

For our scam, we already knew that the restaurant took cash to the bank every Friday after lunch, and since Thursday evening and Friday lunch are traditionally very busy in London, we knew there would be a lot of cash in play. I therefore needed two things:

1. A way to combine my money with theirs that would not arouse suspicion.
2. A package big enough to contain everything.

The solution was a large, plastic envelope with a locking zipper used for bank deposits. I arrived at the end of lunch and asked a member of the staff if he could place my envelope behind the bar for safekeeping. In conversation, I mentioned that I was heading to the bank afterward, but just as the manager was about to send someone to the same branch with the restaurant's takings, I pretended to receive a phone call about an urgent problem at my store.

Everything had been building to this moment and all I needed was a simple gesture from the staff, an offer of help. Concerned, I asked for my envelope, and as they handed it to me, I asked if they might be passing my branch on the way to their own bank. Of course, I already knew that my bank and theirs was the same, but I acted surprised when they confirmed this.

"Could you possibly do me a huge favor?" I asked.

"What is it?"

"I've got to put this money into my business account," I said as I unzipped the envelope and flashed a large amount of cash and a deposit slip. "If you could just hand this in for me, it would be a lifesaver. A water pipe has burst at my shop and I need to deal with it right away."

She needed a little convincing but soon agreed to help. Another member of the staff arrived with the restaurant's money envelope and I asked if they could keep everything together. The mark was now holding the restaurant takings but uncertain about my request. Without hesitating, I simply took the envelope from her hands, dropped it into my own, and zipped. I then offered her the combined package, which was still filled with money. I was ready to make the switch, but it is essential to do so naturally, without raising suspicion, so just as she was about to take the envelope I said, "Just don't carry it in the open, like this—put it inside your coat or in a handbag, if you don't mind."

She took the envelope and assured me she would look after it, and I rushed out to deal with an imaginary problem in my imaginary shop. Later, she would swear that the envelope never left her sight, but at the moment I said "put it inside your coat" I briefly placed the entire package inside my own jacket to illustrate and switched it for the duplicate that was trapped under my arm. The moment and timing had been perfect, and because they felt that they already knew me, there was no inherent suspicion to overcome.

There seems to be an inexhaustible number of scams that separate and steal in this way. As times change, new stories, methods, and opportunities are quickly adapted to this type of con and old methods such as the Murphy Game, the Jamaican Switch, the Flue, the Jackpot, and the Broken Heart are constantly being re-invented.

Opportunities, Not

When engaging someone on a more personal level, creating the illusion of good fortune is a common and effective ploy. In the Pigeon Drop (where the mark and a hustler seemingly find a bag of money), the victim believes he has stumbled upon a windfall and pays dearly to hold onto the prize. Similar scams place the mark in a position where he needs to invest a large amount of money, certain that he will make much more in the long run.

The Lost Ring Game is a perfect example of a manufactured opportunity. A pretty girl claims to have lost a diamond from her engagement ring in a bar or restaurant. She shows the manager the empty setting in her ring and claims that the missing stone is worth thousands of dollars. A brief search proves fruitless, so the girl leaves her number and promises to pay five hundred dollars to anyone who finds the diamond.

Shortly after, her fellow con artist pretends to happen upon the stone but refuses to give it to the manager or wait for the owner to return. This situation forces the mark to either let the diamond go or offer to share the reward. In most cases, if the mark is well chosen, he will offer to pay a low amount himself in the hope of keeping the rest of the reward—which is exactly what the hustlers are counting on. The aim of this scam is to convince the mark to pay two hundred dollars for a worthless piece of glass because he expects to receive five hundred dollars from its distraught owner.

A clever variation of the gold brick scam employs victims to act as a go-between for two con artists, where one is trying to sell something of great value to the other, but for some reason, the mark is needed to help communicate between the two parties. This man in the middle scenario forces the victim to relay information between the two hustlers and therefore repeat and represent everything he is being told.

On *The Real Hustle*, we targeted a Greek businessman and created a scenario where Alex needed the mark to translate for him (Alex is part Greek and speaks the language fluently). Across a restaurant table, Alex and I tried to negotiate a deal but because we didn't trust each other, the mark suddenly found himself in a position to help facilitate the transaction and make a lot of money in the process. All he needed to do was buy the item from Alex and then sell it to me. This would satisfy Alex's concerns while I was happy to pay whatever was necessary.

This strategy could be used with anyone acting as an intermediary, because the key to this scam is that it forces the mark to unknowingly repeat a *credible* lie and ultimately accept it for himself. Once the mark himself is convinced that the prize is real, the idea of taking advantage of this situation will soon become obvious to him.

Sales Scams

Opportunity scams come in all shapes and sizes with a few managing to technically stay on the right side of the law. These scams all rely on creating the illusion that the mark can make a lot of money in return for a small investment. The simplest example might be a boiler room scam, where victims are made to believe they can buy shares that are somehow guaranteed to make money but prove to be completely worthless, perhaps even nonexistent. This type of con depends on convincing the mark that an opportunity is genuine before applying enormous pressure to force a decision.

High-pressure sales tactics are often used by people who are fully aware that they are tricking people, but instead of leaving them with nothing, they sell items for much more than they are worth. The objective is to badger people until they commit, and the techniques used are reminiscent of a jam auction being played out in people's homes.

These companies don't just con their customers; the people who work for them are often being manipulated too. A certain air-filtration/vacuum cleaner company employs people with the promise of hourly wages or shared profits, depending on which is greater, but the employee induction process has been cleverly designed to avoid paying most applicants. First there's the training, for which no one is paid, but after which, everyone is given the opportunity to jump ahead and begin earning commission by simply organizing ten or more presentations for family and friends. The scam is simple and depends entirely on people being able to secure a few sales from their own contacts in the belief that this will catapult them into a real job with a genuine commission. Almost no one is able to sell enough products to be paid, and if they do, they will soon run out of friends and family willing to buy overpriced carpet cleaners.

None of this proves that the manufacturer of these machines does anything to encourage such practices, but I noticed on their website a large red notice, warning potential buyers not to purchase their products from any source other than approved dealers and that any models being sold on the Internet are guaranteed to be fake. I question this statement and am forced to wonder if its placement on the site is just another layer to aid their high-pressure door-to-door salesmen. While researching this company (which shall remain nameless), I found an interesting claim on one review site regarding one of their most popular air-cleaners. This particular model uses an expensive filter and there is a warning light to signal when this needs to be replaced. According to the reviewer, this light actually works on a timer! This means that, no matter how much you use the device or the quality of your air, the warning light will flash after eleven months then stay on until an expensive new filter has been installed.

A friend explained this employment scam to me several years ago. He once worked for his father, who had successfully operated one of these franchises for many years around the Midwest. He told me that the business depended on victims selling a small number of devices in the hope of getting a real job, which was always given to someone else, usually my friend who pretended to be one of the applicants. Anyone who stayed with the company did so on a commission-only basis, but despite promises to the contrary, were required to generate their own leads. One highly questionable method used by some franchises was to post familiar-looking brown and yellow slips of paper to people, claiming that a package was being held for them. Anyone falling for this tactic would quickly start receiving regular marketing calls until they agreed to an in-home demonstration.

Last I heard, my friend's father was still running the business. I found it interesting that in addition to being a salesman with highly questionable business ethics, he is also a popular preacher with a large congregation.

The Panic Principle

At one point, the Jury Duty Scam was considered to be one of the most common in the United States. People would receive a phone call from the clerk of their local court demanding to know why they hadn't appeared for jury selection. The victim would immediately state that they never received any notification, but the clerk would tell them that it was already too late; a warrant had been issued by the judge for them to appear before the end of the day.

By now, the mark is angry or upset so the clerk offers them a ray of hope. He can pay a fine and sign a form to state they received no communication from the court, and if it's simply been a clerical error, their money will be returned. The alternative is to appear before the judge and there's a chance the mark might need to wait for hours and could even be detained if the judge sees fit. Most people choose the easy way out and a "courier" is quickly sent to pick up their money and have them sign a few fake documents.

One of the most powerful lessons I learned while writing and producing *The Real Hustle* and *Scammed* is that people are much easier to manipulate when maneuvered into a compromising situation. This tactic has the benefit of both sinking and cooling out a mark who's willing to give anything to get out of a jam or help a loved one. The setup is simple: convince a mark that he or someone he cares about is in trouble and offer him a resolution that will quickly expire.

It's easy to see how anyone might agree to pay a fine to avoid facing an angry judge or spending the day waiting at the courthouse, and this scam works because the situation is so plausible that the mark's reaction is predictable, which is the key to many successful con games. If you heard that a loved one had been hurt or arrested while on vacation, how much money would you send to help? If you were suddenly found in a compromising position with someone, what would you pay to avoid shame or scandal?

The panic principle is the basis of many scams, but it is also a powerful technique to sink or cool out a mark. In the black money scam, another buyer might appear offering to buy everything and forcing the mark to make a decision, or the mark might be threatened with legal consequences for attempting to buy "cancelled money." In any situation where people tend to just react rather than stop and consider their options, con artists are able to anticipate and take advantage.

Trust Abuse

Trust can be grown, it can be earned, it can be assumed, and it can be stolen.

No one visiting one of London's most prestigious department stores would think to question anyone who appeared to work there, but one year, a team of hustlers installed their own cash register in a quiet corner of the store, then directed members of the public who were paying cash to use that till. It's easy to assume that security or other staff members would quickly stumble upon this scam, but during the pre-Christmas period large stores can hire up to two thousand seasonal workers—it's easy to blend in and claim to be a temp. The hard part is walking in and out with your own cash register, but as a professional grifter told me after watching us pull this scam on *The Real Hustle*, once you make enough money, you only need to walk out with the cash. In a store like Selfridges or Harrods, scammers might make tens of thousands of pounds on a busy day, and everyone conned into buying goods at their register is technically stealing since they haven't paid the store for anything!

This scam takes advantage of implied trust, where someone is assumed to be part of a well-known company or institution. It's exactly the same principle that I used to steal innocent people's money for parking by wearing the appropriate attire. In this case, each of the customers who uses the fake register is a victim of a simple short con. Most will never know they were scammed, but the company itself loses tens of thousands of dollars from right under their own noses. It is similar to the van dragging scam and illustrates how fulfilling a simple role allows a scammer to borrow legitimacy by blending into their surroundings.

Con artists often pose as people in authority or respectable members of society. They might even claim to be a real person if the mark is easily persuaded or impressed. In the late nineteenth century, Cassie Chadwick conned several banks out of millions of dollars simply by claiming to be the daughter of Andrew Carnegie, and one hundred years later Christophe Rocancourt successfully pulled the same scam by pretending to be a French member of the Rockefeller family. By borrowing the reputation of others and leeching legitimacy from well-known names and institutions, scammers have been able to steal billions over the years. Frank Abagnale Jr. specialized in passing forged or bad checks and was very successful thanks to his habit of posing as a pilot or a member of some other respected profession that the banks wouldn't question.

Mixing Up

Many con games employ several of those principles or marry scams together when attempting longer cons. The Bank Examiner scam, for example, takes advantage of people's respect for authority and secures trust by impersonating the police, security, or some other official supposedly employed by the financial industry. Once a mark is convinced by their story and fake credentials, the scammers will either ask him to help with an investigation or convince the mark that he is somehow under suspicion of helping to pass counterfeit money. When accused, innocent people will often go to any lengths to prove their virtue, so to prove their innocence, they are asked to help catch a crooked bank teller in the act.

Whether by the victim's willingness to help or their need to escape suspicion, the con is the same. The mark is asked to withdraw a large sum of money from his bank and given strict instructions about which teller he should use. Later, when the hustlers examine the cash, they claim that it is all counterfeit and must be kept as evidence, exchanging the sucker's money for a worthless receipt. Eventually, the victim realizes the truth but even then, the con may not be over.

A few months later, the mark is approached by two more grifters pretending that they want to set up a sting to catch the people who stole the mark's money. Eager for retribution, the mark often falls for the same scam twice. The pigeon is made to believe he is helping the real police catch the impostors in the act of taking his money for a second time. They might even make an act out of pretending to arrest the dastardly con men before keeping the mark's money as evidence again!

Not only do these principles work, with a slight twist on the story they can even be repeated on the exact same victims. This is one of the most important lessons I can pass on about the nature of cons and scams. Not only do they continue to change and adapt to the times, they can be easily tailored to any victim. The more that a story connects with a mark, the harder it is for them to see the deception—even if they've seen or heard the same scam before. The bank examiner scam works because people want to help the authorities or prove their innocence; it works a second time because they want retribution for the first scam. Though the mark is motivated differently, the principles of the two scams are identical.

It is the story that hooks the mark, convinces him over time, and ultimately causes him to commit. Once distracted by this fiction, it is extremely difficult, perhaps impossible, to recognize deception. The more beautiful and beguiling the rose, the easier to forget the thorns.

Going Long

Confidence tricks like the Spanish Prisoner often engage a mark over greater periods of time, and as they evolve into long cons, the stakes become much higher. Deeper conviction results in a larger commitment to the lie, but the scams remain essentially the same, perhaps combining elements from different cons.

Yellow Kid Weil's Boxing Scam was an ingenious combination of principles. It started with a real estate deal that the victim was easily able to verify as genuine, but while working on this deal, the mark became aware that his new business associates were involved in a colorful affair where a former champion boxer was planning to take a fall during a private boxing match. The mark soon demanded to be "let in" on the action and Yellow Kid and his partners agreed on one condition—that the mark place all of their money in one large bet.

On the night of the boxing match, the sucker added a huge amount of his own money to that bet, and while waiting for their fighter to take a fall, the mark, brimming with confidence, even agreed to a much larger wager. Unfortunately, before he could pretend to get knocked out, the "ringer" scored a lucky punch that lifted his opponent clear off the canvas, killing him instantly.

As blood poured onto the canvas, it suddenly dawned on the mark, with a little encouragement from Yellow Kid, that this was an illegal boxing match and that everyone in the room might be arrested as accomplices to murder. The mark didn't need any help finding the exit and was soon on his way home, a poorer man but grateful to get away.

Notice how this beautifully crafted con game uses several principles to hook the mark, manipulate him with the line, then sink him and eventually cool him out. It uses several strategies to create a concert of connivery:

- *Bait and Switch*: The real estate deal was legitimate but was only intended to get the victim involved with Yellow Kid and his team of hustlers. Their real objective was to let him find out about the fixed boxing match, knowing he was exactly the kind of mark who would relish the idea of easy money. Had they tried to approach him directly about the match, his suspicion might easily be aroused.

- *Abuse of Trust*: The honest business transaction that Yellow Kid used to get close to his mark required time to complete. While the con man had no intention of completing the deal, it allowed him to develop a level of trust and legitimacy that would become an invaluable ingredient when convincing the mark.

- *Panic Principle and "Separate and Lift"*: The staged death of a fighter during an illegal boxing match in an underground gambling den is a powerful motivation to make just about anyone walk—or run away—no matter how much he has lost, resulting in a complex but effective "separate and lift."

- *The Cool-Out*: Once the mark had left his money behind, it was almost certain he would never return, and convinced by the scam, there was little danger of him calling the police. Yellow Kid's plan was for the mark to catch the first train home to try to forget the whole affair and that's exactly what he did. But his ordeal was far from over.

During the match, the sucker had agreed to commit to a larger bet, so a few months later, someone posing as a money collector would demand that the debt be paid with interest. In fact, the victim might have been blackmailed for months or years after the con, but the scam soon collapsed. With so many people involved in the charade, it was inevitable that someone would attract the attention of the law. Brilliant as the scam was, it proved too dangerous and ultimately cost the life or liberty of several players when the police caught up with them.

With most scams it is the mark who dictates how a con should be played. As time progresses, hustlers identify new angles and there seem to be no depths to which they won't sink. Charity scams are all too common, especially after a well-publicized disaster or tragic event, but I see nothing particularly clever in this type of fraud. It's simply taking advantage of the public's instinct to help people and there's little or no art in it.

Con games are just as despicable as these fake charities and con artists are no better than their lying, bottom-feeding cousins, but there's an inherent ingenuity to these scams that sets them apart from other crimes. It's difficult to appreciate how effective they are or why they work, because there is a powerful element at work in more sophisticated scams: emotion.

In essence, con games are a seduction, and it takes experience to know when or how to introduce the idea of commitment. Come on too strong or too soon and the mark is likely to resist or walk away. Long cons allow con artists to build a relationship, foster trust, and gradually manipulate the mark. A long con is played over a greater period of time, potentially for much bigger stakes. The result is a higher return for the hustlers and a deeper, more damaging impact on the victim. In this sense, a confidence trick is like a one-night stand, while a long con is a passionate affair that becomes devastating when it proves to be a lie.

CHEATING HEARTS

I lost another hand and watched as SM pulled more of my chips toward himself, adding them to his growing stack. Soon, we would be evenly matched; it was obvious that my luck had taken a turn for the worse.

The air was thick with smoke that clung to the ceiling in dark gray clouds as about a dozen people sat or stood around the table to see who would win the tournament. In another room, several cash games were under way, and I knew SM was keen to join them. After the previous player was knocked out, SM quickly offered to share the prize money for our table—a built-in option—but I had refused, partly because, despite having far fewer chips than me, he insisted on an even split, but mostly because I despised the prick. I wasn't alone in this regard, and most onlookers were watching in the hope that I would beat him, but it seemed that the cards had turned against me.

The game was hosted in a large Glasgow apartment with several rooms filled with folding chairs and card tables. The players were all invited from local casinos; a rogues gallery of crooks, businessmen, gambling addicts, and poker enthusiasts. The games were self-dealt, with cards that were about ten years old, passed from player to player to deal, but no one had tried any kind of sleight or false shuffle until that night, when I decided to take SM down.

Seven Card Stud has never been my strongest game. I had spent some time studying the odds and learning a few plays, but I was probably more of a danger to myself than a player like SM. Nevertheless I'd gotten this far by luck, some good decisions, and a few well-timed maneuvers. I knew that skill could eventually turn the tide in SM's favor. It was my turn to deal, and I gave the cards a legitimate shuffle and a cut. I dealt each of us three cards—two face down and a third face up. With each additional card, SM increased the pressure, constantly raising while I continued to call.

As I picked up the deck to deal us each a seventh card, I was faced with a decision to either bluff or fold after the next raise. I was holding two pairs but SM had four hearts face up and was acting like he already had the flush. Someone made a joke and SM reacted, looking away for just a second, and in that instant, I secretly peeked at the top card of the deck. It was exactly what I needed to make a full house! If SM really had his flush, he was sure to go all the way, but the top card was meant for his hand, not mine. As far as I could tell, I was about to lose unless I could somehow keep that top card for myself.

As it happened, I could.

With everyone's eyes on me, I broke the cardinal rule: never move when the heat is on. I drew my left thumb to the edge of the deck and pushed what looked like a single card to the right. In fact it was two cards, perfectly aligned, and as my right hand approached, the left thumb quickly drew back the uppermost card leaving the second card protruding with my right fingers contacting its face. Then, with the aid of my right thumb, I spun the second toward SM.

Performed well, a second deal can hide among several fair deals, emulating the honest action almost exactly. As a single deal it needs to be absolutely perfect and performed without hesitation. The slightest variation in handling might attract attention or, in the worst possible scenario, the second card might not come, and remain protruding underneath the top card. This is known as "catching a hanger" and is usually followed by "going to the hospital." Dealing a second under these conditions doesn't just take great skill; it requires huge, brass balls.

The second card sailed toward SM and landed softly as I fairly dealt the card I had just stolen for myself and gauged the room to determine if anyone suspected. Nothing had changed. I was free and clear. All I had to do was take SM's money. But things don't always work out the way we plan them.

SM was a poker cheat. For years I'd found myself sitting across from him and his two partners at final tables after hours of play, only to be squeezed out as all three played from the same pocket. Their method was to keep each other in the game by passing chips whenever only two of them remained in a hand. They would each add chips to the pot until the last round where the weaker of the two would raise whatever he had left and the other would fold, no matter what cards he had. This was blatant collusion, but even though everyone knew it was happening, they all felt that it was impossible to prove.

SM was also an aggressive player, constantly badgering people into making poor decisions and regularly being admonished for his bad behavior. I have no idea if SM had ever dealt from the bottom or stacked a cooler (set up a deck in advance), but he and his partners were cheats, and when given the chance to turn the tables, I didn't hesitate. Unfortunately, fate had other plans.

Sleight of hand had rewarded me with a full house but had also given SM the exact card he was hoping for. He was only holding four hearts until my second deal gave him not just a fifth heart (a flush) but the exact card he needed for an unbeatable *straight flush*. Unaware of this, I bet everything on my full house and walked right into a trap of my own making. Had I dealt honestly, I might have won the hand fair and square, but instead, I used a lifetime of practice to gut myself.

Later, as I sat in my car feeling the sting of a self-made bad beat, I resolved to take this experience as a sign that the universe didn't want me to cheat and that I had better find a more productive outlet for these skills.

Cheating methods teach us that, with enough determination, anything might be possible, and hustlers will go to incredible lengths to get the money. Volumes could be written about cheaters and their practices, but there's an important lesson to be learned from the sheer number of cheating methods and devices that exist: If there's anything worth stealing, thieves, hustlers, and con men will find a way to steal it. Dismissing the idea of deception simply because it seems difficult or unlikely is a common mistake at both the gaming table and in life.

Consider the term "loaded dice." For most people, this refers to opaque, numbered cubes that are weighted on one side to force a favorable roll. In fact, there are many types of gaffed dice, all of which might be called "loaded dice" by the laity: tops, where numbers have been changed to affect the odds; shapes, where each die has been shaved to favor preferred sides; spinners that help hustlers to control the dice; and juice, where each die contains magnetic material mixed with the painted spots on one side.

With weighted dice, the loads can be so subtle that they simply increase the percentage of a preferred outcome and so small and flat they can be hidden under the spots of a clear casino cube. There are loaded dice that can be set on or off thanks to an internal mechanism with a tiny weight that shifts when the die is tapped. There are even perfectly balanced dice that roll fairly but contain electronic sensors that transmit from inside a dice cup to tell cheaters which side is up in games like Pai Gow.

Delving deeper we might discuss the different combinations of mis-spotted dice, how to stamp loaded dice with casino logos before switching them into a live craps game, or the best ways to use a magnet. Eventually you might learn about controlled dice shots where an expert cheater can throw legitimate dice and have a definite effect on the outcome. The further you delve, the more variations and methods you will find because loaded dice, like all forms of deception, are designed to beat games, break rules, and solve problems.

In this chapter I will illustrate just how far a card mechanic will go, in terms of skill, to beat the game of poker and show that, when expert sleight of hand is combined with ingenious concealed devices, the results can be devastating. My intention is not to teach you how to spot these methods, because many can be completely invisible. Instead, it is important to understand that they are possible and that they are often easier to deduce than detect.

Beating the Cut

One of the main obstacles for a mechanic* in a poker game is the cut. After the shuffle, the cards must be presented to the person sitting on the dealer's right, who cuts the cards before they are dealt. This would normally ruin any setup unless the cut could somehow be defeated. In fact, the cut *can* be beaten, and the methods used range from the surprisingly simple to the fantastically difficult.

An obvious solution is to palm away a small number of cards before the deck is cut and replace them on the top or bottom as the cards are returned for the deal. Players usually practice "holding out" when they are not dealing and little attention is directed toward them; it remains a practical way to keep control of cards if the cheater has the required skill to palm cards without attracting suspicion.

A completely invisible method is when another hustler is seated to the right of the mechanic. The cheat can then set a

---

* A professional cheater and expert in sleight of hand.

tiny step in the cards after the shuffle, which his partner can easily cut to. This can also be attempted without an accomplice by bridging the upper portion of the deck before presenting the cards to be cut. This creates a natural point for the cards to break and, if the mark cuts in a consistent fashion, he can often be manipulated to break at the desired position.

A more direct approach is the "hop" or "shift," where the cards are simply re-cut in the action of taking them into the dealing hand. This is a big risk—and not for the faint of heart—but expert mechanics can solve most problems with the cut and there are dozens of methods to accomplish this move. Many use both hands and a few can even be performed with just one, but all require great skill and expert timing. A much easier method is a bluff hop where the bottom half is picked up first, followed by the original top half. You might think this would appear obvious, but by performing some action between picking up each of the halves, such as tossing in a chip or moving a drink, the deception is rarely noticed and if caught, can easily be passed off as a mistake.

A few years ago, a wealthy businessman explained to me a procedure for passing the cards in his high-stakes private poker games. The deck was shuffled by the player to the dealer's right and cut by the player to the dealer's left, meaning that the person who actually dealt the cards had no control over the position of any cards in the deck. This is not an uncommon procedure to prevent cheating but it is a pointless one if two hustlers get into the game. All they need to do is sit either side of one sucker and they can easily locate cards, false shuffle, and false cut before letting the man in the middle deal the cards after they are stacked. When demonstrating these techniques to my clients, it soon becomes clear that there are many ways to beat any game no matter the conditions. I can think of hundreds of ways to beat the cut, but the most fascinating is a method that can be watched closely and does not break the cutting procedure. It requires the greatest skill imaginable.

Dealing cards from the bottom requires many years of practice and a high degree of dexterity, but in the hands of an expert, it can look exactly like the dealer is taking cards from the top. You could watch a gifted mechanic for hours without ever suspecting that he was dealing from the basement. The cut is the biggest problem for these cheaters because, if there's too much heat to move,* culled (secretly located) cards are sent to the middle and all of the work required to set up would be wasted. This was true until Allen Kennedy, a grifter from Pleasant Hill, Missouri, invented a brilliant, seemingly impossible solution: the center deal.

The idea was simple. Instead of reversing the cut, a tiny brief was held between the two halves of the deck and maintained during the deal. Then, instead of taking cards from the bottom, Kennedy would squeeze them right out of the middle and into his right hand as he pretended to take the top card. If this sounds impossible, you're almost right! In fact, the technique is so difficult that almost everyone who heard about it thought it must be some sort of pasteboard fantasy. Even today, only a

---

* That is, too much attention or suspicion from other players.

handful of experts can perform the deal deceptively because of the high level of skill necessary. Many performers have learned to fake the second deal for their demonstrations, but few, if any, would risk their neck on dealing from the middle in a live game.

Any cheater willing to perfect and use such a move would certainly have a powerful weapon at his disposal, but as one mechanic told me, the only guy who ever used the sleight was probably Allen Kennedy! Nevertheless, the mere fact that such a sleight exists shows us that card thieves, like con artists, will go to any lengths to get the money.

Up the Sleeve

The cheater's arsenal is filled with ingenious sleight of hand designed to overcome almost any obstacle. Over time, countless mechanical solutions have been invented to aid hustlers and sold through supposedly secret catalogs. Many of these contraptions claimed to replace traditional sleight of hand, but while a few were genuinely useful, they required the operator to master a new set of skills to avoid suspicion.

The 1932 issue of H. C. Evans's "Secret Blue Book" contains everything one might need to open and operate a small gambling joint or medium-size back-room casino. From cards, dice, wheels of fortune, and chuck-a-luck cages to cash boxes, measuring equipment, tables, and printed chips, Evans's catalog was a one-stop shop for all your underground or gambling needs. In the same book, among the legitimate paraphernalia, you would also find a fascinating selection of crooked dice, marked cards, machines to pull cards into your sleeve, and specially shaped spinning tops for the game of put and take.

At the time that this edition of the blue book was published, H. C. Evans & Company were in their fortieth year of successfully supplying games both fair and false and had a strong clientele on both sides of the table. Much of their merchandise was designed to give dishonest gaming establishments an unfair or unbeatable edge (there are six pages dedicated to hidden electromagnets), and a few items were sold purely for players to beat fair games, but the majority of the crooked confections were intended for gamblers to cheat each other. The truth was that many of the items being sold were fanciful contraptions with as much practical value as a pair of x-ray specs from the back pages of a comic book, but a few ingenious devices were (and still are) genuinely used by grifters and con men.

The variety of cheating devices is staggering and a few collectors have been able to build breathtaking assortments of now-rare items. In a handful of glass cabinets scattered across the globe, the catalogs of H. C. Evans, the K.C. Card Company, and others come to life and the toys and tools that were once sold from those pages can be handled and used. My own collection is tiny by comparison and visiting these secret museums can be a roller coaster ride of wonder and envy.

Most of these contraptions were impractical, but a few remain genuinely useful if the cheater is willing to master the necessary skills. "Bugs," for example, are a simple method for hiding a card under the table and are usually nothing more than a spring or clip that would hold a card in place until needed. I own several bespoke bugs. They're about as effective as another method: sticking a plastic spoon to the underside of a table so a card can be held out by the bowl of the spoon. A close friend uses cheap plastic clips that come with their own glue spot, ready to stick anywhere. No matter what method of holding a card is being used, the cheat must still learn to invisibly remove cards from the table and insert them into the bug, which takes both gall and skill—neither of which can be purchased from a catalog.

The wide selection of "hold-out" devices perfectly illustrates the variety of methods and ideas that serve the same purpose: to steal a card, hide it, and then secretly return it to play. "Bean shooters" are made of flexible plastic with a long, thin wire that can be threaded into the lining of a jacket at the mouth of the sleeve. A length of elastic is attached and pinned near the shoulder to create constant tension, so when the bean shooter is slid out of the sleeve and a card is inserted into the clip, it automatically returns to its hiding position. This simple device allows a cheater to turn any garment with a suitable sleeve into a seemingly practical hiding place for stolen cards. In truth, the bean shooter is an incredibly difficult gadget to operate. To consistently be able to extract the apparatus so that it meets the palmed card reliably takes practice, and even in the hands of an expert, the action required to steal or return a card can easily be spotted.

More elaborate machines appear to solve these problems by extending a metal plate called a "thief" out of the sleeve and back again, and the arm-pressure holdout features a switch that the cheater can operate by merely leaning on the table so that the lever is squeezed, extending a metal arm until the thief has been loaded. Elastic bands then return the device to the safety of the sleeve. I love this machine; I own one and often include it in my demonstrations, but I would never use one for real. It might have been worn in real games by a few brave souls, but as pleasing as this Jacob's-ladder contraption might be, it is more likely to put a bullet in your head than an ace up your sleeve.

With a holdout device the cheat must learn to palm cards so that the machine can steal and return them to the same position, but many hustlers hold out without devices, simply keeping a card palmed until they find an opportunity to use it. One technique even allows a hustler to place his hand flat on the table with his fingers spread; I've even seen security footage of someone sitting for over fifteen minutes with his hand apparently glued to the same spot until he finally got the cards he was waiting for! With a machine the hands are almost always clean (empty), and when used by an expert, the secret action is completely invisible. The 1932 edition of Evans's "Secret Blue Book" contains a dozen methods to accomplish this but only one that has endured and that I have actually seen used during play.

Examining the wide selection of holdout devices offered in the Evans catalog, it is obvious there was clearly a great deal of interest in all these crooked devices. Many were intended to be nothing more than expensive novelties, especially once buyers realized the dangers of trying to use them under fire (in a live game with genuine danger of being caught). However, the Kepplinger device, named after its inventor, was a clear exception.

J. P. Kepplinger was so successful with his invention that in the late nineteenth century he became known in California as "The Lucky Dutchman." His machine allowed him to move cards in and out of play invisibly and with much higher precision than other methods. The secret was a series of lines and pulleys, contained within a combination of bespoke narrow tubes and hinges that allowed the wearer to control the thief with a

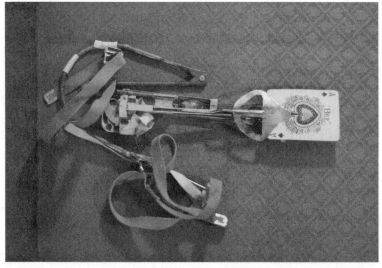

A Kepplinger/Martin "hold out" machine. With this, players can go either straight to the bank or the hospital.

line of tight chord suspended between the knees. By opening and closing one's legs under the table, the action of the holdout can be imperceptible.

Kepplinger made so much money that he eventually became complacent, taking too much from the same group of players until they became sure he was cheating; unable to see any evidence from across the table, they resorted to violence. In the middle of a big hand, Kepplinger was suddenly grabbed from behind and lifted out of his chair. When his coat was removed, the device was discovered. All seemed lost for the card shark until his attackers demanded that he make three more machines for them to use! The group teamed up and were soon the scourge of San Francisco's card rooms.

The Kepplinger concept became a powerful utility device that is still used today. Whereas the original device was sewn into a jacket, variations like the Martin holdout allow the machine to be strapped to the arm and worn under the wearer's shirt. Modern versions are operated by the foot, so there is no need to cut holes near the knees. This variation is known as a "toe-spread" (as opposed to a "knee-spread"), a name that once caused great pain to a close friend of mine.

After waiting years to find a working device, BF called me and asked if I could fly out and give him a lesson on how to operate it. Since I'm not a professional card shark, I had never used one under fire, but I could show him how to set it up and the sleight of hand required to position cards for the steal. Since it was intended for use in a magic trick, I agreed to help and jumped on the next plane to Madrid. When I arrived at his apartment, BF was limping. Since talking to me, he had been experimenting with his machine but complained that operating it hurt so badly, he was ready to give up and sell the damned thing. Confused, I asked him to demonstrate what he had been doing, and by the time he had finished setting up the machine, I was laughing so hard I could barely breathe.

My friend had figured out how to strap the apparatus to his arm and how to wear it under his clothes, but when it came to operating it with his foot, BF took off his sock to reveal a big toe that had turned completely black. He looped the wire around the same toe and then pushed his foot gently into a shoe. Grimacing, BF proceeded to demonstrate, but the amount of pressure required to operate the thief was so high that BF was literally strangling his toe to death! Had I not intervened it might have fallen off before he figured out that the wire was supposed to be placed over the outside of his shoe. In fact, many holdout men wear cowboy boots because the pointed toe is easier to use than a rounded one.

Gambling devices rarely come with instructions, so knowledge is often sold or traded between individuals. The prospective cheater then retires to practice for many hours a day until he or she can move without being detected. BF went on to use his machine in front of an audience, inviting them to stare at his hands as cards vanished and appeared before their eyes. If a magician can use a Kepplinger machine under those closely watched conditions, what chance would you have of spotting one in a game?

While the mechanics of this particular holdout have changed little since 1888, there are several ingenious variations on how and why it is used. One idea is to replace the thief with a mirror, angled to give the operator a table-level view of the cards being dealt, revealing enough information to gain a powerful advantage. A modern version of the same idea uses a tiny camera that is extended to see cards being dealt from a shoe. An even more sophisticated scam recorded the indices (the value and suit in the corner) of cards as the cheater rubbed a plastic cut-card along eight decks before inserting it for the dealer to cut. The rubbing action opened the deck just enough for the camera to see each card riffling off the plastic cut-card. This information was played back so the hustlers were essentially playing from a stacked deck. The "Secret Blue Book" also features shiners (mirrors) hidden in stacks of chips that allowed a crooked dealer to see every card he dealt. Modern variations contain tiny cameras and transmitters that can peek at cards being dealt by almost anyone at the table.

In 2010, security at Foxwoods Resort Casino in Connecticut became suspicious of two baccarat players who had been consistently winning and behaving in a way that suggested deception. When they removed the players from the casino floor, one was found to be wearing a modified version of the Kepplinger machine. He had been using the device while his partner covered any suspicious actions by waving a scorecard to distract the dealer. The casino's security team was experienced enough to suspect that something was wrong; this consistent form of misdirection created a pattern they could identify, but the machine itself was almost undetectable. This one-hundred-year-old contraption was used to steal almost one million dollars from a modern casino, and while these two jokers got caught, more sophisticated hustlers are almost certainly getting away with the same scam elsewhere.

The old gaming catalogs record a point in time where there seemed to be a way to cheat almost any game. Some of these methods were so practical that they are still being used today, but as technology has continued to develop, cheating devices have become much more sophisticated. Computer software, used to process information for advantage players, can now be run on a smartphone and hidden in plain sight, instead of being taped under the player's clothes with a network of wires. Crooked devices or gaffed apparatus alone don't get cheaters very far. They all require skill—especially physical dexterity—to use successfully.

Hop

Gambling sleight of hand is all about getting the money and can vary from crude concealments to feats of skill so fantastic they are almost impossible to believe until you've seen them with your own eyes. In the last four hundred years, countless cheating techniques have been invented to achieve almost any outcome with an ordinary pack of cards. I have personally dedicated almost forty years to mastering hundreds of moves, and there is a growing community of magicians and cheating aficionados who collect and learn these methods without ever intending to use them. For a grifter, one good sleight, perfectly executed, can be the foundation of a cheating career. Very few are adept at more than a handful of techniques.

One exception was Roderick Dee, aka Rod The Hop.

I met Rod in 1997 and we quickly became friends. Whenever I was in Las Vegas, we would spend long nights trading secrets in The Peppermill restaurant on Las Vegas Boulevard. As a child, Rod was a keen amateur magician with a gift for difficult sleight of hand. As a teenager, his interest drifted toward cheating and he was soon using his talents to steal from small money games. By the time we met, Rod was an expert mechanic but spent most of his time as a slot thief, using the latest technology to beat slot machines around Las Vegas.

With a deck of cards, Rod was unmatched. He preferred the smaller, plastic cards used in most card rooms at the time and could execute moves with frightening speed and accuracy. I had little to share in terms of cheating other than my personal methods and a couple of Gin Rummy moves I'd invented, but Rod had a voracious appetite for any form of deception. He loved good magic and we once spent several weeks improving conjuror's moves by combining his approach as a cheat with mine as a magician.

Over the years that I knew him, Rod was in and out of prison, thanks to his addiction to easy money. He was always on the cutting edge of cheating devices for slot machines and at one point was using a method to register a one-dollar bill as a hundred, which the casinos insisted was impossible. That device was the last in a long line of doohickeys that included bright LEDs at the end of a long piece of plastic and stiff wire bent into the perfect shape to reach internal mechanisms, with countless variations adapted to different models of slot machine. Eventually, he returned to the card table as a mechanic for hire and was flown around the United States to deal winning hands for his employers. Not all of these were shady back-room games. Many were held in expensive homes owned by the rich and famous and Hop often found himself busting-out (beating) famous actors or sports personalities.

For Rod, his relationship with magicians proved to be a lifeline—an opportunity to use his skills to entertain. On several occasions he performed demonstrations of card table artifice for private groups. His close friendship with Jason England, a magician and expert on crooked gambling, helped Rod to stay out of trouble until Rod passed away in December 2013. Without Jason, I think Rod would have died in prison, because his love for conjuring was a powerful, positive influence on his life. For Jason and me, cheating is a world that we both might easily have slipped into, but knowing Rod has given us a valuable insight into what happens when you steal for a living. I might not believe in karma, but in my experience, cheating rarely has a positive effect on one's life. Rod made hundreds of thousands of dollars in his career, but it was soon gone and his life was filled with troubles. For me, Rod was a dear friend, a confidant, and a constant reminder of the reality of being a cheat.

Rod differed from his contemporaries because he was genuinely fascinated by the art of sleight of hand. While many cheaters only care about a move that will make them money, Rod collected sleights he thought were clever and could perform most of them effortlessly. Hop also liked to adapt old methods or invent new ones for the games he was playing, and over time, he taught me that no gaming procedure was completely safe or impossible to simulate.

Perhaps Rod's most amazing skill was his ability to operate a Kepplinger-style holdout. A few months before his death, a handful of Rod's friends gathered at Jason's house to watch him demonstrate and expose his technique. With the machine Rod was able to move cards in and out of his sleeve without the slightest flash or tell, but this was not the device that Rod would go on to use in high-stakes poker games. Before being diagnosed with terminal cancer, Rod was hired to deal private games where even though he never needed to make a secret move, his partners could play every hand as if it came from a stacked deck.

As technology advances, cheats are constantly looking for new ways to win. Marked cards have evolved from simple adjustments to standard back designs and special inks that can only be seen with a trained eye to systems that use special glasses or contact lenses to see markings that are invisible without them. The introduction of tiny hidden cameras has allowed grifters to push deeper into the infrared spectrum until their marks can be completely invisible without the right equipment. The simplest application of this is a hidden camera that transmits an IR image to one of the hustlers. When combined with a computer program, this method of marking cards can be devastating.

Rod was hired to perform an honest shuffle and to position the cards, completely squared, in front of a tiny camera that would read the edge of the deck, which was secretly marked with IR ink. To the camera, the ink on the edge of the deck formed a barcode that revealed the exact location of every card in the deck, which the computer would then use to predict who would win that hand and what cards each player would receive. This information was simultaneously sent to one of the players who would use it to good advantage.* The system Rod used can now be bought online for a few thousand dollars, available to anyone who cares to take the risk. All the dealer needs to do is square the deck and place it in the exact position required to get a read, but there are other issues with this system that require skill to overcome. First, the cheaters need to be able to play well enough to use the information without making it obvious they have advanced knowledge. Knowing that a seven-two off-suit will prove to be the best hand is of little use if the other suckers start to wonder why anyone would play those cards. Second, the device can be unstable and often breaks down, which is why Rod was hired to deal; whenever the machine malfunctioned, Rod would start cheating the old-fashioned way. Lastly, Rod was able to assist the device and deliver better quality hands to his partners using false deals that were dictated by the computer.

Even with this kind of system, it takes patience to get the marks' money and many hustlers usually resort to switching decks to save time. A hustler once told me that he was brought in to fill a seat at a private game where the host was the only mark and everyone else at the table was there to cheat him. When the sucker went to the bathroom, one of the cheaters reached over and stole hundreds of dollars from the victim's pile of chips.

---

* I'm deliberately being vague about how this information is captured or received, but if you stop to think how much technology is already at the table in the shape of smartphones, you might be able to piece together the system.

"What are you doing?" my friend asked.

"Saving time!" the hustler replied.

Just because something seems highly unlikely, even impossible, it doesn't mean it can't be done by someone with the time to practice or build a working solution. When it comes to cheating games of chance, some people will go to fantastic lengths to steal. Some methods require nothing more than a willingness to take the shot, regardless of risk or danger; other techniques take years of practice to perfect seemingly fantastic feats of skill that no one would suspect, let alone detect.

It would be impossible to describe more than a tiny sample from the spectrum of cheating methods, but I hope to have illustrated enough of their ingenuity, perspicacity, and tenacity to prove that no game is safe when it can be played for money.

ADVANTAGE PLAY

I could barely breathe. Panic was trying to take over as the sweat ran down my back to the electronic device secretly taped to my skin. Everyone at the table was looking at me expectantly, waiting for an answer. I waved my hand to signal "no more cards," the dealer moved on, and the game continued while I surveyed the room. Everyone on my team was leaving, picking up their chips and cashing out. In a matter of minutes I would be alone in the casino with a hidden computer on my back and a keypad strapped to my leg.

It was my first night working at the tables in a live game. After weeks of perfecting how to enter every card dealt into a computer using binary code, this was my audition for the team who hoped to profit from lax shuffling procedures that were endemic in the UK at that time. We were spread across several tables, recording cards from each round of play and then telling the computer whether or not the dealer employed a weak or a strong shuffle. When the shuffle was weak, we could predict the next round of play with incredible accuracy; but even when it was strong, the odds were still on our side.

As the players would track each round of cards, occasionally rotating to take breaks or keep things moving, a "Big Player" would walk from table to table, seemingly at random but actually guided by his crew. When the odds were in our favor, the computer told me via a tiny earpiece and I would make a signal to bring the Big Player in. Once at the table, the Big Player's earpiece would pick up the signal from my computer and start following its advice. A voice synthesizer would reveal where the aces were most likely to hit and the Big Player would bet more money on those spots, before moving to the next table, where another member of the team was tracking that game.

It was a simple system that required a great deal of work and preparation to execute. No one, it seemed, would believe that five people might be working the tables with complex electronics under their pants. Nevertheless, we had strict rules on how to behave in the event that staff might become suspicious. The most important thing was to never try to make a run for it. Security would hit first and ask questions later. Running was as good as admitting guilt before any questions were even asked.

Just as we had a system for beating the games, there was a strict method for making an exit in the event of heat from the house. First, there was the signal: an open hand running fingers through the hair from front to back. Once this was seen, players would begin taking their chips to the cage and cash out before leaving. We would then meet at the hotel suite rented by our Big Player, who also ran the crew.

I had missed the signal and had no idea when or why it was given. Focused on the game, I had no idea how long we had been in danger and only noticed there was a problem when the Big Player caught my eye from across the room and glanced toward the last member of our team as he left the cashier. Once he had my attention, the Big Player walked to the door and shook hands with the manager as he left. Suddenly, I was alone.

My shirt was soaking wet by the time I stepped off the stool and collected my chips. Each breath I took was a conscious effort to remain calm while the cashier counted out my money; as I walked to the door, my imagination was on fire, terrified that I'd feel a hand on my shoulder just as I was about to reach freedom. Nothing happened. I walked to the curb, hailed a taxi, and told the driver to take me to our hotel.

As I entered the suite, the room fell silent. Everyone turned to stare at me as I walked in, fully expecting to be reprimanded for not spotting the signal. No one spoke.

"What happened?" I asked.

The Big Player stood up. "You don't know?"

I shook my head. "I didn't see anything."

"Nothing?"

"I didn't see a thing. Who gave the signal?"

"You did."

There was an uncomfortable pause as everyone began to realize what had just happened. It turns out that, when under pressure, I had a nervous, unconscious habit of running my fingers through my hair, from front to back. The room erupted in laughter and I felt like a complete idiot. Within the week we were all back at the tables, with a brand new "get out" signal and a powerful, probably legal, advantage against the house.

A talent for deception and an eye for opportunity are not limited to those of a purely crooked disposition. In the world of casino gaming, there is a fascinating middle ground that remains mostly on the right side of the law. Advantage players seek out weaknesses in game procedures, looking for opportunities to gain an edge against the house. Their methods can shift the balance of odds dramatically, but despite being technically legal, the casino industry spends millions of dollars to identify and prevent these strategies.

Employing an advantage is a negative proposition for the house, so it's understandable that they don't take kindly to players who have an edge over them. Las Vegas was built on tiny percentages that keep the odds firmly in favor of the enormous casino resorts that created a thriving city in the middle of the Nevada desert. As Penn and Teller used to point out in their show, the entire city depends on bad math, and major casinos advertise 98 percent return on their slot machines as if this was a good thing.

In all aspects of life, it is possible to find yourself taken advantage of, or to have an advantage hidden or denied to you. To a con artist, life is just a game where rules are for suckers. It's all a matter of who's the player and who's being played.

By far, the most well-known Blackjack system is card counting. Many people think this is an illegal strategy that somehow breaks the rules, but it is completely above board. Counting cards is about observing the outcome of previous rounds of play and using that information to determine the quality of cards that remain to be dealt. Since some cards are more beneficial to players than others, if we can track how many of those cards have been removed from the deck then we can easily gauge how many remain. The number of good cards compared to the size of the deck that is still to be played tells us how attractive the game is at that moment in terms of positive or negative expectation.

Even though this is a simple concept, it can be difficult to understand because most people just don't think this way. Most casual players approach a casino table to gamble until their stake is gone or fortune smiles upon them. Many do not even employ the optimum strategy for each hand, and those who do are sometimes berated or harassed by fellow gamblers who believe purely in luck. How you choose to play is up to you, but with any transaction, if you really want to win, luck alone rarely does it—and a deeper understanding of the game is essential.

As a useful example of how to regard any game, let's put ourselves in the role of a blackjack player and figure out the best way to invest our money at the table.

First, we need to know the basic strategy for every hand we might be dealt. There is a mathematically proven way to play that we need to memorize long before we approach the table.

The casino depends on players to either ignore this strategy or play it so poorly that it becomes irrelevant.

Basic strategy in blackjack does not require any information other than the cards you're dealt and the dealer's "up card," but it can improve your odds significantly. Despite this, many players simply don't take the time, or do the work required to learn it. Perhaps this is because they're just hoping to have a good time, and if they're prepared to lose every penny then I have no problem with that. However, if that money is not disposable, then why on earth would someone ignore their best chances of winning?

Returning to the blackjack table, let's assume that we have memorized and mastered basic strategy (found in countless books and websites) so that we are always making the best decisions at the table. How else can we improve our chances?

For each round, the cards are dealt face up and played, then placed aside into a small plastic tray to the dealer's right. This continues until the dealer decides to shuffle all of the cards, which is usually determined by a plastic "cut card" inserted into the deck after the shuffle. Up until this point, we have been shown every card that was dealt, so if we were willing to do some more work, we could track these cards to determine what is left in the balance of the deck. Basic card counting simply monitors the overall quality of the deck and whether it contains more or less valuable, potentially profitable cards for the player. Knowing this can help us to adjust basic strategy and increase our bets when the quality of the deck is higher. Put simply, we know when the cards are in our favor and bet accordingly.

This all requires a high level of concentration on the player's part, but for some of us, this was always part of the attraction to this game. The very fact that we can mentally improve our chances of winning is fascinating, but for the casinos, it turns a profitable game into a losing one, especially when dealing with effective card counters. When players become better organized, develop more sophisticated systems, and play with deeper pockets, their slight mathematical edge could possibly dig a serious hole in the house margin. Fortunately, there are far fewer expert players out there than the casinos like to think. Most players who take a shot at card counting are ill prepared or poorly trained and have probably more than compensated over time for some of the losses made to professional teams. The majority of 21 players simply haven't the dedication or determination necessary to employ this kind of system, but since most people are only playing the game intermittently, hopefully as entertainment, learning pages of odds just isn't worthwhile. If a player is determined enough to turn their game into a profitable endeavor, they can and should go to any legal lengths available to them.

Sometimes a line is crossed and a perfectly good strategy becomes a felony. While playing in the UK and Europe, I was part of a team that used concealed computers and keypads to record and process data from several tables so that our Big Player could seemingly walk from game to game and bet large sums with a huge advantage. At this time there were no laws against these devices, but over time, we learned that this alone offers no protection to players using them. In the UK particularly, the legal system usually takes the side of the casino and has jailed players who simply processed information available to anyone watching the game. By using electronics these teams enjoyed a huge advantage but created a tangible threat to the game that could be used against them in court. In Nevada, any device that can be shown to assist the player when making decisions is illegal and there's a harsh penalty for anyone caught using one. To my mind, devices are too risky and no amount of money is worth spending time behind bars, but professional (and not-so-professional) teams continue to use technology in the hope of making a big score. For them, perhaps it's worth the risk.

The term advantage player typically refers to someone who avoids crossing that line and remains within the law, but casinos dedicate a great deal of energy to weeding these players out and barring them from the tables. It's true that a well-organized group with a solid system can take a lot of money, but any money actually lost over time is dwarfed by the amount spent to defend against those few effective players, and this itself might be insignificant compared to the amount lost by slowing down games and limiting how much ordinary players can gamble every hour.

Not all deception is criminal. Approaching any situation or transaction as a game or problem to be solved is similar to the mindset of a con artist, who is always searching for an angle or way to take an advantage. This perspective often reveals flaws or opportunities in social or business scenarios, which can be used or abused depending on one's motives. An understanding of how to interpret the world in this way can be a powerful defense and a useful skill in the right circumstances. Lines can be crossed in everyday life when someone sees a way to up their profits or ensure success at all costs. The loser might be you, and out here in the real world, it could be your house that's on the line. Learning how to identify an off-balance or crooked proposition would certainly be valuable, but I believe it's more productive to simply understand that these scenarios exist rather than having to know about every type of deception. Smart casinos will politely back a player off the game even when they can't identify what he's doing, usually telling him that he's "too good." There's no reason you can't do the same if you feel out of your depth or don't have enough information to make an informed decision.

Finding the Edge

Some businesses deliberately design their procedures or interfaces to mislead or misdirect the consumer. Sharp practice is the art of staying on the right side of the law while offering a transaction or deal that places the customer into a situation that is either unfair, more costly, or deliberately manipulative of expectations. Payday loans, cellular contracts, investment deals, and business "opportunities" are well-known territory for clever wording, misleading figures, and concealed terms.

Terms and conditions are everywhere and most people have become trained not to read them simply because they are now comically long and deliberately complicated. How many times online have you clicked that button without even opening the window, even to just look at what you're agreeing to? In any interaction where money is involved, one party usually makes more and this is almost always because their position or strategy is preferable. For example, a loan company makes a profit and their customers lose money, but this is a fair trade-off if the cost of the loan is acceptable in return for access to an agreed amount. The loan company takes a risk, but this is mitigated by their diligence when processing each applicant. The customer chooses from whom to borrow by estimating who is offering the best deal, but in some cases, loan companies obfuscate the details of their product in order to encourage people to underestimate the cost. This is by no means universal. Legislation in some countries has forced lenders to be more transparent, but even when horrific repayment plans or harsh penalties are clearly illustrated, a person's need for the loan focuses them solely on the amount they hope to borrow, *not* how much it will cost them in the long run. This might explain why a lot of advertising concentrates on how easy it is to get the loan, rather than how difficult it will be to pay back.

The smart borrower understands that he or she has a negative expectation and takes the time to minimize their losses within the law, while the lenders do all they can to avoid this. Credit cards can be managed by switching from one card to another, taking advantage of deals for new customers in order to cut the percentage being charged. Depending on what deals are available, it might be possible to save a considerable amount over time, but the credit card companies would prefer you to ignore these options and continue paying them in a timely fashion. To this end they offer deals to encourage loyalty and penalties to restrict your options, so most people simply go with the flow and pay their bills; just as most blackjack players take whatever cards they're dealt and let Lady Luck do the rest.

In the end, this is simply capitalism at work and it's perfectly fair and above board most of the time. Even when a level of transparency is enforced, the focus is firmly directed to what the customer wants, rather than what it will cost him in the long run. When deception of any kind is employed, even subtly, then I believe this becomes sharp practice to varying degrees.

There's an old joke about a traveling salesman and his amazing watch that could do anything. Carrying two heavy suitcases, he approaches a man on the street and asks if he would be interested in owning a miracle of modern technology. Pulling back his sleeve, the salesman reveals an impressive device strapped to his wrist. "It tells time in every country, you just say the name. Japan." The digital display changes to reveal the exact time in Tokyo. "London," he says and the watch changes again to reflect Greenwich Mean Time. "It does much more than that. It can scan any document with this camera and can send and receive faxes—there's even a tiny roll of paper inside. It can display TV channels from any network in the world. It can tell you your exact geographical position down to half an inch either way and it can store thousands of your favorite films, music, or TV shows. It even has a tiny projector built into the side. Best of all, it only costs five hundred bucks!" The impressed stranger immediately reaches for his wallet and hands over five one-hundred-dollar bills and the salesman removes the watch and puts it onto the other man's wrist. Satisfied, the man is about to walk away when the salesman calls him back and hands him both of the heavy suitcases, saying "don't forget the batteries!"

I first heard that story in the early eighties, and those two suitcases tend to remind me of the lengthy contracts most people sign in order to own the latest and greatest gadget or gizmo.

The Monty Hall Problem

As human beings, we often see complexity where there is none, or ignore a simple solution while searching for something more satisfying. Magicians know this well. Our best secrets are often devilishly simple, sometimes counterintuitive, but mostly disappointing if the method is revealed. Con games are all about finding or creating opportunities where the hustler secretly has the upper hand, but it's possible to find an edge in legitimate situations so you can identify the best way to play. To that end, we're going to look at a classic game scenario where the best strategy has proven difficult for many people to understand.

In the well-known "Monty Hall Problem,"* the optimum strategy is often difficult to accept because the worst strategy appears to make more sense.

---

* Monty Hall was the host of *Let's Make a Deal,* a popular game show that aired in the 1960s and 1970s.

It's highly unlikely you'll ever find yourself in this exact scenario, but we can use this to illustrate that a powerful advantage can exist without being immediately obvious.

Briefly, the Monty Hall Problem works like this:

You are playing a game of three-card monte. On the table are three face down cards: one red queen of hearts and two random black cards. If you choose the queen, then you win a dollar.

You're the player and the person running the game is the performer. This is nothing more than a one-in-three guess but once you choose a card, the performer will offer a second choice.

Once you have nominated a card, the performer will turn over one of the remaining two. The card he turns over will always be a losing black card because he will *always know where the queen is.*

Once a black card has been turned face up, you are given the chance to stick with your original choice or switch to the other unseen card.

Many people believe, when presented with the second choice, that this is now a fifty/fifty proposition and that it makes no difference whether they switch or not. In fact, the odds of winning are doubled if you switch.

The problem is that most people reject this idea once the second choice is offered. They started with one in three but, once one of the losing cards is revealed, only two choices remain and those appear to each have a fifty-fifty chance of being the winner.

As with many magic effects, con games, or puzzles, it's all about how you look at it. In all variations of the classic Monty

Hall problem, there are three choices consisting of two losers and one winner: in other words, one chance in three. It is important, however, to remember that the performer who is offering you this choice knows *exactly* where the winner is and will only reveal losing options. At this point the player is offered the chance to switch, but this second choice is definitely not a fifty-fifty proposition.

Let's stick with playing cards but change the numbers. Instead of one winning card and two losing cards, let's add eight more losing black cards. Now there are eleven cards on the table but there's still only *one* winner.

The rules are the same. One card can be selected but, before it is turned over, the performer will remove nine losing cards from the remainder and turn them over, leaving *just one card* from the group you *did not* choose. That card could be either the winning red card or just another black card.

If I offered you the chance to switch in this example, would you stick with your original choice? Do you still think this is just a fifty-fifty chance of getting it right?

You know that there was one red card in the packet and that the first card you took had a one in eleven chance of being that red card, so it should be obvious that the red card is much more likely to be among the other ten cards. Hopefully this makes the switching strategy more obvious.

It is the actions of the performer who's running the game that determines the odds, because he will always remove nine losing cards leaving either a tenth loser or the winning card. The remaining card will only be a losing black card *if* you happened to select the red card as your first choice, which we know is the least likely outcome.

If you chose one of the majority black cards first, then the remaining card from the other group (after nine black cards have been removed by the performer) will be the red winner *ten times* out of eleven!

This is because the procedure reverses the odds *against* the player on the first round, becoming *for* the player on the second round *if he switches*.

This is a result of the conscious intervention by the performer, who removes all but one of the remaining options because the cards he removes will always be losing options. If the winning card is in the remaining ten, the performer is forced to leave it in play. Therefore, when you make that first choice, you are isolating a card that is more likely to be a loser and will then trade it for a card that is more likely to be a winner.

If a second person enters the game after the losing cards have been turned over, they would see only two choices and their chances are fifty-fifty of picking the right card because they do not have the same information as you. This is an excellent example of playing a game according to the information available to the player. You have been involved since the start of the game, so the above strategy allows you to double your odds of success by switching. You know that one card was part of the group that had a much better chance of containing the winner, that this other card retains those positive odds and is therefore the better choice. The new player knows none of this and might as well flip a coin and take his chances.

This is where people often get tripped up because they put themselves into the position of that second player. It's important to remember that the card you first selected had the odds against it and that the remaining card (and its group) had the odds in its favor.

In case it's still not clear, imagine the entire deck is in play and that only the queen of hearts was the winner. If I let you choose one at random (unseen) and I then threw away fifty cards that definitely were not the queen of hearts, leaving just one—what are the chances that the only card I didn't throw away is the winning queen? Do you think I've got the queen or do you think it's more likely that you managed to somehow pick it from the fifty-two options at the beginning? Now would you switch?

The bigger the number of losing cards, the clearer it should be that switching in the second round is the best strategy.

Now let's return to the classic version with just three choices. As with the examples above, there are more losers than winners. Once you make your initial choice, there are two cards remaining and the odds clearly state that the winner is more likely to be one of the other two. Think of your own choice as an isolated group and the remaining cards as a second group. A moment ago, you knew that the other group had double the odds of containing the winner and now, thanks to the intervention of the performer, the losing options from the other group have been identified, leaving just one card that retains the same odds of *being a winner* as the entire group had of *containing the winner.*

The conscious nature of the performer's procedure ensures that only losing cards are turned over after your initial selection, but if this was a random selection by the performer, switching offers no advantage because one time in three, the randomly flipped card will be a queen. It is only when the performer knows which card to expose that the advantage exists.

Once the performer has intervened and revealed a losing option in that other group, he has given you a huge advantage, but only if you understand how and why to take it. As the Monty Hall Problem shows, it would be very easy to tell a player that sticking with their original choice is as good as switching. Even mathematicians have struggled to recognize why changing doubles the odds of success. This makes that lie easy to believe and that's a powerful tool for a con artist or under-handed business.

On the Internet a related form of chicanery has become so common that most of us encounter examples on a daily basis. By playing online transactions as a game, options can be restricted, choices manipulated, and positive outcomes for the customer disguised by companies taking an unfair advantage.

Sound familiar?

The term "Dark Patterns" refers to user interfaces that are deliberately designed to trick people. Some of the largest companies in the world employ subtle methods to misdirect users from certain choices on a page or build those pages with the intent of concealing certain elements while technically including legally required options or notices.

These ploys have evolved from blatant deceptions into subtle arrangements based on knowing how people interact with a form or page, the order in which their attention is directed, and how elements become more or less noticeable.

As a rule, people tend to take the easiest option when confronted with any unfamiliar interface; their choices are usually guided by the clearest, most obvious path, from the beginning to the end of a process.

Any procedure where additional costs can be incurred or choices restricted is susceptible to these questionable techniques. Online forms for services like insurance, air travel, car rental, and subscriptions will often try to deliberately manipulate the user toward a preferred outcome. Even extremely savvy users can miss an option that has either been preselected or camouflaged.

A simple example would be an option to receive newsletters that is preselected as "yes" but the "tick box" option is placed after the "continue" button that advances the user to the next page. Designers might claim this as an innocent mistake; that they didn't consider people who tend to follow a linear path and would click "continue" before examining the rest of the page. Great care goes into the design of every website at that level and very little happens by accident.

Sometimes advertisements are disguised to look like part of the site they inhabit in order to sucker people into clicking onto other pages. If you have ever tried to download software from certain sites, you will have encountered the bogus "download" button. In one example I found eight identical green download buttons on one page and only one of them was for the software I actually wanted. The others were for products I definitely did not want. I would caution anybody about using any services from any company who needs to trick people into installing their software.

Many people will accept a three-dollar charge rather than spend a little extra time locating the correct button or drop-down menu, because the simplest path is usually the most attractive (as con artists know well). Large companies can make huge profits from small variations in prices, so any way they can build an advantage into these processes is worthwhile.

The website www.darkpatterns.org lists dozens of examples, categorized with names such as "bait and switch," "misdirection," and "trick questions." The practice has become more sophisticated over time. On many sites it's likely that an option is hidden in plain sight or strategically placed to be ignored. It's a clear example of an advantage play on the part of companies that employ such methods. They are increasing the odds of making higher profits simply by observing how people navigate and placing elements accordingly.

The ability to look at any transaction as a game to be won or lost is invaluable; your first question should always be "what is the best way to secure a positive outcome?" In a casino, it's possible to win even when the odds are against you (and of course, vice-versa), but in the real world, it's easier to predict how things should work out. Your second question should be, "who has the best of it?" As a customer, that will usually be the provider since their job is to make a profit, and there's nothing wrong with this unless they are consciously trying to make more than is reasonable.

As consumers, we can learn to identify the most beneficial options in any marketplace. In most cases, this is a matter of balancing cost and commitment or comparing offers to find the best deal. The trick is to spot the advantages being played against us and to negotiate the best possible variation based on the options available.

There is a point where some deals cross the bridge between grift and graft. I start to become concerned when a company wants me to believe that I have the edge, since any business that gives away its profit margin is doomed to fail. In these circumstances I always look for the catch that will reverse my fortune or throw me into a deep hole without a rope to climb out.

DIGITAL DECEPTION

---

*A*lex approached our fifth mark as he left the store, showed him a fake ID, and claimed to be a member of the Metropolitan Police. Immediately, the mark was keen to comply or resolve any misunderstanding; Alex walked him over to me so I could feed him the story.

"Did you use your credit card today, sir?" I asked.

"Yes."

"We are currently monitoring this store because a member of staff is suspected of stealing customer's details . . ."

At this point, Jess called over the radio to ask if we had intercepted someone of the mark's description. She was pretending to be another officer inside the store but was actually sitting in a van across the parking lot, simply describing whomever we had stopped at that time. The mark heard this and any suspicion that we were not the real police quickly evaporated.

"This is just a formality," I continued, "but we need anyone who used their card at the suspect's register to give us their details so we can ensure your information doesn't go online and so we can determine whether your details have been stolen when we make the arrest."

The victim nodded as I handed him a clipboard, requesting that he fill out a form with all of the pertinent details. Meanwhile, Alex found another victim and brought him over so we could repeat the con.

We were emulating a scam that is all too common online and has cost banks, credit card companies, and their customers billions of dollars. After a few minutes we had credit card numbers, security codes, and addresses from a dozen people, not one of whom ever questioned our legitimacy. Our real-live reconstruction targeting real victims was so successful that within a few minutes we had more marks than we could possibly use on the show; it remains one of the simplest scams that I've ever filmed.

The objective of *The Real Hustle*, as stated at the beginning of every episode, was to reveal and expose scams that have actually happened. In this case, I seriously doubt that credit card numbers would be stolen by two hustlers dressed in suits outside the Home Depot, because it's too exposed and is almost certain to result in the perpetrators being arrested or pursued.

Our reconstruction of this online scam had the benefit of being able to secure confidence quickly with suits, a radio, and some fake IDs just as some scammers spoof web pages to look exactly like real sites operated by well-known companies or institutions. As we discovered, people are quick to accept something on face value, especially when plunged into a worrying scenario. We could probably have collected people's private information all day, complete with signatures and all the data we would need to steal their money or identity. It was terrifyingly easy.

The evolution of con games has largely depended on certain mechanisms in society: the ways in which people meet and interact. The initial approach has a strong effect on how quickly or easily a potential mark is hooked; as society changes, hustlers must learn to adapt their methods. In the history of cons and scams, the introduction of the Internet as a means to target new victims has been the deceiver's equivalent of the Industrial Revolution. Suddenly, the con game became a numbers game and a new generation of hustlers was born.

A system can only be as strong as its weakest component, and in most cases, the human element is the first link to break. Any form of security needs well-trained and informed people to interact and implement a methodology. Any mistake or failure at the human level might result in the system being compromised. While many hackers target software or hardware to identify flaws, the "meatware" (people) is where crooks usually find the easy money.

On the Internet, people are given access to millions of systems for legitimate purposes, but their means of access can expose both the user and provider when data is stolen and abused. The problem is that complexity is often needed to create more secure procedures, but companies who deal with customers online want to offer convenience and ease of use, thereby reducing the number of steps to access a seemingly secure service. This is clearly at odds with the objective of absolute security since fewer barriers for the user means less information that a scammer needs to steal.

Technically, I am not qualified to discuss the efficacy of modern security platforms or the means by which they might be defeated by hackers directly. Instead, I am interested in cons and scams that have migrated onto the Internet and how they have been adapted to this relatively new arena.

This new age of deception has introduced a new term to the art of deception: social engineering. Kevin Mitnick coined the phrase and has written a great deal about how he gained access to computer systems by targeting the people who operated or maintained them. Mitnick's ingenious strategies were deceptively simple and shockingly effective as described in his book *The Art of Deception*, which effectively illustrated the need for companies to better train their employees to recognize and avoid these types of attacks.

Many times, the human factor is the weakest part of a security system and is easily targeted using techniques taken straight out of the con artist's playbook. Social engineering targets human beings with strategies designed to cause people to give away valuable information or unknowingly perform tasks that aid an outsider. A simple example would be to call someone pretending to be from their own company's help desk and coach that person into downloading harmful software or revealing vital information.

At the annual DEFCON convention in Las Vegas, thousands of hackers gather to share and learn new ideas. Anyone near the convention center would be unwise to use Wi-Fi or cellular services as almost every data signal is being monitored or generated by the attendees. In a small conference room, Chris

Hadnagy and his "Social Engineering Org" team host an annual competition where individuals must call a random company, usually a well-known name, and convince whomever they speak with to give up as much data as possible. For obvious reasons, the type of information they're attempting to extract is completely innocuous, but it's fascinating to hear just how much people will volunteer to a stranger on the phone.

Contestants sit in what looks like a homemade clear plastic game show booth to protect them from audience noise as they call complete strangers at their work, using creative pretexts to coax them into revealing data or to perform simple tasks. Every call is played via speaker to the entire room as each contestant attempts to translate age-old scam techniques to a modern playing field. Incredibly, almost all of the people they call will comply unless they have been properly trained not to do so. In these cases, the questions are usually reflected back to the caller in order to verify that they are who they say they are. Any requests are deflected to a manager or specialist and the social engineer soon has to find a way out of the call without inviting suspicion.

Speaking to Chris after the event, he told me that there were several companies that had clearly trained all of their staff not to reveal any information on the phone, but the vast majority remained easy pickings for a charming or inventive human-hacker. The sad truth is that it would be extremely easy for all businesses to educate their staff with a few simple role-playing exercises.

The same methods used by Mitnick and his contemporaries are also used to trick individuals into revealing personal data that seems unimportant. Other times, it is freely given once the scammer has secured the victim's trust. These techniques can be used to target millions of people, a small group, or a specific individual. A prime example of this is appropriately referred to as "phishing."

Give a Man a Phish...

Phishing is, by now, a well-known term among the computer-literate and refers to an attempt to encourage, trick, or force someone to reveal information such as credit card numbers or bank details that can compromise a person's privacy or finances. Usually delivered by e-mail, phishing attacks can be sent to millions of potential marks at once, so that even a tiny percentage success rate can represent a substantial score to scammers.

"Spear-phishing" uses similar methods to target specific individuals or groups using information harvested from social media or other public resources to tailor that message. The resulting communiqué therefore appears less generic and more credible from the outset.

These attempts to initiate contact sometimes develop into a direct communication between the online hustler and his intended mark. The hustler often tries to direct victims to a website that will try to steal information or install harmful software on the mark's device that might capture and transmit anything of value.

A common tactic is to try to scare or panic the recipient into responding by clicking on a link or downloading harmful software. Hustlers might send one million e-mails claiming to be from a well-known bank and stating that someone has been using the mark's bank account. Panicked, many people quickly click on the link in that e-mail and try to log into their account. This would fail on the first attempt, but on the second they would find that their balance is as expected until twenty-four hours later when all of their money will have been sent elsewhere. That first click took the victim to a spoofed website made to look and function exactly like the one they are used to, and similar tactics have been used to make people download malware that's used to steal data, corrupt files, or destroy computers.

Initiating fear or panic is just one of many ways to force people to react without thinking, and new methods appear almost daily. You've no doubt seen hundreds of these e-mails in your own inbox, and I suspect we've all fallen for at least one in our lifetime. Viruses are often spread by accessing a victim's e-mail address book and sending everyone they know a link to trojan software, and because that link appears to come from a known or trusted source, many people click on it without thinking. These e-mails can be obvious, but many are simple and say very little other than "Check this out!" A clever variation says something like "I found this picture of you. Who's that with you?" or "I can't believe what this is saying about you. Is this true?" These simple sentences could come from almost anyone and many people would click the link automatically.

"Vishing" uses phone calls or VoIP interfaces to convince a mark that the caller represents a company or service, often a technical help desk. If the victim accepts the scammer's story, he is conned into typing harmful commands on his device or downloading malware. Ian Kendall, a close friend with Asperger's syndrome and a passion for pedantry, takes great pleasure in tormenting bogus help-desk callers, often toying with them for hours in an effort to waste their time. For Ian, their lack of actual technical knowledge is obvious but to the uninitiated, they can easily sound convincing.

Spamface

Lottery scams, psychic messages, and romantic propositions are common online scam tactics, and once someone takes the bait he is groomed and clipped just as he would be in a face-to-face swindle. Spam mail, which was once sent to victims by the sack-load, quickly migrated to the Internet; as the older generation of potential victims passes, scammers now find their quarry electronically and con people using fake identities or stolen credibility. The same methods used for decades to entice the desperate or unwary remain just as effective in an e-mail—and now they can be sent to millions of potential marks at once. E-mail junk filters quickly learn to weed out obvious ploys, but as new schemes appear, a few slip the net and find their way to our inboxes.

Social media offers a convenient window into people's lives, revealing addresses, dates of birth, phone numbers, and all sorts of useful trivia for crooks to use and abuse. Just by "friending" a potential mark, a con artist can learn a great deal about him. By hacking into someone's account, scammers can pretend to be that person in order to then target his friends and family. In fact, social media is one of the most powerful and useful tools for a hustler to connect with fresh fish.

I honestly don't think it's possible to be completely safe online. If targeted by sophisticated hackers, no one's data is secure. The best we can do is to observe best practices, be less impulsive, and learn to detect online deception whenever possible.

Another *Real Hustle* scam was based on websites that conned people into filling out forms requesting dangerous amounts of personal data. We created a bogus employment agency and invited hopeful clients to fill out a long form that required them to share details that could ultimately be used to steal their identity, including a credit card number to "verify" each applicant. Only one of our potential marks refused to give any information that would compromise her security. As I watched her type each section of the form, she quickly ignored anything that asked for sensitive data. Later, during our interview, I asked why she hadn't completed the form. She explained her concerns, accurately stating how each item of information might be used illegally. As it turned out, our "mark" had spent years working for the police as a victims' counselor and had helped many people deal with the repercussions of identity theft.

If we could all learn to be as vigilant without the need to experience or witness these scams firsthand, it would be much easier to avoid becoming a target. Sadly, none of us are perfect; we are all prone to moments of weakness or thoughtlessness and technology often moves faster than the means to protect us.

Fresh Fields

Technology continues to advance at blistering speeds, with manufacturers racing to release the latest products before their competitors. The speed of these advances is too much for many security methods to keep up, and gaps in the fence are widened as it stretches to cover new ground. Hackers have a knack for spotting an opening before it can be anticipated by developers, and whenever a new device or software is released, the race to break down its defenses begins.

As a confirmed tech-addict, I am all too aware of the dangers posed by new ways to carry or interpret my personal data. Simply by observing best practices we can all maintain a certain level of security, but the platforms we use online or the devices we buy often turn out to have their own flaws that compromise our digital safety.

New developments present new opportunities for all kinds of con artists. Remember the fake cash register in a London store during the holiday season? In many shops, staff now carry a portable device with a tiny plastic card reader. Many of these are well-known smartphones or tablets, and it would be a simple matter to walk into any large store with the same device, pretend to be a member of the staff, and steal credit card details during a busy period.

In most major cities, people carry their digital lives in their pockets, communicating and sharing through the ether and interacting with those devices hundreds of times a day. As we move from cell tower to cell tower and Wi-Fi to Wi-Fi, our information bleeds constantly, leaving a trail that can be followed or intercepted. Wi-Fi signals are particularly susceptible—it is an easy matter to create a hotspot with a common name and attract people to take advantage of free Internet access. Public Wi-Fi can be cloned or used to monitor data being transmitted by other users. Trapping user details and passwords sent to secure sites is unnecessary if the access key that is sent back from the site (a "cookie"*—a piece of code that allows your device to remain logged into a secure site) is unencrypted and easy to intercept, then paste onto the hacker's own computer. This form of attack gives criminals full access to a secure page—such as e-mail or banking sites—so long as the victim doesn't log out, which can be prevented if the hacker has the means to block the mark from doing so. This is just one way to intercept our data, but there are many more.

Bluetooth can be used to take over some devices, switch them on, send messages, monitor conversations, or even to dial expensive premium rate phone numbers. A hacker in the UK once demonstrated how a very common model of cell phone could easily be forced to switch on and transmit anything the

---

* When you log into a secure site, your browser is sent a "cookie"—a piece of code that allows you to remain logged into that site so long as that code is detected by the site. If this cookie is not encrypted, then it can be intercepted and copied into the hacker's browser to grant the same access. This code expires whenever the user logs out of the site. If they fail to do so or are prevented from doing so, the code remains active.

microphone heard. The phone was incredibly easy to hack and at that time was one of the most popular devices among British government employees, who often work with highly sensitive information. Theoretically, a hacker with a large enough antenna could scan the houses of Parliament for vulnerable phones and listen in to any conversation nearby. The manufacturer of the cell phone had been notified of this weakness, but as is typical of many large corporations, the threat of bad publicity was of greater concern and the weakness was never publicized.

It would be impossible to know every conceivable method to compromise technology, so as users, we need to follow some simple guidelines to avoid becoming an easy target:

1. *Be careful about what you share online and where you share it.* You should always be aware of what information about you is available on the Internet. Your social media page should not have your phone number or your address; in fact, I would even avoid giving your true birthday online, which can be incredibly useful to identity thieves. I also monitor and remember what can be deduced by accessing my profile. Should someone find a way to use that information or present themselves to me with nothing but facts they've collated from known sources, I might be able to recognize this. Remember that information on the

Internet can be accessed by anyone with enough time and motivation and that anything you say or do online could one day be used against you.

2. *Do not accept anything on face value.* An unsolicited e-mail from a friend asking you to visit a website or download a file should automatically be treated with suspicion. Look at the wording, consider the circumstances, and unless you are absolutely certain about its nature, don't click on anything. I don't trust secure websites unless I type the URL and visit them directly, and even then, it's possible to redirect my request and send me to a spoofed page depending on how and where I am accessing the Internet.

3. *Take great care in how you access the Internet and avoid logging into secure pages or sending sensitive data on unsecured or unknown networks.* Caution should always be exercised, even at home or when using cellular services. I personally try to avoid buying anything via public Wi-Fi or with my cell phone.

4. *Try to remember that opportunity rarely knocks and that fabulous prizes are incredibly rare—even when we actually take part in a lottery or contest!* Any windfall that arrives by e-mail or instant message is far more likely to be a scam than a gift of fortune. Act accordingly. Even if there's genuine reason to think something might be true, proceed with caution.

5. *Take a few extra steps to protect your online presence.* Buy software to manage passwords, protect yourself from viruses, always log out of any site you access publicly,

and spend a few minutes every week monitoring your own activity to see if there's anything you don't recognize. Of course, nothing is completely safe; the objective is to avoid common pitfalls rather than needlessly restrict your online activity. Remember, the more you have to lose, the more steps you need to take to protect your online presence.

The digital domain may be the biggest playground of all time for con artists and scammers. It's an ethereal land of opportunity where potential victims are still blind to many of the dangers that exist when sharing information. Prevention is the best way to protect your online presence, and it's important to maintain a functioning level of knowledge about security and best practices, which are changing all the time. Complacency and ignorance are commonplace and are the primary reasons why online scams succeed. By investing a little time and taking a few simple steps, anyone can avoid becoming an easy target.

IN SECURITY

---

*M*G stood at the roulette table and made a few inexpensive bets while he waited for the next spin. His wife, SG, was at the other end of the table sipping a soft drink as the other players dropped chips on and around the numbers printed on the green baize.

The dealer reached into the large wooden tub and plucked the white ball from the still-spinning rotor. As the numbers continued to spin, the ball was pressed hard against the well-worn runway inside lip of the tub and snapped with familiar skill so it spun at high speed around the inner rim. As the ball hummed, MG found the tiny button sewn into his sleeve and began to press it in time with the ball as it passed a fixed point on the wheel. In his pocket, a PDA* running a secret computer program recorded each button-press and calculated the speed of the ball compared to the spinning wheel before transmitting a single number to the earpiece being worn by MG's wife.

Instantly, SG passed her hands smoothly over the layout, dropping chips with well-practiced accuracy on a memorized

---

* Personal Digital Assistant—a palmtop computer for managing data.

pattern of numbers. The ball slowed, then fell into the tub and onto the rotating wheel. After a few bounces, it landed on a winning number. MG smiled as his wife collected another large stack of chips.

MG had spent months testing his system, which had finally started to pay off after he taught the program to adjust its predictions for bounce patterns and human error. The losing bets were cleared away as MG prepared himself for the next spin, but from the corner of his eye, he spotted trouble.

Just as the dealer was preparing for the next spin, the head of security approached and asked MG if he would mind stepping away from the table.

Smiling, MG followed the head of security to the bar, where the casino manager was waiting. At the roulette table, SG continued to play without the aid of their advantage while glancing over nervously at her husband as he spoke to the manager and his security officer. After a few minutes, MG returned in time for another spin of the wheel. Without hesitation, he continued to clock the wheel and send the predicted number to his wife who expertly dropped her chips before the dealer called "no more bets."

"Everything okay?" she asked.

"All fine," MG replied. "We've been invited to dinner. The manager likes to take care of his best customers."

SG looked over at the bar and waved to the manager who smiled back and returned the gesture as the ball landed on another winner.

With MG and his wife, the casino fell victim to an ingenious system that was far more advanced than anything previously seen within the industry. Because of this, any indication that a system might be behind MG's success was completely ignored. MG always watched the ball closely and his wife constantly made several bets at the last moment, but the casino ignored all of this because, at that time, clockers were thought to work alone or with physical signals. The idea that MG's wife was being sent the information wirelessly didn't occur to them because this was 1999, and Bluetooth technology was still relatively unknown.

Fifteen years later, casino security continues to fall victim to a lack of knowledge and understanding. In 2012, one of the world's most successful gamblers negotiated playing conditions that allowed him to selectively rotate the casino's cards during play until certain values pointed in opposite directions. He was able to do this thanks to a common flaw in almost all playing card back designs, which allows an advantage player to identify the orientation of known cards. Keen to attract his business, the casino easily agreed to an unusual procedure where the player was able to see each card before dictating how it should be turned face up. As a result of this tactic, the player earned almost thirteen million dollars, which the casino then refused to pay.

What shocks me is that the casino took so long to identify the ruse. Any genuine expert on cheating would consider this to be almost obvious, but advantage players have been successfully using the ploy all over the world. On the face of it, the strategy appears to rely on a tiny printing flaw; in fact, I believe that it depends entirely on the ignorance of casino managers and their staff who agree to these requests.

Sadly, instead of accepting their mistake, the casinos decided to blame the player for asking to improve his chances, have refused to pay his winnings, *and* have taken legal action against him. If a gaming establishment is willing to bend or break their own procedures to attract big-money gamblers, they are solely responsible for any advantage they might be giving away.

I could easily name a dozen casinos in Las Vegas where "playing the turn" in this way should never work because the people they employ have taken an active interest in how games can be beaten in this manner, and if there's anything they don't know, there are experts who can easily advise them.

I've had many dealings with casino security over the years. Most meetings have been pleasant and enjoyable, but in almost every interaction there is an air of defensiveness, a feeling that they don't wish to appear weak or foolish. This is natural since their job is to monitor and protect their company's interests. Any obvious lack of knowledge on their part might be seen as a weakness that could one day be used against them. Nevertheless, a more productive solution would be to actively educate themselves with the help of some genuine cheating experts.

This attitude is not isolated to the casino industry. Airport security, particularly in the United States, is almost belligerent in its certainty that their procedures are effective. In fact, it is my opinion that most of their practices are actually not just pointless but detrimental to the objective of genuinely protecting passengers. Security expert Bruce Schneier often uses the term "security theater" to describe unnecessary processes such as removing shoes or screening passengers with unproven, insufficiently tested body scanners. These slow down the lines but provide little defense against an intelligent or creative attack.

Ben Gurion Airport in Tel Aviv is an excellent example of a well-run security system that monitors and interacts with passengers closely. They use technology effectively to screen baggage and protect the perimeters of the airport, but the key to their success is simplicity. At Ben Gurion, security personnel are highly trained and extremely knowledgeable. This does not appear to be true in many of the airports that are protected by the TSA, where poorly educated staff often focus all of their efforts on finding forgotten containers of harmless liquid instead of engaging with passengers to identify a potential threat.

The Tel Aviv model has been successful because it examines people just as closely as their property, whereas the TSA model (and many others) spend too much time looking at luggage, shoes, and small bags filled with shampoo and cosmetics. Ben Gurion staff talk to people and observe their behavior, looking for any reaction or signal that would indicate stress or deception. A bomb might be hidden so perfectly it could easily go undetected, but a few friendly questions to the person intending to use that device might quickly alert a trained individual that something is amiss. Real terrorists do not behave as coolly and calmly as they do in the movies. They tend to be nervous, distracted, or unable to communicate normally.

With the TSA, I have noticed a change in the last few years. Now, there is greater interaction when passengers present their ID. I hope those officers have learned what to look for, but beyond this point, staff are still shouting at passengers or distracting one another with gossip while failing to exercise basic common sense in many situations. It continues to surprise me that management regularly fails to resolve conflicts at the security area because they give support to their staff instead of giving them what they need: leadership.

This type of machismo is counterproductive and fosters ignorance. The really smart security managers (and I've met many) maintain a more open posture. They listen more, consider all possibilities, and are constantly looking for new danger. The opposite of this approach is to build a secure environment, then fail to maintain it over time. Many successful incursions, whether physical or digital, depend on defenses that had not evolved as quickly as possible means of attack. Resting on the laurels of a well-built system is an all too common mistake, because it's not a matter of if your walls will be breached, but when. The biggest concern is not how long it takes to defeat a system but how long it takes before that breach is detected.

Let's imagine that a castle hires a company of experts to build a moat. Typically, a moat surrounds the structure in order to better protect it from invading forces and to add a powerful layer of defense to the outer wall. Even if the castle hires the best moat builders in the world, concessions will need to be made in the construction of the moat itself or in how the castle will operate in the future. Now let's imagine that the marketing department of our castle dictates the width of the moat based on aesthetics, rather than the most difficult distance for an army to cross during an assault. Normally, a moat would restrict access to all sides, but catering demands that there's a back entrance for them to better manage their food supplies and the king and queen require a secret tunnel to escape without being seen. Next, the castle's design team dictates that the moat should be filled with clear water and expensive koi fish for visitors to appreciate so the depth of the moat is now severely limited. To the untrained eye, this property is protected by a moat, but to anyone who has studied how to breach the outer defenses of a castle, the compromises made during installation suggest many opportunities for attack.

In the casino world, this is akin to spending millions of dollars to provide and protect a particular game only to have a player negotiate his own conditions of play in return for risking a higher amount of money at the table. As already discussed, this has certainly happened many times and smart players have been able to adjust the order of play in order to give themselves a huge advantage without the need to cheat or conceal their actions. In the past, poorly designed games have been installed in large casinos that attract herds of advantage players eager to grab every penny they can before the house wakes up and pulls the game off the floor.

Most people have an area of expertise or a field of interest in which they are able to see past the surface with a deeper understanding than others. Whether it be a business or a hobby, there's something you know well enough to spot an opportunity other people might miss. This is the heart of the advantage player's approach. It's not just a matter of spotting a lucky gap in the fence. An advantage-oriented outlook often depends on a deep understanding of a subject so that profitable patterns might emerge when observing that subject in the real world.

It's important to understand that people who build walls think differently from those who break them down, and many attackers find ways to pass under, over, around, or through that wall invisibly. Only by maintaining an active, fluid posture can we be prepared for any attempted incursion.

I often say that if you want to know how vulnerable your home is, place a saucepan of milk on the stove, turn up the heat, and lock yourself out. Now try to get back in before the milk boils over.

For security professionals, I recommend taking the same approach by constantly testing defenses in the hope of identifying a weakness before it can be abused. Unfortunately, this is often frowned upon in an industry where any flaw is treated as a failure and saving face is all too important.

These issues are not isolated to the casino industry or airport security. Large corporations have often been guilty of complacency and have regularly fallen victim to hackers who are one step ahead in terms of technology and how to use it.

In the hacking community, the term "white hat" refers to experts who often use their abilities to identify vulnerabilities on behalf of companies and individuals. This is opposed to their "black hat" cousins who might exploit any weakness from the outside or share it with others. Many of these ethical "white hat" hackers are part of the expanding penetration testing industry that is employed to test systems for susceptibility, but many more are lone wolves, exploring the digisphere for anything that could be taken advantage of.

I am not part of this community, but I've spent a lot of time in their company learning about new ways information can be intercepted or stolen. I recognize in them the same passion for deception and cleverness that first drove me to study cheating and con games. I also see, on a larger scale, the same problems and suspicions that this passion can attract.

In the casino business, no one likes to be "schooled" by outsiders, and anyone who knows how to beat their games is regarded with distrust. I know a few genuine cheating experts in the industry, but unless they play the corporate game in terms of how they interact with management, interpret evidence, and present ideas, casinos often prefer—to their detriment—industry insiders who have a small interest and a little knowledge in cheating or advantage play.

The same appears to be true for businesses that rely on an image of impenetrable security. Banks, credit card companies, department stores, investment firms, and communications giants all claim to protect their customers' information, but as we've seen many times, all are vulnerable. In some cases, millions of lines of sensitive data can be lost before a breach is detected. I believe that failures in security are inevitable. Companies need to do more to monitor and evaluate their defenses. "Pentesting" (penetration testing), where expert consultants are hired to evaluate potential dangers, is one way to actively assess security, but it is not nearly enough. Education of users at all levels is essential to create stronger, more flexible systems.

Companies also need to build a means to interact with freelance hackers who are willing to share their findings fairly. This suggestion will no doubt infuriate many security experts who feel targeted by aggressive "white hats" who threaten to expose any weaknesses if they aren't compensated. This practice is far from ethical and hackers who constantly probe exposed systems in this way have been described as "gray hats." I believe that, with a little creativity, the industry can find a model that uses well-informed professionals to test their level of resistance while finding a way to interact with and reward anyone who finds a weak spot from the outside.

The closed-minded nature of security departments in all industries is merely a magnified reflection of human nature. As a rule, we tend to be defensive and most people think they are too smart to be cheated or conned. The truth is that most of us haven't been conned because we've been lucky up till now! As I've tried to illustrate, deception can target anyone at any time and knowledge remains the only consistent defense.

Demonstrating cons and scams is a powerful way to teach and cultivate greater understanding about the art of deception. The only way to fully comprehend an idea is to experience it firsthand. For this reason, during seminars, I encourage my audience to split into pairs and try to con one another using simple scams as role-playing tools. The objective is not to protect against these particular con games but to learn the patterns of a scam that they might now recognize in the future.

One such exercise is the change raising scam (described in chapter nine). Using pieces of paper, audience members take turns playing the hustler and the cashier until they fully understand the principle of forcing a victim to perform two transactions at the same time. Next, I invite someone to take part in a simple social engineering exercise that uses exactly the same principle to embed a dangerous mistake into a series of innocuous tasks. During this procedure, the person helping me would test cables, check their Internet speed, and log in and out of their e-mail account. The mistake is in how they are directed to their e-mail provider, because the Internet speed test is a bogus page with links to a spoofed website. This is all acted out as a role-playing game before and after the change-raising exercise. Only after experiencing a few scams from the hustler's perspective does the audience immediately recognize the deception in that role-playing scenario.

Education is the single most effective means of protecting against all forms of deception. In today's world, it's a downhill race to keep up with ever-changing possibilities; if the enemy gets too far ahead, by the time your business catches up, it will likely be too late. For casinos, corporations, and individuals, it is better to identify any harmful vulnerability before it can be exploited. The most effective strategy is to fully accept that we are all potential targets and that it's only a matter of time before our defenses need to be repaired or rebuilt.

In essence: Confidence is the opposite of vigilance.

WISE UP

I never anticipated how much I would learn from my experiences writing and executing con games for television. Soon after starting, I began to recognize the opportunity to study my lifelong passion from the hustler's perspective without risking life or liberty in the process.

My initial observations were focused on the scams, which sometimes seemed to work automatically. I soon identified the three key phases and borrowed the terms "hook, line, and sinker"; as I delved deeper, I began to see that these were merely objectives on the path toward deception. How each hustler achieves these goals can vary wildly depending on talent or audacity. I soon began to question why victims were vulnerable and how scams worked from their perspective.

I'm not a psychologist, but I am naturally interested in many aspects of psychology, especially when it applies to deception. While much of it is fascinating, I disagree with many of its conclusions about scams. I'm certainly not qualified to challenge these academically, but I often find myself frustrated or infuriated by attempts to define scams as either this sequence of events or that list of ingredients.

It's easy to correlate "optimism bias" with the hook and "confirmation bias" with the line and for the sinker there are aspects of "sunk-cost fallacy," where people are inclined to allow previous investments of time and money to influence their decision about whether or not to commit. Personally, I am reluctant to overly simplify or confine any aspect of con games because con artists adapt and their preferred methods can vary wildly.

By their very nature, con games *have no rules* and they don't belong in a box.

One can identify objectives and elements of different cons, but successful scams vary in style, content, order, and execution. It can be an expression of the con artist or a response to the personality of the mark. It's more difficult to understand something that shifts and changes depending on unknown factors like thoughts and feelings, but this is the nature of con games; they depend on human interaction and that is fluid by nature. It's one of the things that makes them so resilient. Hustlers learn to adapt proven strategies to each scenario and through experience, they develop a toolkit of lies and tricks to achieve their goal.

As I noted at the outset, every one of us is a potential mark. Con artists often select their victims in an attempt to find the most vulnerable targets, but the truth is that we can all be susceptible to a well-timed scam or confidence trick.

Eradicating cons and scams completely would be impossible, but as a society, we can do so much more to defend against crimes of deception.

Knowledge, Empathy, and Acceptance

Con games prey on our hopes and fears, and unless we shed all emotion and learn to regard all of life's interactions with cold logic, there will always be new ways to play old scams. Con artists depend on human nature; to give up those qualities that make us who we are would be a far greater loss than any amount of money, property, or self-respect.

Trust is an important aspect of a successful and productive society, and it would be impossible for a community to thrive without some faith in authority or in each other, and to regard all situations with automatic suspicion could be as damaging as blindly accepting anything we hear. The wheels of civilization need a little oil to keep turning or the machine will quickly break down.

Protecting ourselves and others from deception is important and there are three steps we can take that would quickly make con games more difficult and dangerous for those who would attempt them: spread the word, stop blaming the victim, and be honest with yourself.

Spread the Word

If you are willing to steal from others, you will quickly learn or devise any con game that is likely to work in your personal situation. The first question a smart grifter would ask is whether the public is aware of the con he is planning. The more a scam is in the public's consciousness, the less effective it will be for potential scammers. Hence the con artist's motto, "Never wise-up a mark."

It is therefore important that, whenever a con game turns up, the public is quickly informed. The more people know about a new scam, the more difficult it becomes to safely hook new marks. This forces hustlers to adapt more quickly and the sooner any new twist is shared with the public, the sooner people will learn to identify further variations.

In the age of information there are many ways to share knowledge, but with so much digital noise, it is almost impossible to reach everyone. On the Internet there are many useful resources that discuss cons and scams for those who care to look, but not all of the information is accurate. There are many books that describe and expose con games, and occasionally there are entertaining TV shows that reveal scams in a memorable fashion. The problem is that none of these reach a large enough audience to have a significant impact on real hustlers.

Until we find a way to communicate with a larger percentage of the population, hustlers will continue to easily find victims who are unaware of their methods. Fraud and deception should be a regular feature on local, network, and cable news shows. There's no shortage of heartbreaking, shocking, or ingenious stories, and if presented properly, with respect to the victims and in a manner that is entertaining and memorable, it could have a genuine, positive effect for the audience.

People understand the world in terms of stories, and when a scam is re-invented, it is the *story* that attracts and distracts the mark from the hustler's true objective. It's a common mistake when exposing con games to focus on the details of a scam, rather than the underlying strategy. The Spanish Prisoner game has evolved over time but the principles remain the same. Whether it's a ship loaded with gold or a Nigerian bank account waiting to be transferred, the victim is convinced to pay a large amount in return for a king's ransom. When exposing a con game, it should be described in terms of story, which is constantly changing, and objective, which is almost always the same. Once people learn to recognize the ingredients of a scam, no matter how it is presented, the sooner that scam will cease to be effective.

Stop Blaming the Victim

In 2009 I co-authored an academic paper with Professor Frank Stajano of Cambridge University's computer laboratory, which had been studying con games in an effort to find a correlation with aspects of computer security. The similarities between scams and social engineering were obvious, but Professor Stajano went on to find strategies from my world that were clearly applicable in his. A key component of our study was the perspective of the intended victim.

Using con games from *The Real Hustle*, we were able to identify seven principles that illustrate why people succumb to deception; we used these to explain patterns in human behavior that have been exploited by hustlers for centuries. Our objective was to help designers of security platforms to understand the human element in order to anticipate possible weaknesses that often prove to be the most vulnerable aspect of any system.

Once we published our paper, the interest in our findings was surprising. We found the paper being widely circulated online with our list of scam principles often reprinted or summarized. It proved to me that there was enormous interest in the subject; more important, it showed me there was an opportunity to encourage greater empathy for victims, which is an important step toward protecting the public.

Con games can have a powerful, damaging effect on a mark. Loss of money or property is amplified by a loss of faith or self-respect. Because of this, few victims are motivated to admit what's happened to them. Their primary fear is that they will be regarded as foolish, naive, greedy, or gullible. These are normal human frailties that are preyed upon by con men, and when the ride is over, the victim is suddenly faced with a naked truth that can cut deeper than any knife.

It is therefore essential that society learns to treat victims with greater understanding and to be supportive of those who come forward. Friends, family, and authorities need to show genuine empathy. Once a scam has been successful, marks are only able to describe their own perspective—how things unfolded through their eyes. It is extremely difficult for them to convey the confidence they had in a lie once they know the truth, so to rely on the victims to explain why they were conned is pointless. Instead we can accept that they were deceived and perhaps learn how. With the benefit of hindsight, it is nearly impossible to fully comprehend how real a story might have originally seemed from the mark's perspective.

How many times have you re-told a joke only to receive a polite reaction, but when you originally heard it, the audience cried tears of laughter? A con game takes experience, timing, and talent, and no victim will ever be able to tell a lie as convincingly as they heard it. We need to learn that con games prey on human nature and accept that we can all be fallible.

In our academic paper, Professor Stajano and I listed seven principles. This was never intended to be a complete list; in fact I have added three more since we published the original paper. Instead, I hope the list serves as a guide to understanding why and how people are deceived.

1. Distraction
Thieves use this as a tool to misdirect and steal belongings. In a con game, victims are focused on the bait or prize and distracted by their own desire. Hustlers manipulate perception by carefully directing the mark toward anything that builds confidence and encourages commitment.

2. Social Compliance
People are often predictable in common situations. When presented with authority, many will automatically comply or can eventually be convinced to do so. Scammers often take advantage of social conventions to play on people's good nature or fear of confrontation. A con man might "play the victim" or act offended to manipulate a mark.

3. Herd Instinct
When we are part of a group, there is a powerful urge to follow the crowd in terms of action and direction. Scams like the jam auction condition people to behave in a certain way and

respond to learned stimuli, encouraged by those around them (many of whom are stooges).

4. Dishonesty
We all have a streak of larceny that might one day inspire us to do something foolish or indiscreet. Sometimes it is used to explain the circumstances of an unlikely scenario such as cheap merchandise that may be stolen. In other cases it might be a questionable proposition that could leave the mark in a compromising situation after the sting. People are motivated by powerful, natural desires and might easily be persuaded to do something they might later regret.

5. Deception
Clearly, this is the foundation of all con games, but it's important to understand and accept that hustlers are experts at making something seem real that might otherwise be easily dismissed. We need to accept that no matter how obvious or unlikely an idea or scheme might appear to be in hindsight or from a distance, inside the "con bubble," it feels very real to the victim.

6. Need and Greed
Once a con artist knows what you want, he can take everything you have. We are often blinded by our desires, but it is a mistake to assume that most victims fall victim solely to greed. Scammers constantly target people with real needs, knowing that desperation can easily be used as a means to manipulate.

7. Time Pressure

A common way to secure commitment is to narrow a victim's opportunity to think and consider his options. In retrospect, when a mark untangles everything that led to a sting, it can be difficult to understand how he was so easily fooled, but in the heat of the moment, it feels natural to him.

Throughout this book, I have illustrated how these principles are used, but I would like to add three more to our original list:

8. Situation

Individual needs and desires are often dictated by our position in life. Knowing what people want gives a hustler a powerful advantage, and an experienced con artist can assume a mark's needs with a quick glance at him and his situation. This is why so many scammers target the elderly or those in obvious need. It might seem difficult to understand why anyone would respond to an e-mail from an African prince, but if you were consumed by desperation, prayed to God every night for help, and were willing to jump at any opportunity, that e-mail might seem like the answer to your prayers. We should always consider the conditions that contribute to a victim's state of mind and judge not only what people believe but *why they might be in a position to believe it.*

9. Self-Image

Hustlers are natural psychologists and often have a knack for identifying how people regard themselves. Playing on this can be a powerful tool in the hands of a gifted deceiver. On my show

Scammed, I deliberately played on Uncle Barry's ego, which ultimately proved to be the best leverage I had. However, if this is done carelessly, a mark might easily recognize a clumsy attempt to pander or patronize. When connecting with a victim's inner self, a hustler can foster strong emotions and genuine commitment. Romance scams or cons where a victim's hopes and dreams are shattered can be the most painful because the mark feels a genuine sense of loss when abandoned by someone who seemed to truly understand him.

10. Denial

I've met many who have refused to believe they were being scammed. Once a mark is inside the con bubble, it's very difficult to convince him that everything he believes might not be real. So powerful is this resistance to the truth that victims have allowed themselves to be scammed several times in the fading hope that a story might prove to be legitimate. Even if a mark begins to suspect trickery, he might persist in the hope of being mistaken.

Each of these principles applies to an aspect of human nature, and it's important to accept that people can be easily manipulated in the right circumstances. If we can create a society that supports victims without shame or ridicule, then crimes of deception will be more difficult to commit and easier to eradicate.

Be Honest (with Yourself)

Sharing knowledge and understanding victims are two sure ways to protect our communities, but as individuals, there is one important step each of us can take to make ourselves much more difficult to con.

I always tell my clients "if you think you can't be conned, you're just the person I want to meet!" As any good magician will tell you, it's often easier to fool someone who thinks he can't be fooled. Con artists prefer an easy mark, but a self-proclaimed expert or puffed up know-it-all might be just as ripe in the proper circumstances.

Confidence is what a con man tries to give his mark, and any sucker who already has a rich supply could prove easier to take down. Once a self-assured victim is on the hook, he might never admit to being conned (to himself or others), which in itself makes them an attractive mark.

The simplest and most effective step anyone can take toward self-defense against deception is to fully accept that he could one day be deceived. It can happen to anyone and whoever you are, I guarantee that smarter people than you have been stung by the simplest of scams.

Con games are about objectives: stepping stones toward a desired outcome. How someone is hooked, the line he is given, and when he is finally sunk all depend on how a hustler engages with that particular mark. Even though a victim's actions might ultimately be predictable, a con artist must manipulate circumstances to achieve the desired result. This takes talent, skill, and experience. It also requires an ability to lie without hesitation and steal without remorse.

Understanding these goals and the principles employed to achieve them helps us to protect ourselves and those we care about. It can make con games more difficult and less profitable.

Eventually, scams evolve to adapt to new conditions, and there's just no way to be constantly on guard without locking ourselves in the proverbial basement. There will eventually be some weakness or vulnerability that a professional deceiver can find or some advantage worth playing upon.

Con artists have been compared to method actors, but I believe that being a successful scammer requires a natural talent for duplicity and a mind for deception. Intelligence can also be important, but I've met many professional liars who can appear completely convincing without being able to generate a single original thought. Whether he's a grifter or a gold digger, a hustler's willingness to say or do anything to get what he wants will ultimately determine his success.

A con game can hit like a falling piano or creep up like an expanding waistline, but once entangled in the con man's web, it's easy to become wrapped up in the lie. Waking up to a scam is extremely difficult because the mark must reject not only what they have come to believe but their own feelings of desire, commitment, and self-worth.

Deception is not a single thing. By nature, it is amorphous, adapting to each scenario depending on interaction between human beings. It is affected by the past, the present, and perceived notions of the future. Emotion, expression, and expectation can all determine what we might believe and even the simplest of scams can be a singular combination of elements derived from any particular moment. Ultimately, it is impossible to define a comprehensive theory of deception. Instead, we can accept that it is effective and observe the elements and principles that deceivers use to achieve their goals.

An artist can express his or her own thoughts and feelings but cannot reveal or delineate the nature of all art. The artist's objectives are easier to define—to inspire emotion, to make a statement, or to sell for money.

Hustlers are as individual as the people they prey upon, and while each might follow a long-established line of actions and reactions, how they dance around that line before the music stops is impossible to define or predict. The art of the con, like any other art, is full of contradiction; simple objectives are achieved by complex actions, contrived situations seem natural or ordinary, and intelligent people are easily manipulated.

Learning to think like a con artist might one day help to protect you, your business, or your family; if you study the principles and understand the craft, you might know it when you see it.

There is no golden rule or surefire way to defend against all forms of deception. Instead we can be better informed so that even if we cannot anticipate every type of scam, we might be able to detect one before it's too late. Whether you find yourself dealing with a criminal mastermind or being preyed upon by deceitful dunces, there *is* one aspect of all con games that can be easily recognized. All you have to do is to stop, think, and look in the mirror.

A Note on Sources

The contents and conclusions of this book are the culmination of thirty-six years of fascination and obsession. Ten of those years have been spent exploring and experimenting with every conceivable type of con game from street scams to casino take-downs. Along the way I have met and befriended people on both sides of the law. I've cheated myself (literally), I've watched criminals at work, and I've spent great amounts of time and money to pursue any nugget of information about the art of the con. Some of my sources can be named, others cannot. Often I have decided to use nicknames or initials, but even those might be changed to protect the guilty.

It's true that I've crossed the line a couple of times, but I'm happy to admit that I don't have what it takes to be a real con man. If I did, I'd care only about what works, never how—and the last thing I'd want to do is reveal anything that might get the money.

It's important to emphasize that my perspective has been motivated by a lifetime of study and practice. I came to the BBC show as a producer, director, writer, and expert on the art of deception. My co-stars on *The Real Hustle* were the charming chameleon Alexis Conran (originally an actor, now also a presenter, magician, mentalist, consultant, speaker, commentator, anti-gambling campaigner, and gambler) and the very beautiful Jessica-Jane Clement (model, actress, and presenter). They would certainly have their own opinions about the show based on their personal experiences and motivations. For me it was a chance to experiment and to learn; being on camera was just a means to an end.

My findings are based on hundreds of sources and thousands of hours practicing and studying these methods. The manner in which *The Takedown*, *The Real Hustle*, and *Scammed* were filmed created a unique opportunity for someone with my interests and a willingness to share what I learned. This book is about con games *as I see them* after reviewing and analyzing hundreds of scams that I've performed on television as writer, producer—or hustler.

Acknowledgments

This book would not have been possible without those who shared their secrets over the last thirty-something years.

Thanks to Jason England, Steve Forte, Rod The Hop, Bob Bain, Sonny Day, Timbas, Larry Jennings, Douglas Cameron, James Lewis, Alan Ackerman, Jim Patton, BB (aka The Seldom-Seen Kid), Ronald Wohl, Whit Haydn, Bob Sheets, Doc, Bill Herz, Eric Mead, Michael Weber, Dean Dill, Patrick Page, Moves, Ron Connelly, Darwin Ortiz, MZ, DW, GO, MB, AW (aka Gus), "A," Mark Mason, Sal Piacente, Norm Beck, Marty G, "Alien," The Colonel, "Adam," Marc Rogers, Jeff McBride, Henderson Lynne, Francis, Tony Giorgio, Gene Maze, William Kalush, Juan Tamariz, George Joseph, Phil H, Frenchie The Hawk, and the Farmer's Market gang.

For my "life of crime": Leslie Greif and Adam Reed; Jim Milio, Melissa Jo Peltier, and Mark Hufnail; Andrew O'Connor, Matt Crook, Anthony Owen, and David Britland.

Sincere appreciation to Jason England for providing photographs and for sharing his remarkable collection.

Thanks to Lyons Press and my editor Jon Sternfeld for his enthusiasm, encouragement, and patience.

Thanks also to my agents David Boxerbaum and Laura Nolan (and her assistant Katelyn Dougherty) for making this happen.

Finally, special thanks to Roy Walton for pointing me in the right direction.

INDEX

Index

ABOUT THE AUTHOR

Part investigator and part performer, R. Paul Wilson is one of the world's foremost expert on cons and scams. His hit TV show, *The Real Hustle*, has run for eleven seasons on the BBC and been syndicated in more than forty-five countries. The show is studied by universities and law enforcement agencies to understand confidence games.

Paul was born in Cyprus in 1969, was raised in Singapore, and moved to Scotland in 1977. Since the age of eight he has studied con games, conjuring, and cheating. After college, Paul was recruited by the British Army Intelligence Corps, where he served before being injured and returning to civilian life. He went on to spend ten years as a computer consultant before becoming a professional performer and speaker for clients around the world.

In 2002 Paul moved into film and television as a writer, director, and producer. By 2004 he found himself in front of the camera, exposing con games by performing them for real. In 2012 he presented his unique one-man show "Lie. Cheat. Steal. Confessions of a Real Hustler" at the famed Edinburgh Fringe Festival.

Paul has written and starred in eleven seasons of *The Real Hustle*, created and starred in *The Takedown* for Court TV, and created, produced, and starred in *Scammed* for the History Channel. He has also directed, consulted, and acted in films and TV shows, working with many A-list actors including Sylvester Stallone, Jamie Foxx, Gabriel Byrne, and Jeremy Piven, among others. He has contributed articles to newspapers and reported for the BBC's *Watchdog* and *Crimewatch*.